SPIRIT *of* TRUTH

# THE REVELATION OF CHRIST IN SCRIPTURE

## Student Textbook

FRAMEWORK COURSE I

## About Sophia Institute for Teachers

Sophia Institute for Teachers was launched in 2013 by Sophia Institute to renew and rebuild Catholic culture through service to Catholic education. With the goal of nurturing the spiritual, moral, and cultural life of souls, and an abiding respect for the role and work of teachers, we strive to provide materials and programs that are at once enlightening to the mind and ennobling to the heart; faithful and complete, as well as useful and practical.

Sophia Institute is a 501(c)(3) nonprofit organization founded in 1983.



The Subcommittee on the Catechism, United States Conference of Catholic Bishops, has found that this catechetical high school text, copyright 2019, is in conformity with the Catechism of the Catholic Church and that it fulfills the requirements of Core Course I of the Doctrinal Elements of a Curriculum Framework for the Development of Catechetical Materials for Young People of High School Age.

*Printed in the United States of America*
*Design by Perceptions Design Studio*
*Cover image:* The Transfiguration *by Giulio Cesare Procaccini (1574 – 1625),*
*Church of St. James, Whitehaven, Cumberland / Alamy stock photo.*

***Spirit of Truth: The Revelation of Christ in Scripture Student Textbook***
ISBN: 978-1-64413-401-6
Second printing

# Contents

# Acknowledgments

*Spirit of Truth High School Edition* follows the basic scope and sequence of the *Doctrinal Elements of a Curriculum Framework* set forth by the United States Conference of Catholic Bishops. This course corresponds to **Core Curriculum Course I: The Revelation of Christ in Scripture**.

## Authors

Dominick Albano
Veronica Burchard
Jose Gonzalez
Mike Gutzwiller
Andrew Willard Jones, PhD
Michael McLaughlin
John Meinert PhD
Louis St. Hilaire
Michel Therrien, S.T.L., S.T.D.
Talia Westerby

## Editors

Veronica Burchard
Emily Stimpson Chapman
Mike Gutzwiller
Anna Maria Mendell
Ethan O'Connor

## Catechetical Consultant

Michel Therrien, S.T.L., S.T.D.

## Copyeditors

Kyle Burchard
Jane Cavalina
Janelle Gergen
Katie Takats

## Design

Perceptions Design Studio
Amherst, NH

# *A special thanks*

In grateful recognition of Lawrence Joseph
and Lynn Marie Blanford.

The chapter readings in this textbook were developed in partnership by Sophia Institute and Emmaus Road Publishing, an initiative of the St. Paul Center for Biblical Theology.

The St. Paul Center for Biblical Theology is a non-profit research and educational institute that promotes life-transforming Scripture study in the Catholic tradition. The Center serves clergy and laity, students and scholars, with research and study tools — from books and publications to multimedia and on-line programming.

Sophia Institute is particularly grateful to Dr. Scott Hahn, Ken Baldwin, and Chris Erickson for their generosity and contributions to this textbook. We value their friendship and are grateful for all they do to help people encounter Christ through Scripture and engage in the work of catechesis and evangelization.

UNIT I

# How Do We Know about God?

The *Catechism of the Catholic Church* states in paragraph no. 150: **"Faith is first of all a personal adherence of man to God. At the same time, and inseparably, it is a free assent to the whole truth that God has revealed."** In other words, faith is not just a blind leap. We put our faith in God who has made Himself known to us. Where can we discover this truth that God has revealed in order to be able to assent to it?

Human beings yearn for the infinite. We yearn for something outside ourselves and for the divine. If we pay attention and look closely, we do not have to try very hard to find God. We will discover that He is searching for us and has left us clues to help us encounter Him. Throughout human history God has been active and has revealed Himself to us in a variety of ways.

The first way we can come to know God is through His creation. If we look around at the natural created world we can come to the conclusion that something greater than us designed it. The world and everything in it, including ourselves, are complex, beautiful, and well ordered. This leads us to know that there is a designer behind everything that is.

The second way we can see that God has revealed Himself to us is through the two pillars of divine revelation: Sacred Scripture and Sacred Tradition. Sacred Scripture is the inspired word of God written down and passed on throughout history. Sacred Tradition is the mode of transmission of the Word of God. Jesus, who is the Word of God incarnate, gave to the Apostles all that was necessary for our salvation from sin. The Apostles in turn handed on what they had received to their successors, the bishops. With the help of the Holy Spirit, the Church has kept the Word of God whole and safe over the centuries so we can know and believe in the true Faith today.

## In This Unit

- **Chapter 1:** The Desire for God
- **Chapter 2:** Natural Revelation
- **Chapter 3:** Divine Revelation
- **Chapter 4:** The Transmission of Divine Revelation

Chapter I

# The Desire for God

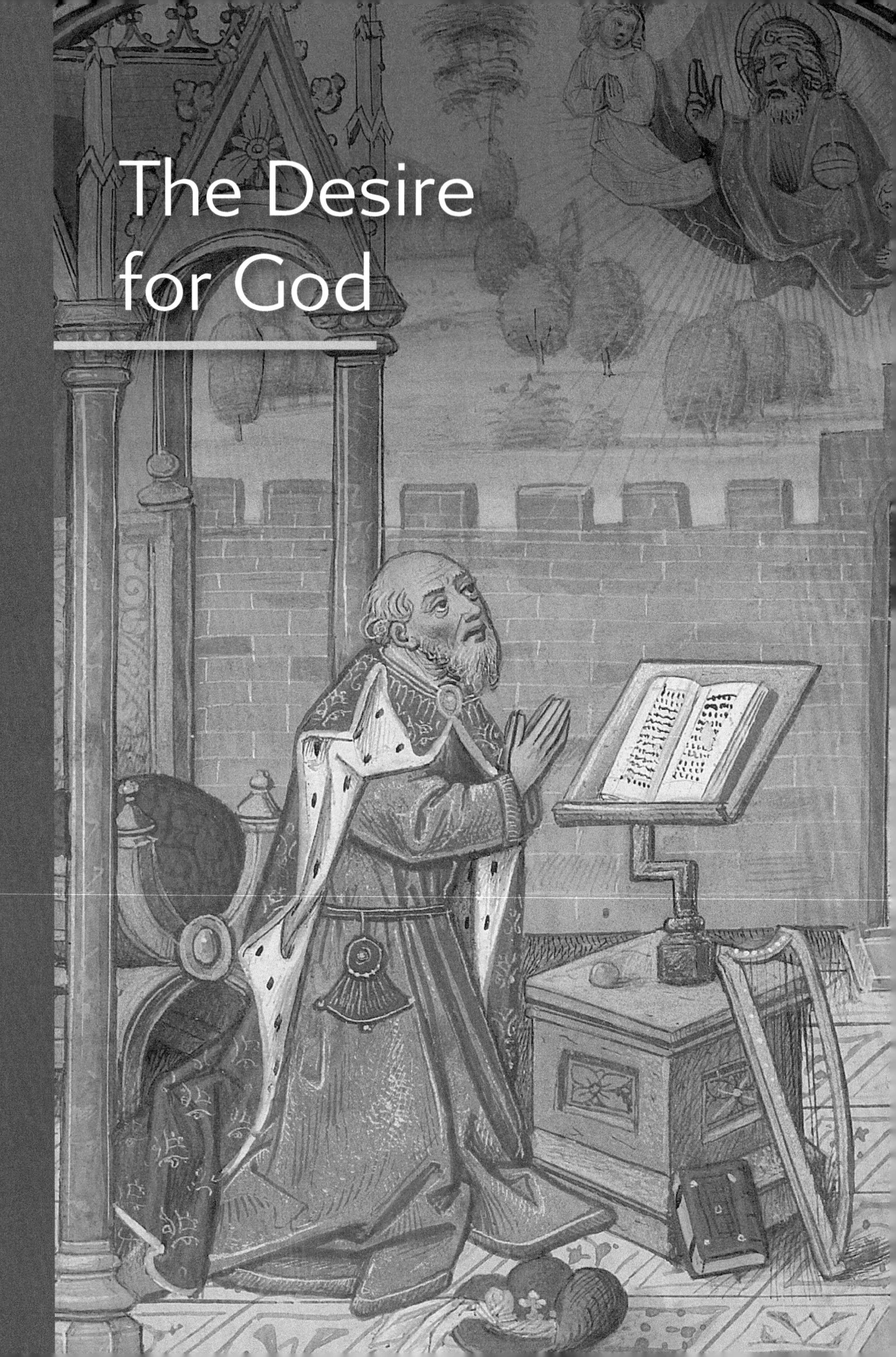

# Chapter Overview

We all desire to know God and to be in relationship with Him. In fact, this is the very purpose for which God made us—to know and love Him and to be loved by Him. Because of sin, our knowledge of God and friendship with Him does not come as easily as He created us to experience. And so, throughout human history, God has made Himself known to us in various ways to call us back to Him and to the purpose for which we were made. This chapter—and this course—are an introduction to God's revelation of Himself, which finds its fullest expression in His Son, Jesus Christ. It is an invitation to you to know Him and find your true purpose in Him.

## In this chapter you will learn that …

- Every human person desires to know God.
- Real happiness is found only in communion with God.
- God made each of us in His image and likeness with the purpose of loving and being loved by Him.
- Our original parents rejected God's love and sinned against Him. All people after them are born with the stain of Original Sin on their souls.
- Throughout human history God has revealed Himself to us to call us back to Him so we can find the happiness for which He created us to enjoy.
- Jesus Christ is the fullness of God's self-revelation.

### Bible Basics

God created mankind in his image; in the image of God he created them; male and female he created them.

GENESIS 1:27

When I see your heavens, the work of your fingers,<br>
  the moon and stars that you set in place—<br>
What is man that you are mindful of him,<br>
  and a son of man that you care for him?<br>
Yet you have made him little less than a god,<br>
  crowned him with glory and honor.<br>
You have given him rule over the works of your hands,<br>
put all things at his feet

PSALM 8:4–7

## The Desire for God

Every human person desires to know God. Every human heart longs for communion with him. Whether we recognize that longing or not, the desire for happiness that we all feel is really a desire for God. It is a desire to be in a relationship with the One who made us and who is the source of all good things. St. Augustine (AD 354–430) expressed this idea in his *Confessions:* "You have made us for yourself, O Lord, and our hearts are restless until they rest in you."

St. Augustine's words are beautiful (and true), but at first glance, they might not correspond to our experience of the world around us. After all, plenty of people exist who do not act interested in God, yet still seem happy. They laugh. They have friends. They do important things. If a relationship with God is the key to happiness, how does the Church account for those people?

In order to answer this question, it is important that we first understand what the Church means when she teaches that happiness is found only in communion with God. When she says that, she is making a statement about what humanity is—about what type of creatures we are. The Church's **anthropology**, or understanding of the human person, is the basis of her understanding of happiness. In order to understand what makes us truly happy, we need to understand what we are.

This is not just true of human beings. A good way to understand anything is to start with its origin. For example, if we want to understand a work of art or architecture, we need to know about the time and place of its creation. We also need to know something about the creator—where he

### Vocabulary

**Anthropology (n.):** The study of the origins and nature of the human person.

▼ All mankind, beginning with Adam, was made to love God and enjoy communion with Him.

*The Creation of Adam* by Michelangelo (1508–1512).

came from or what type of person he was. Consider the Great Pyramids in Egypt. With just a glance, we know the pyramids are astonishing. We can appreciate their grandeur simply by looking at them.

If we want to progress past simple appreciation, however, and truly understand what the pyramids are, we must ask questions, such as, "Who built them?" "When were they built?" and most importantly, "Why were they built?" Through answering these sorts of questions—questions that concern the origin of the object's creation—we move into the realm of understanding.

What is true for architecture is also true for the human person. If we want to understand who we are and why the Church says we can find true happiness only through a relationship with God, then we need to understand our origin. We need to go back to "the beginning."

**"God created mankind in his image; in the image of God he created them; male and female he created them."**

GEN. 1: 27

## In the Beginning

The Book of Genesis is the first book of the Bible. There, we read:

> **God created mankind in his image; in the image of God he created them; male and female he created them. God blessed them and God said to them: Be fertile and multiply; fill the earth and subdue it. Have dominion over the fish of the sea, the birds of the air, and all the living things that crawl on the earth (Gen. 1: 27–28)**

God created every creature in the world, but only man was made in God's image. This means only man was created with a rational soul in addition to a body—with the capacity to reason, choose right from wrong, and make a gift of himself in love. God created us out of pure love, and He created us in His image so that we could love him in return. Therefore, we desire to be close to God; we were made this way. It is part of what it means to be a human being. When we do not have a relationship with Him or are separated from Him in some way, we are not fulfilling our nature, and so, as St. Augustine said, we feel "restless" and, ultimately, unhappy.

What, however, does it mean to fulfill our nature? An illustration from the animal kingdom can be helpful. Dogs, in general, are bred for specific tasks, and Labrador retrievers, in particular, are bred to find and return birds shot by a hunter. For a Labrador, the desire to chase things down and bring them to his master is a part of his makeup. It is his nature. It is a part of what it means to be the kind of thing that he is. As any dog lover knows, Labs are happiest when they are satisfying their desire to retrieve. Many Labs will play fetch until they collapse from exhaustion; that is how much they love it. It makes them happy because it satisfies their nature.

Death is a consequence of Adam and Eve's first sin and rejection of God's love, known as the Fall.

**Aa Vocabulary**

**Garden of Eden (n.):** The place where Adam and Eve originally dwelled in perfect harmony with themselves, with all of creation, and with God. Paradise.

*Expulsion from the Garden of Eden* by Peter Paul Rubens (1620).

In the same sort of way, it is part of our nature to be with God. God made us to love Him and be with Him. When we are close to Him, that satisfies our nature, and we experience a happiness and joy that we never want to end. This experience of endless joy in God's presence is what we were made for, and in the book of Genesis, human beings' initial experience of such joy is fittingly referred to as "Paradise," a word that the New Testament also uses for Heaven (Lk. 23:43; 2 Cor. 12:4). In fact, the redemption Jesus won for us by His Cross, Resurrection, and Ascension into Heaven is not merely a restoration of this Original Holiness, but is an even greater blessing of grace, for, as St. Paul tells us in his letter to the **Romans**, **"where sin increased, grace overflowed all the more" (5:20)**.

## The Fall

The first-time human beings sinned, they lost their place in earthly paradise. They lost the close, intimate friendship with God they experienced in the **Garden of Eden** (Gen. 3:1–7). They wounded their relationship with Him. This is called "**the Fall**." The Fall dramatically changed the relationship between God and man, but it did not change the type of creature man was, and it most certainly did not change God. God created humans so He could love them and be loved by them, and He continues to desire this. After the Fall, Genesis tells us God came to be with Adam and Eve. He walked in the garden, and Adam and Eve hid. God, however, did not give up on them. Instead, he sought them out, calling, **"Where are you?" (Gen. 3:9)**.

This is the situation in which we continue to find ourselves. Because of Adam and Eve's sin, we all are born in a state of **Original Sin**. We are conceived with a nature deprived of the original holiness and justice Adam and Eve enjoyed before the Fall. We have also inherited their tendency to "hide," to turn our backs on God. But God still seeks us out. He wants to walk with us in Paradise, the place of our perfect happiness. From our hiding places, which we are reluctant to leave, we still long to be with God. This paradox is the source of the restlessness of which St. Augustine speaks.

Based on this understanding of humanity, the Church teaches that lasting joy and happiness, both in this life and in the next, can only be found in God. This does not mean that people who do not know God, or even those who reject God, are completely incapable of experiencing any type of happiness. To the extent they love others more than themselves, they are fulfilling their nature and can experience a share of happiness. "Restlessness," however, will never disappear from this kind of worldly happiness. Total happiness, and with it, total peace, are only found when we fulfill our nature by loving God and reflecting the love that He pours out on us. That is Paradise. That is Heaven.

## God Makes Himself Known

Every one of us is made for happiness; we are made to love God. Loving God, however, starts with knowing Him, and, thanks to the Fall, that is not as easy as it was supposed to be. Because of sin, we no longer walk in Paradise with God, so our knowledge of Him does not come effortlessly. We must work at it. If we do, we will find that God still makes Himself known in a number of ways.

First, He shows Himself through His creation. This can be called **natural revelation**. God made the world and everything in it. Although only the human person is made in His image, all of creation, in some way, still reveals something about its maker. By studying the world—its contents and its properties—we can use our reason to discover important truths about God and His nature.

### Aa Vocabulary

**The Fall (n.):** When Adam and Eve, due to the temptation and lies of Satan, disobeyed God and rejected His love. Also called the Fall of Man.

**Original Sin (n.):** The state of human nature deprived of the original holiness and justice Adam and Eve enjoyed before the fall.

**Natural Revelation (n.):** God's communication of Himself to us through the created order.

**Divine Revelation (n.):** God's communication of Himself, by which He makes known the mystery of His divine plan by deeds and words over time, and most fully by sending His Son, Jesus Christ.

 Lives of Faith

## St. Paul the Apostle

What do you do when you are torn in two directions?

How do you choose when the seasons overlap for the two sports you love to play, and you have to pick one? How do you choose when you got into your top two choices for college and now you have to pick between them? How do you choose when some of your friends are going to the movies on Friday night while others are going to have a bonfire and you are invited to both? How do you choose when you are staring at the menus for your two favorite take-out restaurants and you cannot pick which one to order dinner from?

Admittedly, some of our choices are bigger than others, but very often we are presented with choices that pull us in two very different directions.

St. Paul the Apostle faced this situation for almost the entire second half of his life. The story of his conversion to Christianity is one of the most well-known; from his beginnings as a member of the Jewish Sanhedrin, a group of Jewish rabbis who served in a system of courts, to the most prolific and far reaching Christian evangelist in history.

Born in Tarsus with the Jewish name Saul, the Bible tells us Paul persecuted the first Christians, admitting in his own words how he **"persecuted the church of God beyond measure and tried to destroy it" (Gal 1:13)**. One day while Paul was traveling, Jesus Christ appeared to him in a blinding light and asked him directly, **"Saul, Saul, why are you persecuting me?" (Acts 9:4)**.

This visit from Jesus led to a complete and radical transformation of Paul's life. As a Roman citizen, he began using his legal Roman name, Paul, and with the same zeal he persecuted Christians, he began to proclaim the Gospel to the Gentiles. The members of the Sanhedrin who once looked at him as a hero now plotted to kill him. And the people who once feared him now looked to him as a hero of the early Church.

**Jesus Christ ... asked him directly, "Saul, Saul, why do you persecute me?"**

ACTS 9:4

Paul's new life was marked by his travels to plant new Christian communities. His is a true adventure story of what God has in store for those who will boldly follow him. Paul's letters constitute thirteen books in the New Testament.

In his letter to the Christian community in Philippi, St. Paul writes about being torn in two directions. After his conversion, Paul had a firm and set desire to be with Jesus Christ. But he also had a firm desire to serve Him by sharing the Gospel.

**"I am caught between the two"** he tells us in **Phillipans 1:23–25**. **"I long to depart this life and be with Christ, [for] that is far better. Yet that I remain [in] the flesh is more necessary for your benefit. And this I know with confidence, that I shall remain and continue in the service of all of you for your progress and joy in the faith".**

Whether we are aware of it or not, the deepest desire of the human heart is to be with God. Paul spent the first half of his life ignorant to that desire, but after his conversion the desire burned so passionately in him that death no longer scared him.

So, what do you do when you are torn in two directions? A good rule of thumb is to ask yourself which desire leads you closer to Christ. As St. Paul puts it, **"[f]or to me life is Christ, and death is gain" (Phil 1:21)**. In the end, nothing will make you happier than a life with Christ.

*The Transfiguration of Christ* by Peter Paul Rubens (1605).

Jesus, the ultimate exemplar of God's revelation of Himself to mankind, revealed His divine glory to three of His disciples in the Transfiguration.

God, however, does not just ask us to look for Him in the world using reason. He also comes to us, revealing Himself directly to humanity. This is called divine revelation. There are two phases of **Divine Revelation**, which are recorded in writing in **Sacred Scripture**, or the Bible. Sacred Scripture is composed of two parts: the **Old Testament** and the **New Testament**. In the Old Testament, we learn how God revealed Himself to the people of Israel and established a covenant with them. Then, **"when the fullness of time had come" (Gal. 4:4)**, God revealed Himself intimately to humanity by sending His only Son, Jesus Christ, to become a man. We call this the **Incarnation**. The Incarnation is the ultimate example of God coming to us, making Himself totally known to us, and asking us to join Him in happiness. The events surrounding the Incarnation are recorded in the New Testament.

In the next chapter, we are going to explore God's revelation to mankind and how the content of this revelation is transmitted to us. In other words, we are going to seek to answer the question: how do we know who God is?

## Aa Vocabulary

**Sacred Scripture (n.):** The written record of God's revelation of Himself contained in the Old and New Testaments. It was composed by human authors inspired by the Holy Spirit. The Bible. The Word of God.

**Old Testament (n.):** The 46 books of the Bible, which record the history of salvation from creation through the old covenant with Israel, in preparation for the appearance of Christ as Savior of the World.

**New Testament (n.):** The 27 books of the Bible written by the sacred authors in apostolic times, which have Jesus Christ, the incarnate Son of God as their central theme.

**Incarnation (n.):** The fact that the Son of God assumed human nature and became man in order to accomplish our salvation. Jesus Christ, the Son of God, the second Person of the Trinity, is both true God and true man.

# The Truth Is…

St. Augustine's observation that our hearts are restless until they rest in God is just as true today—if not more so—as it was nearly 1700 years ago when he wrote it. We live in a restless time when so many people struggle with finding their place in the world, with depression, anxiety and all sorts of other mental illness, with self-esteem, and with countless personal, social, and political conflicts. This restlessness of our hearts is real and the things of this world—wealth, power, money, fame—will never truly satisfy us.

But there is good news! God has made each one of us for so much more. He knows you, He loves you, and He wants your heart to find rest in Him. Our restlessness has a solution and it is found in God. God has made Himself known so that you can find Him. This course has been written to invite you to find and understand your purpose as a son or daughter of God and to live that purpose—to love and be loved by God and to live His love in the world around you. The Catholic Church always and without ceasing proposes the Good News of Jesus Christ who has made God known to us. And that Good News will ultimately lead you to find the joy and happiness that you were created for in this life. As you begin this journey of learning about the revelation of Jesus Christ in Scripture, may your heart and mind be open to what God is inviting you to discover.

Chapter 1

# Focus and Reflection Questions

1. What is the desire of every human heart, whether they know it or not?

2. What do we need to understand first in order to know what will make us truly happy?

3. What does it mean that human beings are made in God's image?

4. Why do we desire to be close to God?

5. How do we fulfill the purpose for which we were made? What happens when we are fulfilling our purpose? What is this experience called?

6. What happened to Adam and Eve as a result of the Fall? How did their sin affect the rest of humanity?

7. What is the only way we can find total happiness and peace?

8. How does God reveal Himself to us through natural revelation?

9. What is divine revelation? What are the two phases of divine revelation and where are they recorded?

10. What is the Incarnation and what is it the ultimate example of?

11. Between what two things did St. Paul say he was caught? Why?

# Straight to the Source

ADDITIONAL READINGS FROM PRIMARY SOURCES

## Excerpt from St. Augustine's *Confessions*

Great are you, O Lord, and greatly to be praised; great is your power, and of your wisdom there is no end. And man, being a part of your creation, desires to praise you—man, who bears about with him his mortality, the witness of his sin, even the witness that you resist the proud,—yet man, this part of your creation, desires to praise you. You move us to delight in praising you; for you have made us for yourself, and our hearts are restless until they rest in you.

1. We have encountered this quote from St. Augustine a few times throughout this chapter: "You have made us for yourself, and our hearts are restless until they rest in you." Why do you think this is such an appropriate quote for the main idea of this chapter?
2. Many people in our world today seem restless—that is, they seem to be unhappy, dissatisfied, and searching for something that will make them happy and satisfied without ever really finding it. Considering what you have learned in this chapter, what might you say to someone who feels "restless" in this way?

## *Rerum Novarum* 40: An encyclical letter of Pope Leo XIII, May 15, 1891

Life on earth, however good and desirable in itself, is not the final purpose for which man is created; it is only the way and the means to that attainment of truth and that love of goodness in which the full life of the soul consists. It is the soul which is made after the image and likeness of God; it is in the soul that the sovereignty resides in virtue whereof man is commanded to rule the creatures below him and to use all the earth and the ocean for his profit and advantage. "Fill the earth and subdue it; and rule over the fishes of the sea, and the fowls of the air, and all living creatures that move upon the earth." In this respect all men are equal; there is here no difference between rich and poor, master and servant, ruler and ruled, "for the same is Lord over all." No man may with impunity outrage that human dignity which God Himself treats with great reverence, nor stand in the way of that higher life which is the preparation of the eternal life of heaven. Nay, more; no man has in this matter power over himself. To consent to any treatment which is calculated to defeat the end and purpose of his being is beyond his right; he cannot give up his soul to servitude, for it is not man's own rights which are here in question, but the rights of God, the most sacred and inviolable of rights.

1. Why does Pope Leo argue that the soul of man is so important?
2. Rerum Novarum is an important document in the history of the Church. In it, Pope Leo XIII lays out what has become the beginnings of modern Catholic Social Teaching. In other words, the document addresses the relationship and duties between individual persons, employers, governments, and society in general. The Church has always understood these intertwined relationships to be rooted in the fundamental truths about human nature. Considering what you have learned in this chapter and what Pope Leo says in this quote from Rerum Novarum, what do you think is the fundamental truth about human nature that all other rights and responsibilities are based upon?

# Straight to the Source

ADDITIONAL READINGS FROM PRIMARY SOURCES

### *Gaudium et Spes* 12–13, Pastoral Constitution on the Church in the Modern World, December 7, 1965

For Sacred Scripture teaches that man was created "to the image of God," is capable of knowing and loving his Creator, and was appointed by Him as master of all earthly creatures that he might subdue them and use them to God's glory "What is man that you should care for him? You have made him little less than the angels, and crowned him with glory and honor. You have given him rule over the works of your hands, putting all things under his feet" (Ps 8:5–7).

But God did not create man as a solitary, for from the beginning "male and female he created them" (Gen 1:27). Their companionship produces the primary form of interpersonal communion. For by his innermost nature man is a social being, and unless he relates himself to others he can neither live nor develop his potential.

Therefore, as we read elsewhere in Holy Scripture God saw "all that he had made, and it was very good" (Gen 1:31).

Although he was made by God in a state of holiness, from the very onset of his history man abused his liberty, at the urging of the Evil One. Man set himself against God and sought to attain his goal apart from God. Although they knew God, they did not glorify Him as God, but their senseless minds were darkened and they served the creature rather than the Creator. What divine revelation makes known to us agrees with experience. Examining his heart, man finds that he has inclinations toward evil too, and is engulfed by manifold ills which cannot come from his good Creator. Often refusing to acknowledge God as his beginning, man has disrupted also his proper relationship to his own ultimate goal as well as his whole relationship toward himself and others and all created things.

Therefore man is split within himself. As a result, all of human life, whether individual or collective, shows itself to be a dramatic struggle between good and evil, between light and darkness. Indeed, man finds that by himself he is incapable of battling the assaults of evil successfully, so that everyone feels as though he is bound by chains. But the Lord Himself came to free and strengthen man, renewing him inwardly and casting out that "prince of this world" (John 12:31) who held him in the bondage of sin. For sin has diminished man, blocking his path to fulfillment.

The call to grandeur and the depths of misery, both of which are a part of human experience, find their ultimate and simultaneous explanation in the light of this revelation.

1. This quote from the Second Vatican Council in many ways summarizes the main idea of this chapter. In your own words, describe the main idea of both this chapter and this quote.
2. Re-read the final sentence of this quote (beginning with "The call to grandeur…). Do you agree or disagree with this claim? Why?

Chapter 2

# Natural Revelation

# Chapter Overview

God has made Himself known to us through the created world. This can be called natural revelation. We can come to sure knowledge of God's existence by the use of human reason in consideration of what He has made. This knowledge of God is available to all people everywhere. St. Thomas Aquinas set forth perhaps the most well-known and well-thought-out arguments for God's existence using human reason rooted in what can be observed about the created order. These "proofs" for God's existence, along with other proofs, continue to assert the reasonableness of belief in God in our world today.

## In this chapter you will learn that …

- God has revealed Himself to us through the created order.
- Natural revelation is accessible to everyone, not just Christians.
- St. Paul and the early Fathers of the Church appealed to knowledge of God through creation as a means of telling people about God.
- St. Thomas Aquinas summarized five arguments for the existence of God that are rooted in human reason and what can be observed in the world around us.
- The Catholic Church teaches that God can be known with certainty by the light of human reason by means of created things.

### Bible Basics

For from the greatness and the beauty of created things their original author, by analogy, is seen.
WISDOM 13:5

Ever since the creation of the world, his invisible attributes of eternal power and divinity have been able to be understood and perceived in what he has made.
ROMANS 1:20

### Connections to the *Catechism*

CCC 32 (page 20)
CCC 33 (page 26)

## Natural Revelation

The first way God has revealed Himself to us is through the created world. St. Francis of Assisi (c. 1181–1226) famously praised the beauty of all creation and God's presence throughout it in his "Canticle of the Sun":

> Praised be You my Lord with all Your creatures,
> especially Sir Brother Sun,
> Who is the day through whom You give us light.
> And he is beautiful and radiant with great splendor,
> Of You Most High, he bears the likeness.

In poem and prayer, St. Francis expresses what every person has experienced; namely, a realization of the beauty, complexity, and wonder of creation. Like Francis, when we experience something in nature and stand in awe of it, we are not just encountering creation; we are encountering its Creator. We are seeing His handiwork, and that helps us to see something about God.

## God's Self-Expression

The created world is a form of revelation from God. It is His creation. Just as we can learn about an artist from the way he expresses himself in his art, we can learn about God from His art: the universe. The world around us is a form of His self-expression. Therefore the Church has always taught that God is knowable through our experience of the created world. This revelation of God through the created order can be called natural revelation.

**[T]he Church has always taught that God is knowable through our experience of the created world.**

Importantly, you do not have to be a Christian to understand this revelation. The wonder of creation is so great that human beings in every age have looked to it for meaning. Some have even gone so far as to worship the sun, the wind, the trees, or the oceans. These people have seen traces of the divine—signs of the Creator—in created things. They are right to recognize the goodness of those things, goodness which comes from God. Their mistake, however, is confusing creation with the Creator. As the book of Wisdom 13:1–9 teaches, the wonder of creation is not something to be worshipped. Rather, it is evidence of God, who created it and, as such, it should lead us to Him.

> **Now if out of joy in their beauty they thought them gods, let them know how far more excellent is the Lord than these; for the original source of beauty fashioned them. Or if they were struck by their might and energy, let them realize from these things how much more powerful is the one who made them. For from the greatness and the beauty of created things their original author, by analogy, is seen (Wis. 13:3–5).**

*A Harvest Scene with Workers Loading Hay onto a Farm Wagon* by James Ward (ca. 1800).

▲ God reveals Himself to us through the created world; we participate in His divine order by being good stewards of the earth.

### *Natural Revelation and Sacred Scripture*

Natural revelation took on new importance in the New Testament, as the Apostles began to preach the Gospel to non-Jewish peoples (the **Gentiles**). As we will learn in the next chapter on divine revelation, God prepared Israel to receive Jesus by revealing Himself to them in a special way and promising to send them the **Messiah**. But the Good News about Jesus was not meant only for Israel; it was meant for all people, and God prepared them to receive the Gospel as well, by showing Himself to them through His creation:

> **For what can be known about God is evident to them, because God made it evident to them. Ever since the creation of the world, his invisible attributes of eternal power and divinity have been able to be understood and perceived in what he has made (Rom. 1:19–20).**

Because of this, when St. Paul preached to the people of Athens, he could appeal to their own religious searching, even though they knew nothing yet of the God of Israel:

> **He made from one the whole human race to dwell on the entire surface of the earth, and he fixed the ordered seasons and the boundaries of their regions, so that people might seek God, even perhaps grope for him and find him, though indeed he is not far from any one of us. For "In him we live and move and have our being," as even some of your poets have said, "For we too are his offspring" (Acts 17:26–28).**

**Aa Vocabulary**

**Gentile (n.):** A person of non-Jewish ethnicity.

**Messiah (n.):** The Hebrew word for "anointed one" and the title given to the Savior God promised to the people of Israel.

The beauty and order of the created world raises our minds to its author: God.

*Pastoral Scene* by Nicolaes Berchem (1679).

**Aa Vocabulary**

**Fathers of the Church (n.):** The bishops and teachers of the early Church.

**Pagan (n.):** A person who practices polytheism, or the worship of many gods.

**Creed (n.):** A brief summary or profession of our Christian Faith, such as the Nicene Creed and the Apostles' Creed.

## Patristic Testimony

Following the teaching of the Scriptures and the example of St. Paul, through the centuries the Church has continued to teach that God can be known through His creation. We see this as early as the first centuries after Christ when the Church faced persecution and misunderstanding as it worked to evangelize the world of Rome. Like St. Paul, the early bishops and teachers of the Church (whom we call **Fathers of the Church**), appealed to natural revelation in their discussions with **pagan** critics.

St. Augustine wrote that the beauty of the earth and the heavens is a "profession," almost like the profession of faith we make when we recite the **Creed** at Mass:

> **Question the beauty of the earth, question the beauty of the sea, question the beauty of the air distending and diffusing itself, question the beauty of the sky … question all these realities. All respond: "See, we are beautiful." Their beauty is a profession [*confessio*]. These beauties are subject to change. Who made them if not the Beautiful One [Pulcher] who is not subject to change? (quoted in the *Catechism of the Catholic Church* no. 32, hereafter cited in text as CCC).**

In sunsets and oceans, butterflies and daisies, glimpses of God's great beauty are revealed. But they are only a glimpse. No matter how great the beauty of a mountaintop or forest might be, it is changeable. At some point in the past it did not exist, and at some point in the future, it will cease to be. These things can be damaged or destroyed. This is how it is supposed to be. These created things were not made to show us all there is to see of beauty. Rather, they were made to make us look deeper, to look for the source of their beauty, and to point us to a beauty that is unchanging and eternal.

**Created things were made to make us look deeper, to look for the source of their beauty, and to point us to a beauty that is unchanging and eternal.**

### *Five Ways of Knowing God*

The writings of St. Augustine and the other Fathers of the Church influenced and formed the framework through which the Church understood natural revelation for many centuries. Then, in the High Middle Ages (1100–1300), a renewed study of ancient Greek philosophy introduced a new way of approaching the subject. The thinkers of this period sought to build a philosophical foundation for both the Scriptures' and Church Fathers' claims that God is knowable through creation. The most important of these thinkers is St. Thomas Aquinas (1225–1274).

A Dominican priest from Italy who studied in Paris with St. Albert the Great, St. Thomas is recognized as one of the greatest intellects the Church has ever known. Through his work, he sought to integrate philosophical method and Christianity in order to describe and explain revealed truth. His method is known as **Scholasticism**. We can see Thomas' characteristic style of argumentation at work in his **five proofs for the existence of God**. In these five approaches to God's existence, Aquinas illustrates the power of the light of human reason and its ability to prove the existence of God from the things the human intellect perceives in the physical world. He also answers common objections against the arguments for God's existence in order to show their strength. The fascinating result shows one of the greatest minds of all time at work.

The "five ways" can be summarized like this:

1. *Argument from Motion*: As Thomas states, "Whatever is in motion is put in motion by another." For example, a ball does not roll by itself, nor does a seed plant itself. Someone (or something) had to start it moving or growing. What is true for a ball or a plant, St. Thomas observes, must be true for the world and life itself. If you trace the movements of the universe back through their various causes, there must be a single and first (or a prime) mover. This mover is God.
2. *Argument from Causation*: The existence of everything temporal has been passed on through a series of causes and effects.

**Aa Vocabulary**

**Scholasticism (n.):** An intellectual method originating in medieval Europe that sought to integrate classical philosophy and Christian thought in order to understand and explain revealed truths.

**Five Proofs for the Existence of God (n.):** Arguments developed by St. Thomas Aquinas that use human reason and observation of the created world to conclude that God exists. Also called the "five ways."

### Lives of Faith

## St. Francis of Assisi

"*I can't believe what I am seeing*," the man thought as he gazed wide-eyed at the people around him.

He stood at the back of the crowd and watched as grown men and women gathered around the statue in the middle of the town square. Some laid down flowers. Others comforted their friends and family. Some of the women and many of the young children had tears running down their faces. This scene was not unusual for a funeral, but highly unusual for the funeral of a wolf!

"There are some strange folks in this town," he told his companion as they sat in the corner of the tavern later that night. The man was a travelling merchant and he had seen his fair share of oddities in his travels, but never anything like this. "How does a whole town cry over a dead stray?"

"I do not really know," his companion replied, "but I think it might not be about the wolf at all. I think it might be about the man who tamed the wolf."

If you ask most people what they think of when they hear the name St. Francis of Assisi, they will have one answer: animals. Their grandma had a bird bath that was a statue of St. Francis or they took their beloved family dog to Church for a pet blessing on his feast day. Even people who are not Christian can usually recognize the robed saint with birds on his arms and rabbits gathering around his feet.

It is true, the 12th and 13th century Saint loved animals. But he did not love animals the way some people love their pets. No, St. Francis loved animals because he loved all of God's creation. When he saw an animal, he saw the creative power and goodness of God.

When he saw beautiful birds while traveling a forest road one day, he called out to the birds and told them to sing praise to God for His goodness in giving them such splendid clothes and the gift of flight. When he saw a fish in a stream, he would tell it to make sure it did not get caught and to give thanks to God for its life.

**St. Francis loved animals because he loved all of God's creation.**

In one town, the villagers told him of a wolf that was terrorizing the people, attacking and eating the animals and the townspeople alike. The people were so afraid that they would not go with him when St. Francis left the city to confront the wolf. The wolf charged from the forest straight at St. Francis, who simply made the Sign of the Cross and told the wolf to stop.

"Brother wolf," St. Francis said, "it is time to make peace between you and the people of the town. You will no longer harm them and they will not harm you." St. Francis stuck out his hand, and he and the wolf shook. Then the wolf followed St. Francis into the town, and he was introduced to all the townspeople as Brother Wolf. From that day on, Brother Wolf was a beloved companion to the men, women, and children of the town until the day it died.

The men and women of the town experienced powerful conversions through the witness of St. Francis and Brother Wolf; so powerful, in fact, this story survived hundreds of years as we still tell it today. And all those pet blessings and bird baths of St. Francis—they too remind us of God's goodness and love.

Saint Thomas Aquinas, Protector of the University of Cusco by Unknown Artist (ca. 1695).

St. Thomas Aquinas summarized five arguments for the existence of God using human reason and observation of nature.

**Since existence is a gift that all existing things merely share, but do not possess (nothing can cause itself), there must be a first or uncaused cause. This cause is God.**

Nothing causes itself. A vase exists because of a potter. A painting exists because of an artist. But why does the world exist? St. Thomas answered this dilemma by noting that if you trace the series of causes and effects in the world back, you arrive at the moment of nothingness. And since existence is a gift that all existing things merely share, but do not possess (nothing can cause itself), there must be a first or uncaused cause who is existence and does not receive existence. This cause is God.

3. *Argument from Contingency*: Everything that receives its existence has the real possibility for nonexistence (death proves this). When we humans die, sad as it may be, the world will continue to exist. Its existence does not depend on us. It is not contingent upon us. Rather, we are all contingent beings; we owe our existence to others (parents, grandparents, great-grandparents, etc.). It is impossible that every being, however, is contingent.

Nature displays profound beauty, order, harmony, and efficiency; from these principles St. Thomas Aquinas argued that it is entirely reasonable to conclude God's existence.

*The Garden of Eden* by Thomas Cole (1828).

There must be an absolutely necessary being, a being who is not dependent upon anything else for its existence, but upon whom everything else is contingent—upon whom everything else depends. This necessary being is God.

4. *Argument from Degrees of Perfection*: All created or contingent things have various degrees of perfections, such as being, goodness, truth, and dignity. Levels of being, goodness, truth, and dignity, however, require an absolute standard of being, goodness, truth, and nobility. St. Thomas showed that there must be one being who is being, goodness, truth, and nobility. In other words, there must be a cause which is itself all perfection and whose perfection is the standard by which everything else receives their perfections. This being who is himself being, goodness, truth, and nobility is God.
5. *Argument from Design*: If you found a watch on a beach and picked it up, you would never think it was something formed by the sea, wind, and waves. You would see all of its intricate systems and know someone had made it intentionally, carefully, and intelligently. This, St. Thomas explained, is even more true

of the world. All creatures are so intricate, ordered, and perfect that they demonstrate a supreme intelligence as their cause. This intelligence cannot be accounted for by any intelligence we know, nor is random chance a reasonable assumption. Rather, because of the order that saturates each being and all of reality, we must conclude that there exists a supremely intelligent and powerful being who is the author of all that exists. This author is God.

## The Ongoing Witness of Natural Revelation

### *Vatican I*

Even in the changing cultural and social contexts of the modern era, the Church has continued to affirm definitively that human reason can obtain knowledge of God. At the First Vatican Council (an **Ecumenical Council** held from 1868 to 1870), the Church responded to the skeptical philosophies that developed in the modern world following the **Enlightenment** (late 17th–18th century) by insisting that God's existence can be known with certitude by reasoning from His creation: "The same holy Mother Church holds and teaches that God, the beginning and end of all things, may be certainly known by the natural light of human reason by means of created things …" (*Dei Filius* 2).

While some would limit the use of human reason to only what can be known by the natural sciences, arguing that reason cannot tell us anything about God, human nature, or the meaning of our existence, Vatican I restates the teaching of the Book of Wisdom and the great Fathers and teachers of the Church. Human reason, the Church reminds us, reflects the intelligence of the Creator, and the mind of man—who was created in God's image and likeness—is capable of tracing the things it observes in the world back to the God who created them. Indeed, human reason craves knowledge of God just as it seeks knowledge of the natural world.

In a way, this assertion about the relation of humanity and the natural world to God is a restatement of the Church's anthropology we discussed in chapter 1. The longings of our heart for happiness and the wonder we experience at creation are there because God put them there. They are there because we are made to know God. We are made to love Him and glorify Him, both in this world and the next. This purpose gives every man and woman a dignity beyond measure. It is why every human life matters and why the Church, in the twentieth century, stood firm against the nightmares of atheist Communism and racist Fascism, both of which denied the inherent dignity of the human person and the fundamental rationality of the world in which we live.

**Aa Vocabulary**

**Ecumenical Council (n.):** A meeting of all the world's bishops together in union with the pope.

**Enlightenment (n.):** A philosophical movement of the eighteenth century that denied the value of faith and maintained that reason alone leads us to truth and holds the potential to solve the problem of evil.

## Responding to Relativism

In the twenty-first century, the Church continues to assert the ability of humanity to ascertain real truth about reality. Now, however, she does so in the face of **relativism**, which asserts that human reason is not capable of knowing either truth or God.

Some Christian thinkers, when making the case for God's existence in an age of relativism, take the physical world as their starting point; they contend we can come to know of the existence of God because of what we objectively observe around us. Another line of argumentation takes the human person as its starting point. This is a subjective approach. The *Catechism* puts it like this:

> **The *human person*: with his openness to truth and beauty, his sense of moral goodness, his freedom and the voice of his conscience, with his longings for the infinite and for happiness, man questions himself about God's existence. In all this he discerns signs of his spiritual soul. The soul, the "seed of eternity we bear in ourselves, irreducible to the merely material", can have its origin only in God. (CCC 33)**

Let us return again to the wonder of creation we discussed earlier. Have you ever been awed by the beauty of the natural world? Have you ever seen a mountain, a landscape, or a sunset that took your breath away? That made you feel like you were seeing something profoundly special? That gave you the sensation you were somehow standing outside of space and time? These can be powerful experiences, moments we never forget, memories that stay with us for a lifetime. Now ask yourself, if human beings were just animals in a world of simple material objects, why would we be capable of such experiences? What biological advantage does our ability to be awestruck by beauty offer us? The answer is none.

From a Christian understanding of the human person, these experiences make sense. We have a soul so we have a spiritual dimension that draws us into the life of God. God created the world because it pleases Him, and because of our soul, we too are pleased by the world; we can participate in His pleasure. The same holds true for our desire and openness toward truth, goodness, and happiness. They are all aspects of our desire to know and be with God. Through all these intangible, subjective experiences, we become aware of ourselves as spiritual beings, and so we become aware of the existence of God, who alone can satisfy our spiritual longings.

### Aa Vocabulary

**Relativism (n.):** A dangerous philosophy that says moral principles are a matter of individual preference based on personal experience, socioeconomic status, education, and particular culture, rather than based on absolute objective moral truths.

**"The soul, the 'seed of eternity we bear in ourselves, irreducible to the merely material,' can have its origin only in God."**

CCC 33

# The Truth Is...

It is easy in our modern world, with all its technological and scientific advances, to take for granted the questions of whether God exists or not and whether we can know Him or not. As you have learned in this chapter, the Catholic Church teaches His existence can be known with certainty simply by the use of reason—our powers of intellect, of knowing and understanding the world around us. And something about Him can be known in the same way.

The challenge then lies not in the questions themselves of God's existence and knowability, but rather in our motivation to find the answers to these questions. We often make our conclusions about God without ever truly making the effort to find real answers. When was the last time you had a true experience of nature? When was the last time you stood in awe and wonder at the sight of a beautiful sunset, or of the vastness of the ocean? When did you last marvel at the complexity of life, at the interrelated relationships between animals and the rest of nature? When did you last sit in silence and listen for His voice—or have you ever? Before you make up your mind about whether God exists or not and if you can know Him, do your homework. If you truly seek Him, you will not be disappointed.

Chapter 2

# Focus and Reflection Questions

1. What is natural revelation?

2. Do you have to be a Christian to understand natural revelation? Why or why not? What should natural revelation lead to?

3. Who are the Gentiles and how did God prepare them to receive the Gospel?

4. What did St. Augustine explain the beauty of creation professes?

5. Who is St. Thomas Aquinas? What was his thinking influenced by? What is his method known as and what does it do?

6. What do Aquinas' five proofs for the existence of God do?

7. What did the First Vatican Council teach about the relationship between human reason and knowledge of God's existence?

8. Based upon our desire for God, why does it make sense that we are able to know Him through what He has made?

9. What does relativism assert about ability to know God?

10. For what purpose does the author suggest human beings are capable of experiences of wonder and awe at the beauty of creation, moral goodness, freedom and conscience, and longing for the infinite and happiness?

11. How is St. Francis of Assisi's understanding of God's revelation of Himself in creation reflected in the story of St. Francis and the wolf?

# Straight to the Source

ADDITIONAL READINGS FROM PRIMARY SOURCES

## *Canticle of the Sun* by St. Francis of Assisi

Most High, all-powerful, all-good
Lord, All praise is Yours, all glory, all honor and all blessings.

To you alone, Most High, do they belong, and no mortal lips are worthy to pronounce Your Name.

Praised be You my Lord with all Your creatures,
especially Sir Brother Sun,
Who is the day through whom You give us
light.
And he is beautiful and radiant with great
splendor,
Of You Most High, he bears the likeness.

Praised be You, my Lord, through Sister
Moon and the stars,
In the heavens you have made
them bright, precious and fair.

Praised be You, my Lord, through Brothers
Wind and Air,
And fair and stormy, all weather's moods,
by which You cherish all that You have made.

Praised be You my Lord through Sister Water,
So useful, humble, precious and pure.

Praised be You my Lord through Brother Fire,
through whom You light the night and he is
beautiful and playful and robust and strong.

Praised be You my Lord through our Sister,
Mother Earth
who sustains and governs us,
producing varied fruits with colored flowers
and herbs.
Praise be You my Lord through
those who grant pardon for love of
You and bear sickness and trial.

Blessed are those who endure in peace,
By You Most High, they will be crowned.

Praised be You, my Lord through Sister
Death,
from whom no-one living can escape. Woe
to those who die in mortal sin! Blessed
are they She finds doing Your Will.

No second death can do them harm. Praise
and bless my Lord and give Him thanks,
And serve Him with great humility.

1. To whom alone does St. Francis give all praise, glory, honor, and blessing? What reason does he give for doing this?
2. The rest of the prayer is a litany, or a series of petitions or prayers, praising God for the things He has made. One by one, St. Francis praises God for a "brother" or a "sister" in creation. Re-read the prayer and list all of the "brothers" and "sisters" for whom St. Francis gives praise to God. Why do you think St. Francis describes these things of nature as "brother" and "sister"?
3. What else might you add to this list of things to praise God for that which He has made?

# Straight to the Source

ADDITIONAL READINGS FROM PRIMARY SOURCES

### *Fides et Ratio* 17—An encyclical letter of Pope St. John Paul II, September 14, 1998

In their respective worlds, God and the human being are set within a unique relationship. In God there lies the origin of all things, in him is found the fullness of the mystery, and in this his glory consists; to men and women there falls the task of exploring truth with their reason, and in this their nobility consists. The Psalmist adds one final piece to this mosaic when he says in prayer: "How deep to me are your thoughts, O God! How vast is the sum of them! If I try to count them, they are more than the sand. If I come to the end, I am still with you" (139:17-18). The desire for knowledge is so great and it works in such a way that the human heart, despite its experience of insurmountable limitation, yearns for the infinite riches which lie beyond, knowing that there is to be found the satisfying answer to every question as yet unanswered.

1. What is the unique relationship between God and man that Pope St. John Paul II describes?
2. The author of **Psalm 139** writes, **"How deep to me are your thoughts, O God! ... If I try to count them, they are more than the sand."** Is it a comforting thought to know that while we are capable of knowing God, we will never exhaust, or come to the end of all there is to know about Him? Why or why not? How is this similar to what it is like to know your best friend, a boyfriend or girlfriend, or a spouse?

### Excerpt from the General Audience of Pope Benedict XVI, February 6, 2013

With the solemn presentation of the divine work of creation that unfolded over seven days, the first chapter of Genesis in particular occupies a special place. God brought the creation to completion in six days and on the seventh, the sabbath, he did not do anything, but rested: a day of freedom for all, a day of communion with God. Thus, with this image the Book of Genesis tells us that God's first thought was to find a love that would correspond to his love.

Then his second thought was to create a material world in which to place this love, these creatures who respond to him in freedom. This structure therefore results in the text being marked by certain meaningful repetitions. For example, the sentence "God saw that it was good," is repeated six times (vv. 4, 10, 12, 18, 21, 25) and to conclude, the seventh time, after the creation of man: "God saw everything that he had made, and behold, it was very good" (v. 31). Everything that God creates is beautiful and good, steeped in wisdom and love; God's creative action brings order, instills harmony and bestows beauty.

In the narrative of Genesis, therefore, it becomes clear that the Lord created with his word: ten times we read in the text the phrase: "God said" (vv. 3, 6, 9, 11, 14, 20, 24, 26, 28, 29). It is the Word, the Logos of God who is at the origin of the reality of the world, and saying: "God said", it was so, emphasizes the effective power of the divine Word. This is what the Psalmist sings: "By the word of the Lord the heavens were made, and all their host by the breath of his mouth.... For he spoke, and it came to be, he commanded and it stood forth" (33[32]:6, 9). Life springs forth, the world exists, because all things obey the divine Word.

# Straight to the Source

ADDITIONAL READINGS FROM PRIMARY SOURCES

> However our question today is: in the age of science and technology does speaking of creation still make sense? How should we understand the narratives in Genesis? The Bible does not intend to be a natural science manual; rather, it wishes to make the authentic and profound truth of things understood. The fundamental truth that the accounts of Genesis reveal to us is that the world is not a collection of forces that clash with each other; it has its origin and its permanence in the Logos, in God's eternal Reason which continues to sustain the universe.
>
> A plan of the world exists which is conceived by this Reason, by the Creator Spirit. To believe that this is the foundation of all things illuminates every aspect of existence and gives us the courage to face the adventure of life with trust and hope. Therefore, Scripture tells us that the origin of being, of the world, our own origin is not in the irrational or in need, but rather in reason and love and freedom. Consequently, there is this alternative: either the priority of the irrational, of necessity, or the priority of reason, of freedom, of love. We believe in the latter hypothesis.

1. According to Pope Benedict XVI, what does the book of Genesis reveal were God's two thoughts were when He created the world? What do these thoughts tell us about the created world around us?

2. How does the pope argue that it still makes sense in our modern world to speak of creation in this way? Do you agree or disagree with his argument? Why?

Chapter 3

# Divine Revelation

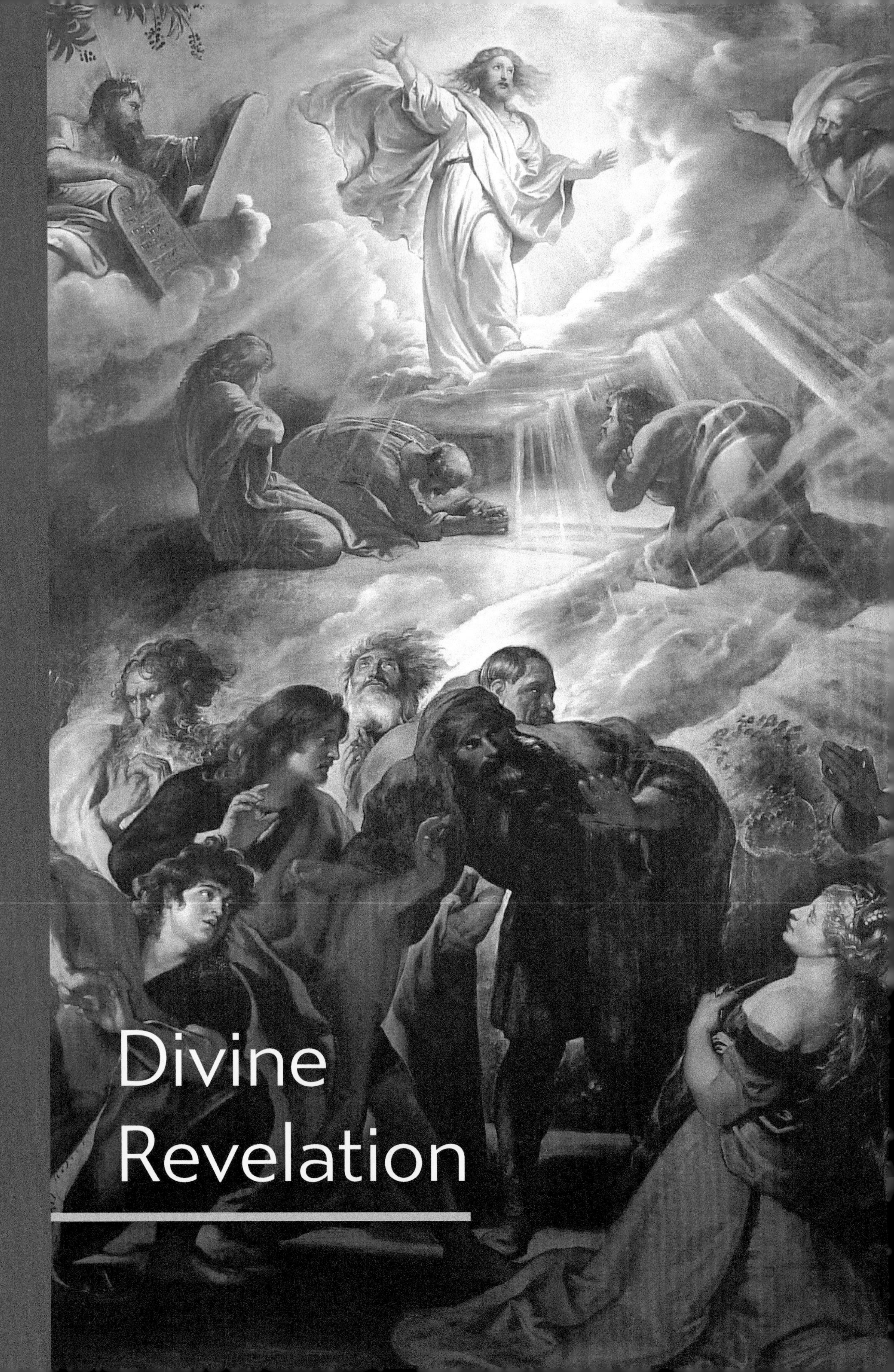

# Chapter Overview

We are capable of knowing with certainty that God exists. We use human reason to know Him from creation. But, there are some things about God, His life, and His will for us, that we could only know if He revealed them to us. And He does! God does not want us just to know that He exists. He wants us to actually *know* Him and be in relationship with Him. So, from the very beginning of human history, God has made Himself known to us in a direct way. We call this divine revelation. After the Fall of Adam and Eve, God called upon Abraham and made three great promises to him that would be handed on through the centuries to His Chosen People. We learn about how God revealed Himself in words and deeds and prepared His People to receive the gift of salvation through the stories of Abraham, Isaac, Jacob, Moses, David, and the prophets, finally culminating in the coming of God's Son, Jesus Christ.

## In this chapter you will learn that …

- God has revealed Himself to us in a direct and personal way; we call this divine revelation.
- God's revelation of Himself occurred in human history.
- God entered into covenants with His Chosen People over the centuries to make Himself known and to prepare them to receive the gift of salvation.
- Divine revelation culminates in the coming of God's Son, Jesus Christ, who is the fullness of God's revelation because He does not just speak about God, but is God Himself.
- Jesus fulfills all the promises of the Old Testament covenants and the prophecies of the prophets and wisdom literature.

### Bible Basics

"You will be to me a kingdom of priests, a holy nation."
EXODUS 19:6

But when the fullness of time had come, God sent his Son, born of a woman, born under the law, to ransom those under the law, so that we might receive adoption. As proof that you are children, God sent the spirit of his Son into our hearts, crying out, "Abba, Father!" So you are no longer a slave but a child, and if a child then also an heir, through God.
GALATIANS 4:4–7

### Connections to the *Catechism*

CCC 60 (page 35)
CCC 62 (page 36)
CCC 64 (page 38)
CCC 523 (page 40)
CCC 2585 (page 40)

## Divine Revelation

To look at the world and know God exists is a wonderful gift. But it is not enough. To know someone exists is not the same as knowing them. It is not the same as loving them, understanding them, and being close to them. God does not want us to simply know that He exists. He wants us to know *Him*. He wants us to be in a relationship with Him. Because of this, God has revealed Himself to us in a personal and intimate way. He also has shown us the plan of salvation by which we can experience a deep friendship with Him. This self-communication of God is called divine revelation.

Aa **Vocabulary**

**Covenant (n.):** A sacred permanent bond of family relationship.

**Israel (n.):** Hebrew word meaning "He who strives with God." God changed Jacob's name to Israel after he wrestled with an angel. God's Chosen People became known as the People of Israel.

## God Reveals Himself in History

### *Abraham, Isaac, and Jacob*

The Bible tells the story of how God revealed Himself and His plan of salvation to us. In the Old Testament, we learn that after the sin of Adam and Eve, God did not abandon humanity, but sought to re-establish friendship with us by forming for Himself a holy people, Israel. Through Israel, God would make Himself known and send His Son to bring salvation to all the world.

The story of Israel began with Abram. God called Abram to leave his home country and go to the land of Canaan, where He promised that Abram would be blessed with many descendants who would become a great nation, that great kings would descend from him, and that his descendants would bless the world (Gen. 12:1–9). Later, God made a **covenant** with Abram and gave him the name "Abraham," which means **"the father of a multitude of nations" (Gen. 17:5)**.

Although God had promised Abraham and his wife, Sarah, that they would have a child, many years passed after that promise was made and through all those years, no child came. The older the couple grew the more impossible it seemed that God could fulfill His promise. But nothing is impossible for God, and even though both Abraham and Sarah were well past child-bearing age, God eventually gave them their son. They named him "Isaac," which means, "he laughs" (Abraham had laughed when God told him Sarah would have a child).

Isaac grew up and became a shepherd. He then married Rebecca, who was the mother of the twins Jacob and Esau. Jacob was the younger of the twins, but with his mother's help, he cheated his brother Esau out of his inheritance (Gen. 33:1–17). God later changed Jacob's name to "**Israel**," meaning "one who strives with God," after Jacob encountered an angel and wrestled with him (Gen. 32:22–32; 35:10).

God's promise to Abraham—that his descendants would become a great nation led by even greater kings—was passed on to Isaac and then

*Jacob Wrestling with the Angel* by Bartholomeus Breenbergh (1639).

▲ After Jacob wrestled with the angel of God he received the new name "Israel", which means "one who strives with God."

to Jacob and then to Jacob's twelve sons, who would become the fathers of twelve tribes that made up the nation of Israel. Abraham, Isaac, and Jacob are called the **Patriarchs**. They are the fathers of the people of Israel. Likewise, because of Abraham's faith in God, he is called the **"father of all the uncircumcised who believe" (Rom. 4:11)**. **"The people descended from Abraham would be the trustees of the promise made to the patriarchs, the chosen people, called to prepare for that day when God would gather all his children into the unity of the Church. They would be the root onto which the Gentiles would be grafted, once they came to believe," (CCC 60).**

Aa **Vocabulary**

**Patriarchs (n.):** The fathers of the People of Israel: Abraham, Isaac, and Jacob.

### *Moses, David, and the Divided Kingdom*

Late in Jacob/Israel's life, a famine forced him, his sons, and their families to leave Canaan and settle in Egypt. Over several generations, their descendants (who came to be known as "the Hebrews" or "Israelites") multiplied. Fearing that the Israelites were becoming too powerful, the Egyptians enslaved them and treated them cruelly. However, in the Book of Exodus, God intervenes. With the help of Moses—an Israelite raised by the Egyptian Pharaoh's daughter—God freed His people from slavery, made a new covenant with them, and promised to lead all twelve tribes back to the promised land of Canaan.

After Moses led God's people out of Egypt, God continued to shape Israel through Moses' leadership. Through Moses, God revealed His name (Ex. 3:13–15), shared his plan of salvation, and gave the Law to Israel. The Law was intended to govern both the Israelites' society and worship, making them into a **"kingdom of priests, a holy nation" (Ex. 19:6)**. Unfortunately, not long after God made His covenant with Israel, the people rebelled. In response, God gave them a new, more stringent Law, which is outlined in the Book of Leviticus.

After receiving this new Law, the Israelites completed their journey to Canaan. However, when they arrived at the Promised Land, the people were too afraid to enter. New inhabitants had taken over their ancestral home, and they did not trust God's promise to take care of them. As punishment, God condemned the Israelites to wander in the desert for forty years. During this time, Moses served them as a great law-giver, judge, and prophet, repeatedly interceding with God for them when they sinned. **"After the patriarchs, God formed Israel as his people by freeing them from slavery in Egypt. He established with them the covenant**

*King David Playing the Harp* by Gerard van Hornthorst (1622).

God promised king David that one of his descendants would sit upon the royal throne forever, and his kingdom would be everlasting.

**of Mount Sinai and, through Moses, gave them his law so that they would recognize him and serve him as the one living and true God, the provident Father and just judge, and so that they would look for the promised Savior," (CCC 62).**

The story from Creation to the Exodus is contained in the first five books of the Old Testament, which are called the **Pentateuch** or Torah. After the Pentateuch, the historical books tell the story of the settlement of the land of Canaan and the development of the Kingdom of Israel under Saul and David. By the time David becomes king, it seemed as if all God's promises to Abraham had been fulfilled: Abraham's descendants resided in the Promised Land; they had become a great nation; and a great king ruled over them.

However, not long after God put David on the throne, He made another promise, which was that a descendent of David would sit on his throne forever: **"[W]hen your days have been completed and you rest with your ancestors, I will raise up your offspring after you, sprung from your loins, and I will establish his kingdom. He it is who shall build a house for my name, and I will establish his royal throne forever" (2 Sam. 7:12–13)**.

God always keeps His promises, but to the ancient Israelites, it almost seemed like He did not keep that one. Shortly after the time of David, the kingdom fell into sin. The kings worshipped other gods, and the kingdom split into two. The Kingdom of Israel was in the north and was centered in Samaria. The Kingdom of Judah was in the south and was centered in Jerusalem. Only Judah was ruled by the descendants of David; the northern kingdom was ruled by a series of pretender kings, most of them wicked.

As the years passed, the two kingdoms wandered further and further away from God. The more they sinned and forgot about their covenant with God, the more they declined until they were conquered by Assyria and Babylon. Their kings were killed, their cities destroyed, and the people taken into exile. By the sixth century B.C., the descendants of David no longer ruled in Jerusalem, and the temple built for God by David's son Solomon had been destroyed.

### *The Prophets and Wisdom Literature*

During this time of decline and exile, prophets emerged in Israel and Judah. At first, before the kingdoms fell, the prophets called the kings and people to repent from idolatry, oppression, and other sins that violated their covenant with God. They warned people of the coming ruin, but no one listened and ruin came. However, in the wake of the kingdoms' collapse, the prophets' message somewhat changed.

**Aa Vocabulary**

**Pentateuch (n.):** The Greek name for the first five books of the Old Testament: Genesis, Exodus, Leviticus, Numbers, and Deuteronomy. Also known as the Books of Moses.

**[The prophets] proclaimed that God had not abandoned Israel or forgotten His promises.**

In addition to calls for repentance, they also had words of hope for God's people. They proclaimed that God had not abandoned Israel or forgotten His promises. In fact, they announced that not only would God end their exile and rebuild Jerusalem and the temple, but He would bring about an even greater redemption: a new covenant and a New Law written not on stone but upon human hearts (Jer. 31:33). With this new covenant, all nations would turn to the God of Israel (Is. 2:2–4) and He would fulfill the promise He made to David, that a descendant of David, a "prince of peace," would reign forever (Is. 9:5–7). The prophets referred to this descendant as the Messiah.

> **"Through the prophets, God forms his people in the hope of salvation, in the expectation of a new and everlasting Covenant intended for all, to be written on their hearts. The prophets proclaim a radical redemption of the People of God, purification from all their infidelities, a salvation which will include all the nations. Above all, the poor and humble of the Lord will bear this hope. Such holy women as Sarah, Rebecca, Rachel, Miriam, Deborah, Hannah, Judith, and Esther kept alive the hope of Israel's salvation. The purest figure among them is Mary," (CCC 64).**

In addition to the Pentateuch, historical books and Prophets, the Old Testament contains the wisdom literature—the books of Job, Psalms, Proverbs, Ecclesiastes, Song of Songs, Wisdom and Sirach. These books—especially Proverbs, Wisdom, and Sirach—are concerned with the pursuit of wisdom, telling us, **"The beginning of Wisdom is fear of the Lord" (Prov. 9:10)**. The wisdom literature contains a variety of writing styles, including poetry.

Throughout the history of Israel, the prophets called the People of God to repentance.

*The Flight of the Prisoners* by James Tissot (between 1896 and 1902).

### Lives of Faith

## St. Faustina

Maureen was not sure if she should believe what she had just heard. She looked around. There were a few others in the church, but none of them seemed to be paying attention to her.

She turned her head and gazed at the small altar in front of her. It was the tomb of Sr. Faustina, and next to it the beautiful painting which Sr. Faustina had shared with the world: Jesus, clothed in white robes, touching the place over his heart where red and white rays of light shone forth. And at the bottom the words, "Jesus, I trust in You."

Maureen had been praying at the tomb thinking about those words when she heard the voice: "Ask for my help and I will help you."

Maureen had come on this trip to pray for healing. It seemed like the only thing left to do. Doctors had performed ten different surgeries and even amputated part of her leg to try to cure the lymphedema that caused her so much pain. They told her there was nothing left to do.

So here she was asking for healing and mercy. And miraculously, the pain was gone.

The healing of Maureen Digan was the first confirmed miracle attributed to Sr. Faustina and paved the way for her to be canonized a Saint.

Born in Poland in 1905, St. Maria Faustina Kowalska of the Blessed Sacrament was a nun who experienced visions of Jesus throughout her life. She first felt the call and desire to be a nun at the age of seven, and desired to enter into the convent immediately after finishing school at 16. But being from a poor family, she had to work as a housekeeper to help make ends meet. However, by 20 she had saved enough money to buy her own habit and entered the convent.

**Jesus appeared to St. Faustina to share with her His message of Divine Mercy.**

Jesus appeared to St. Faustina to share with her His message of Divine Mercy. The Divine Mercy image—described above—is now one of the most famous images of Jesus throughout the world, and represents the overall message of Divine Mercy, namely that Jesus, in all His power and might, desires to have mercy on us.

Under the guidance of her spiritual director, St. Faustina had the Divine Mercy image painted according to Jesus' instructions. He also gave her instructions for praying the Divine Mercy chaplet and for sharing the message of Divine Mercy with the whole world.

Her spiritual director instructed St. Faustina to begin keeping a diary of all her visions of Jesus. Today, this diary is a handbook for devotion to Jesus' Divine Mercy.

St. Faustina was ill throughout her life and died at only 33 years old. Despite her early death, she was chosen to share Jesus' message of Divine Mercy, and it is thanks to her that this message spread to the whole world.

*Appearance of Christ to the People* by Alexander Andreyevich Ivanov (between 1837 and 1857).

▲ John the Baptist was the last of the Old Testament prophets, for Christ, the Messiah, came during his lifetime.

The Book of Psalms contains songs used in the worship of ancient Israel and is **"the masterwork of prayer in the Old Testament" (CCC 2585).** The tradition of the integration of the Psalms into public worship and prayer was carried over into the life of the Church from apostolic times. The praying or singing of the Psalms continues in the Church's worship today, especially in the Liturgy of the Hours, and in the Liturgy of the Word, which is an integral part of the celebration of the sacraments (CCC 1154).

The Old Testament leaves us with the image of God as a loving Father whose patience and guidance of His people was constant, yet not without frustration. Time and again in the Old Testament, God's people went astray. Yet, even as most wandered, a "faithful remnant" soldiered on (see Jer. 23:3, 50:20). As the years passed, this faithful remnant longed for the Messiah promised by the prophets. They believed He would restore the faith of Israel by gathering the tribes into unity, restoring and refreshing the Law, cleansing the temple, and removing every obstacle in the way of union with God.

### *The New Testament*

John the Baptist bridges the gap between the Old Testament and the New Testament.

> **"St. John the Baptist is the Lord's immediate precursor or forerunner, sent to prepare his way. 'Prophet of the Most High,' John surpasses all the prophets, of whom he is the last. He inaugurates the Gospel, already from his mother's womb welcomes the coming of Christ, and rejoices in being 'the friend**

**of the bridegroom,' whom he points out as 'the Lamb of God, who takes away the sin of the world.' Going before Jesus 'in the spirit and power of Elijah,' John bears witness to Christ in his preaching, by his Baptism of conversion, and through his martyrdom," (CCC 523).**

John can be called the last of the Old Testament prophets because he recalls all the Old Testament promises and identifies them with Jesus. Even from the womb, he leapt for joy at the coming of Jesus and was filled with the Holy Spirit. Jesus identified John with the prophet Elijah, who would be the forerunner of the Messiah (Mt. 17:10–13). Through John, the Holy Spirit completed the preparation of Israel for the coming of Jesus. But, as Jesus said, John is even **"more than a prophet" (Lk. 7:26)** because he completed the search of the prophets for the consolation of Israel. He proclaimed the coming of the Messiah and foretold the coming of the Holy Spirit, while his baptism of repentance prefigured the rebirth made possible by the Sacrament of Baptism (CCC 717–720).

### *Jesus Christ: The Fullness of God's Revelation*

**"But when the fullness of time had come, God sent his Son, born of a woman, born under the law, to ransom those under the law, so that we might receive adoption. As proof that you are children, God sent the spirit of his Son into our hearts, crying out, "Abba, Father!" So you are no longer a slave but a child, and if a child then also an heir, through God" (Gal. 4:4–7)**.

The revelation of God through Jesus Christ fulfills all the promises and prophecies of the Old Testament covenants, the patriarchs, the prophets, and wisdom literature. Jesus is the Messiah, the Son of David, and the Prince of Peace. He is, in effect, the summation of all the Scriptures, because, as Hugh of St. Victor states, "all divine Scripture speaks of Christ, and all divine Scripture is fulfilled in Christ" (as quoted in *Verbum Domini* 39). Jesus provides us with more than just information about God; He is God Himself, and through Him, we have intimate, personal knowledge of God. We also have supernatural knowledge.

**The revelation of God through Jesus Christ fulfills all the promises and prophecies of the Old Testament.**

In Jesus Christ, God has fully revealed Himself and provided everything necessary for us to be redeemed and become His adopted sons and daughters (Gal. 4:5). Revelation is complete with Jesus, so there can be no further public revelation that would surpass or correct what God has revealed in Him. Nonetheless, the full significance of revelation becomes more completely understood as the Church reflects on it in faith through the centuries. As part of this, every Christian in every age is called to prayerfully contemplate the mystery revealed in Christ (CCC 66).

# The Truth Is...

God loves you. He wants to tell you about how much He loves you. And He wants you to know how much you are loved. In our modern world, we think of love as a feeling or an emotion. It is something that we fall into, as if we suddenly and blindly step off a cliff. To be sure, as human beings we do have strong feelings of affection for other people, and for things, such as pizza, TV shows, and a new pair of shoes. But this kind of love comes and goes. Just as quickly as we fall into love with someone or something, we can fall out of it. That is just the way feelings work.

The kind of love described above is not how God loves you. His love is who He is. His love is an action. His love is a love that gives solely and unconditionally for your own happiness and fulfillment. His is a love that desires to be with you and to share life with you. And His love is a love that will never go away. How do we know? We know because God has told us. He has made Himself and His love known to us from the very beginning of human history. He continued to make Himself and His love known from those earliest days, throughout the centuries, in big ways and in small, in words and deeds, and in the greatest, self-giving sacrifice of all—the life, suffering, Death, and Resurrection of His Son, Jesus Christ. God loves you and He wants you to know He loves you. All you need to do is open your heart to be loved by Him.

Chapter 3

# Focus and Reflection Questions

1. What is divine revelation? What has He shown us through divine revelation?

2. What do we learn in the Old Testament that God did after the Fall of Adam and Eve?

3. What three things did God promise to Abram (Abraham)?

4. What does the name Israel mean? Why did God change Jacob's name to Israel?

5. Who were the Twelve Tribes of Israel?

6. What was the purpose of the Law that God gave to Israel through Moses?

7. What did God promise to David?

8. What did the prophets proclaim to the people before the fall of the kingdoms? Along with those things, what did they proclaim after the fall of the kingdoms?

9. How is the praying of the Psalms continued in the Church today?

10. How does John the Baptist bridge the gap from the Old Testament to the New Testament?

11. How is the revelation of God through His Son Jesus Christ a summation of all the Scriptures?

12. Why is it true that divine revelation is complete in Jesus Christ? What has been the Church's relationship to divine revelation throughout the ages since the time of Jesus?

13. Jesus shared His message of Divine Mercy with St. Faustina. How do you see Jesus' Divine Mercy present in the story of divine revelation?

# Straight to the Source

ADDITIONAL READINGS FROM PRIMARY SOURCES

*For chapter 3, rather than the usual variety of selections from primary sources, we will look at in close detail the official and dogmatic teaching of the Catholic Church regarding divine revelation that is found in the Vatican II document* Dei Verbum. *You will read all of* Dei Verbum *in this course.*

### *Dei Verbum* 2, 5–6—The Dogmatic Constitution on Divine Revelation from the Second Vatican Council, November 18, 1968

2. In His goodness and wisdom God chose to reveal Himself and to make known to us the hidden purpose of His will (see Eph. 1:9) by which through Christ, the Word made flesh, man might in the Holy Spirit have access to the Father and come to share in the divine nature (see Eph. 2:18; 2 Peter 1:4). Through this revelation, therefore, the invisible God (see Col. 1;15, 1 Tim. 1:17) out of the abundance of His love speaks to men as friends (see Ex. 33:11; John 15:14–15) and lives among them (see Bar. 3:38), so that He may invite and take them into fellowship with Himself. This plan of revelation is realized by deeds and words having an inner unity: the deeds wrought by God in the history of salvation manifest and confirm the teaching and realities signified by the words, while the words proclaim the deeds and clarify the mystery contained in them. By this revelation then, the deepest truth about God and the salvation of man shines out for our sake in Christ, who is both the mediator and the fullness of all revelation.

5. "The obedience of faith" (Rom. 16:26; see 1:5; 2 Cor 10:5–6) "is to be given to God who reveals, an obedience by which man commits his whole self freely to God, offering the full submission of intellect and will to God who reveals," and freely assenting to the truth revealed by Him. To make this act of faith, the grace of God and the interior help of the Holy Spirit must precede and assist, moving the heart and turning it to God, opening the eyes of the mind and giving "joy and ease to everyone in assenting to the truth and believing it." To bring about an ever deeper understanding of revelation the same Holy Spirit constantly brings faith to completion by His gifts.

6. Through divine revelation, God chose to show forth and communicate Himself and the eternal decisions of His will regarding the salvation of men. That is to say, He chose to share with them those divine treasures which totally transcend the understanding of the human mind.

   As a sacred synod has affirmed, God, the beginning and end of all things, can be known with certainty from created reality by the light of human reason (see Rom. 1:20); but teaches that it is through His revelation that those religious truths which are by their nature accessible to human reason can be known by all men with ease, with solid certitude and with no trace of error, even in this present state of the human race.

# Straight to the Source

ADDITIONAL READINGS FROM PRIMARY SOURCES

## Focus Questions

1. What does God do in His goodness and wisdom?
2. Why does God speak to men as friends and live among us?
3. How is God's plan of revelation realized?
4. What is the relationship between God's words and deeds?
5. Who is the mediator and fullness of all revelation?
6. What is the Obedience of Faith?
7. What is needed to make the Obedience of Faith?
8. What did God choose to do?
9. How can God be known with certainty?
10. What does God's divine revelation reveal to us?

## Reflection Question

Given what you have learned about divine revelation in this chapter and from this reading from *Dei Verbum*, why do you think it is so important that God has revealed Himself to us in a direct way?

Chapter 4

# The Transmission of Divine Revelation

# Chapter Overview

Divine revelation is handed on to each generation through Sacred Scripture and Sacred Tradition. Together they form one single Deposit of Faith. The teaching authority of the Church, or the Magisterium, is exercised by all of the world's bishops in union with the pope. Together they guard and protect this sacred deposit and interprets it in the name of Jesus Christ. The Truths of our Faith were given to the Apostles by Jesus Himself through His life and teaching. These Truths have faithfully been handed on through the generations from the Apostles to their successors the bishops. This process has been faithfully continued through today in an unending apostolic succession that will continue until the end of time.

## In this chapter you will learn that …

- The full content of divine revelation is found in the Deposit of Faith, which is the body of Truth about Jesus Christ, passed down through the generations.
- We come to know divine revelation from both Sacred Scripture and Sacred Tradition.
- While different, Sacred Scripture and Sacred Tradition work together and share the same original source, Jesus Himself through the teachings of the Apostles.
- The Apostles were commissioned by Jesus Himself to teach and write down what would become Sacred Scripture, as well as to pass down Sacred Tradition through the succession of popes and bishops.
- We trust the Magisterium, or the teaching authority of the pope and all of the world's bishops in union with pope, to guide us in understanding sacred truth.
- Sacred Scripture, Sacred Tradition and the Magisterium are each essential to the transmission of divine revelation.

### Bible Basics

Then Jesus approached and said to them, "All power in heaven and on earth has been given to me. Go, therefore, and make disciples of all nations, baptizing them in the name of the Father, and of the Son, and of the holy Spirit, teaching them to observe all that I have commanded you. And behold, I am with you always, until the end of the age."
MATTHEW 28:18–20

Therefore, brothers, stand firm and hold fast to the traditions that you were taught, either by an oral statement or by a letter of ours…
2 THESSALONIANS 2:15

### Connections to the *Catechism*

CCC 80 (page 48)
CCC 85 (page 51)
CCC 86 (page 51)
CCC 91 (page 52)
CCC 92 (page 52)
CCC 93 (page 52)

## Vocabulary

**Sacred Tradition (n.):** The living transmission of the Gospel message in the Church.

**Deposit of Faith (n.):** The full content of divine revelation communicated by Christ, contained in Sacred Scripture and Sacred Tradition, handed on in the Church from the time of the Apostles, and from which the Magisterium draws all that it proposes for belief as being divinely revealed.

## The Transmission of Divine Revelation

In Jesus, humanity has met God Himself. However, this revelation, has not just remained in the past. The Church teaches that divine revelation is transmitted to each generation through Sacred Scripture and **Sacred Tradition**. To understand what this means, we need to go back to Jesus' commissioning of His Apostles to spread the Gospel to all nations.

Jesus commanded His Apostles to preach the Gospel. He sent them to teach all they had seen, all He had told them, and all the Holy Spirit would reveal to them. In short, He sent them to preach the full content of divine revelation (Mt. 28:19–20, Mk. 16:15–16, Lk. 24:46–49). This content is called the **Deposit of Faith** and is found in Sacred Tradition and Sacred Scripture as handed on by the Apostles which they themselves received from Christ. **"Sacred Tradition and Sacred Scripture, then, are bound more closely together and communicate one with the other. For both of them, flowing out from the same divine well-spring, come together in some fashion to form one thing and move towards the same goal" (CCC 80).** Like two rivers flowing from the same source, Scripture and Tradition form this Deposit of Faith.

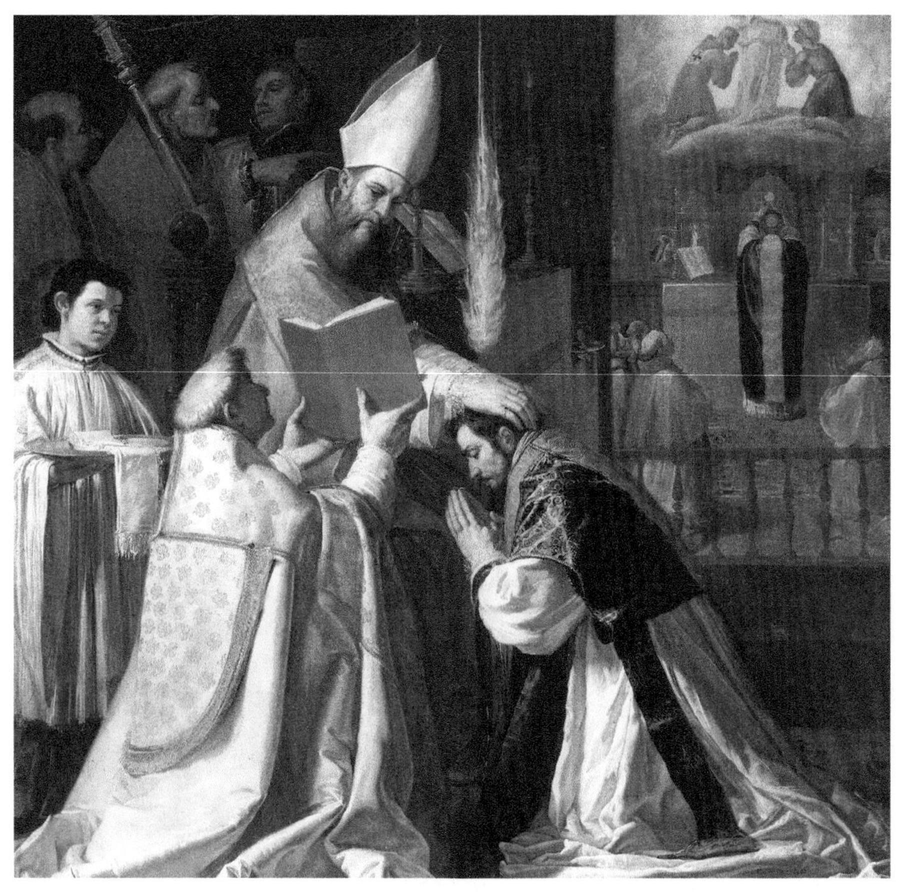

Priestly ordination is a Sacrament and Sacred Tradition of the Holy Catholic Church that has been preserved and transmitted since Christ Himself made His Apostles the first priests.

*Ordination and First Mass of St. John of Mata* by Vincente Carducho (ca. 1635).

The Deposit of Faith was first transmitted to the faithful by the Apostles' preaching, along with the institutions they built and the worship they established. This is normally referred to as the "oral tradition." Some of this oral tradition was quickly written down, either by the Apostles or by men associated with them, under the inspiration of the Holy Spirit. These writings would eventually come to be the New Testament of the Bible (CCC 76).

However, the preaching of the Apostles, was not replaced by Scripture. Rather, Scripture grew out of this preaching and complemented it. The preaching itself continued as Sacred Tradition. This Tradition continued past the age of the Apostles through **apostolic succession**. The Apostles left **bishops** as their successors, who themselves have continued to pass the office from generation to generation. Led by St. Peter's successor, the **pope**, the bishops continue to preach the Gospel in its entirety, just as the Apostles did.

Thus, the Deposit of Faith is handed on from one generation to the next, not through Scripture alone, but also through Sacred Tradition — the living transmission of divine revelation in the doctrine, life, and worship of the Church. Remember that Jesus Himself is the fullness of divine revelation, so the transmission of the Deposit of Faith is not just a matter of handing down a list of teachings and traditions, but of communicating Christ himself. It is one way Jesus fulfills His promise to be with us until the end of the age (Matt. 28:20; CCC 78–79).

Scripture and Tradition are distinct, but also closely connected. In the life of the Church, they work together. They have the same source: the teaching of Christ communicated through the preaching of the Apostles. Together they transmit the same thing: the Deposit of Faith, which was entrusted to the Apostles by Jesus. They also have the same goal, which is communicating God's revelation of Himself in Jesus to every generation. Both are essential: "Therefore both sacred tradition and Sacred Scripture are to be accepted and venerated with the same sense of loyalty and reverence" (DV 9).

### *The Magisterium*

Because Scripture is not easy to interpret or understand, God has entrusted the interpretation of His Word to the teaching authority of the Church, what we call the ***Magisterium***. The Magisterium is comprised of all the bishops in the world in communion with the pope as together they teach on any truth pertaining to faith or morals — any truth God has revealed for our salvation in Jesus Christ. The Magisterium is not the authority on other areas of truth—such as physics, psychology, or economics, for example,

#### Aa Vocabulary

**Apostolic Succession (n.):** The handing on of apostolic preaching and authority from the Apostles to their successors, the bishops, through the laying on of hands, as a permanent office in the Church.

**Bishop (n.):** A successor to the Apostles, who has received the fullness of the Sacrament of Holy Orders. He is the leader of a particular church, or diocese, entrusted to him.

**Pope (n.):** The successor of St. Peter as bishop of Rome and Supreme Pontiff of the universal Catholic Church. The pope exercises a primacy of authority as the vicar of Christ on earth and the shepherd of the whole Church.

**Magisterium (n.):** The living teaching authority of the Catholic Church whose task it is to give authentic interpretation of the Word of God found in Scripture and Tradition, and to ensure the faithfulness of the Church to the teachings of the Apostles in matters of faith and morals. This authority is exercised by all of the world's bishops in union with the pope, and by the pope alone when he defines infallibly a doctrine of faith or morals.

## Lives of Faith

# Pope St. John XXIII

Who do you think has had the greatest impact on the Church in the modern world?

You might say St. Teresa of Calcutta. She started a global movement in service of the poor, gained international fame, and won a Nobel Peace Prize for her work.

You might say Pope St. John Paul II. He changed the way we take the Faith out into the world, became a catalyst for the young people in the Church, and is known as the most photographed man in human history because of his worldwide travels and popularity.

Perhaps you would say Pope Francis. He has gained worldwide attention since being elected Pope in 2013, reemphasized the Church's compassion for the poor and the marginalized, and has changed the way the world views the papacy.

While all of these names are debatable, there is a lesser-known name that might beat out all three: Pope St. John XXIII.

Born as Angelo Giuseppe Roncalli on November 25, 1881 in Lombardy, Italy, Pope St. John XXIII came from humble beginnings. He was the fourth of fourteen children in a very poor family of sharecroppers. At fifteen he was enrolled in seminary, and by 23 he had earned his doctorate in Canon Law and was ordained a priest.

Over the next fifty years, Roncalli assumed various positions of importance in the Church, eventually become a Cardinal and Patriarch of Venice.

He was elected pope on November 4, 1958, choosing the name John. Many believed he would be a sort of "short-term" Pope because of his age. They did not expect him to have much of an impact. They could not have been more wrong.

He immediately started doing things differently. He was the first pope in nearly 100 years to visit the local hospitals, homeless shelters, and prisons around Rome. He gained international acclaim when he offered to broker peace talks between the United States and Russia during the height of the Cold War. He called for reconciliation between the Catholic Church and different Christian and non-Christian groups, and even asked for forgiveness for times he believed the Church had mistakenly persecuted people in the past.

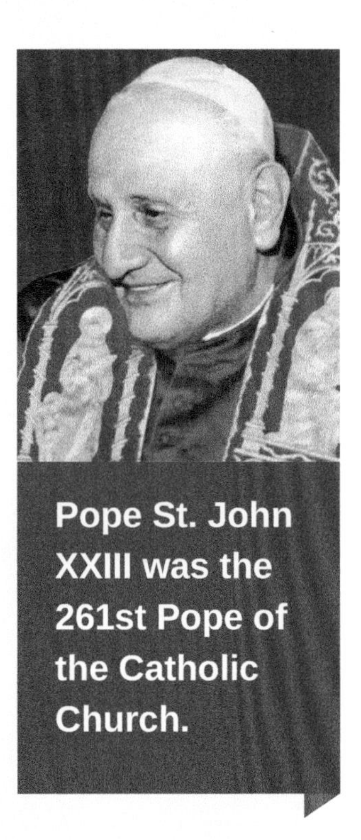

**Pope St. John XXIII was the 261st Pope of the Catholic Church.**

As Pope, John XXIII clarified or re-enforced important moral teachings of the Church. He articulated the Church's position on contraceptives, was an advocate for the unborn and the elderly and strengthened the Church's teachings on human rights. And he emphasized the importance of the family in society in response to rising divorce rates.

But his most pivotal act was calling for the ecumenical council known as Vatican II. In doing so, Pope St. John XXIII encouraged the Church to see the signs of the times and usher the Church into the modern age. "I want to throw open the windows of the church so that we can see out and the people can see in," he said. The Second Vatican Council would bring about profound changes that reformed the way people saw Catholicism and the way we celebrate our Faith.

On June 3, 1963 Pope St. John XXIII died from complications from stomach cancer at the age of 81. His four years and seven months as Pope changed the Church forever by helping it encounter the modern world in new ways.

but only those truths comprised by the faith of the Church — as God has revealed them to His People. On matters of Christian faith, when the Magisterium teaches, it does so **infallibly**, or without error.

The *Catechism* explains it like this:

> **"The task of giving an authentic interpretation of the Word of God, whether in its written form or in the form of Tradition, has been entrusted to the living teaching office of the Church alone. Its authority in this matter is exercised in the name of Jesus Christ. This means that the task of interpretation has been entrusted to the bishops in communion with the successor of Peter, the Bishop of Rome" (CCC 85).**

However, the Magisterium,

> **"is not superior to the Word of God, but is its servant. It teaches only what has been handed on to it. At the divine command and with the help of the Holy Spirit, it listens to this devotedly, guards it with dedication and expounds it faithfully. All that it proposes for belief as being divinely revealed is drawn from this single deposit of faith" (CCC 86).**

Aa **Vocabulary**

**Infallible (n.):** Incapable of error.

**[The Magisterium] is not superior to the Word of God, but is its servant.**

CCC 85

*Delivery of the Keys* by Pietro Perugino (ca. 1482).

When Christ founded His Catholic Church, He bestowed on Peter explicit authority over the Church in His name.

## Why do Catholics hold doctrines that are not in the Bible?

As we have seen, we hold that both Scripture and Tradition are sources of Catholic doctrine. Therefore, if a doctrine is not explicitly found in Scripture, then it was handed down to us through Sacred Tradition. Importantly, nothing about the Catholic faith which we believe from Tradition contradicts Scripture. Scripture and Tradition form a marriage from which we derive the life-giving teaching of the Church. Scripture confirms Tradition: **"Therefore, brothers, stand firm and hold fast to the traditions that you were taught, either by an oral statement or by a letter of ours" (2 Thess. 2:15)**.

**Aa Vocabulary**

***Sensus Fidei* (n.):**The supernatural appreciation of faith on the part of the whole people of God, when, from the bishops to the last of the faithful, they manifest a universal consent in matters of faith and morals and cannot in such a case err in belief. Latin for "sense of the faithful."

The purpose of the Magisterium is to guard and protect the Deposit of Faith, which has remained whole and intact throughout the centuries because of the faithful work of the bishops and popes.

When we are faithful to the whole of God's Word as it has been passed down, the People of God **"cannot err in matters of belief. This characteristic is shown in the supernatural appreciation of faith (*sensus fidei*) on the part of the whole people, when, from the bishops to the last of the faithful, they manifest a universal consent in matters of faith and morals" (CCC 92).**

As the *Catechism* goes on to state,

> **"[b]y this appreciation of the faith, aroused and sustained by the Spirit of truth, the People of God, guided by the sacred teaching authority (*Magisterium*), ... receives ... the faith, once for all delivered to the saints ... The People unfailingly adheres to this faith, penetrates it more deeply with right judgment, and applies it more fully in daily life" (CCC 93).**

This is the case because all the faithful—those who adhere to the faith in mind and heart—**"have received the anointing of the Holy Spirit, who instructs them and guides them into all truth" (CCC 91).** Consequently, through Baptism, all Christians are called to cultivate their own faith and actively hand on the tradition.

The transmission of divine revelation relies entirely upon all three legs of this metaphorical "stool": Apostolic (Sacred) Tradition, the sacred writings of Scripture, and the teaching Magisterium of the Church. When and if any of these has been jettisoned or ignored, the Christian people have been divided by error and sin. Nevertheless, God continues to provide for His Church by sustaining her indefectibly in the power of the Holy Spirit, as the Word of God continues to be proclaimed to all people in every generation.

# The Truth Is...

Scripture is not all there is. While most non-Catholic Christians believe in the Bible alone—that if it is not in the Bible then it is not part of the Christian Faith—Catholics very much do not. Scripture is the Word of God committed to writing, but it is not alone. The Word of God is also brought to us by Sacred Tradition, the handing on of sacred truths through preaching, teaching, practice, and worship. The Bible itself tells us about the importance of Tradition! The ending of John's Gospel claims that Jesus did and said more than what the Gospel contained and that what is contained in the Gospel is there to help us believe, not that it contains everything we need to believe. St. Paul implores Timothy to hold fast to the traditions he had received. In fact, there are numerous other passages throughout Scripture that pertain to the necessity of Sacred Tradition.

So, what does this mean for you and the average believer? It means we cannot sit in our room, alone, with a Bible, and come to know all of God's revelation of Himself and His saving Truth. It means we need the authoritative teaching of the Church, given to her by Jesus Himself, to help guide us in knowing and putting into practice that Truth in an authentic way. It means we need Scripture, Tradition, and the Magisterium to be sure that divine revelation is the revelation God intended us to know and not an imitation, error ridden, or at worst, completely false.

Chapter 4

# Focus and Reflection Questions

1. What command did Jesus give His Apostles before He ascended in to Heaven?

2. What is the Deposit of Faith?

3. How was the Deposit of Faith first transmitted? What happened next?

4. Which came first, Sacred Scripture or Sacred Tradition?

5. What is apostolic succession?

6. What is the shared goal of Sacred Tradition and Sacred Scripture?

7. What is the Magisterium?

8. On what matters does the Magisterium teach infallibly?

9. What is the purpose of the Magisterium?

10. What is the *sensus fidei*?

11. Imagine a three-legged stool. The three legs of this metaphorical stool are Scripture, Tradition, and the Magisterium. What do these three "legs" support? What would happen if one of these "legs" were missing?

12. What was Pope St. John XXIII's most pivotal act and how was it an example of the working of the Magisterium of the Church?

# Straight to the Source

ADDITIONAL READINGS FROM PRIMARY SOURCES

*For chapter 4, rather than the usual variety of selections from primary sources, we will look in close detail at the official and dogmatic teaching of the Catholic Church regarding divine revelation found in the Vatican II document* Dei Verbum. *You will read all of* Dei Verbum *in this course.*

## *Dei Verbum* 7–10—The Dogmatic Constitution on Divine Revelation from the Second Vatican Council, November 18, 1968

7. In His gracious goodness, God has seen to it that what He had revealed for the salvation of all nations would abide perpetually in its full integrity and be handed on to all generations. Therefore Christ the Lord in whom the full revelation of the supreme God is brought to completion (see 2 Cor. 1:20; 3:13; 4:6), commissioned the Apostles to preach to all men that Gospel which is the source of all saving truth and moral teaching, and to impart to them heavenly gifts. This Gospel had been promised in former times through the prophets, and Christ Himself had fulfilled it and promulgated it with His lips. This commission was faithfully fulfilled by the Apostles who, by their oral preaching, by example, and by observances handed on what they had received from the lips of Christ, from living with Him, and from what He did, or what they had learned through the prompting of the Holy Spirit. The commission was fulfilled, too, by those Apostles and apostolic men who under the inspiration of the same Holy Spirit committed the message of salvation to writing.

   But in order to keep the Gospel forever whole and alive within the Church, the Apostles left bishops as their successors, "handing over" to them "the authority to teach in their own place." This sacred tradition, therefore, and Sacred Scripture of both the Old and New Testaments are like a mirror in which the pilgrim Church on earth looks at God, from whom she has received everything, until she is brought finally to see Him as He is, face to face (see 1 John 3:2).

8. And so the apostolic preaching, which is expressed in a special way in the inspired books, was to be preserved by an unending succession of preachers until the end of time. Therefore the Apostles, handing on what they themselves had received, warn the faithful to hold fast to the traditions which they have learned either by word of mouth or by letter (see 2 Thess. 2:15), and to fight in defense of the faith handed on once and for all (see Jude 1:3). Now what was handed on by the Apostles includes everything which contributes toward the holiness of life and increase in faith of the peoples of God; and so the Church, in her teaching, life and worship, perpetuates and hands on to all generations all that she herself is, all that she believes…

9. …Hence there exists a close connection and communication between sacred tradition and Sacred Scripture. For both of them, flowing from the same divine wellspring, in a certain way merge into a unity and tend toward the same end. For Sacred Scripture is the word of God inasmuch as it is consigned

# Straight to the Source

ADDITIONAL READINGS FROM PRIMARY SOURCES

to writing under the inspiration of the divine Spirit, while sacred tradition takes the word of God entrusted by Christ the Lord and the Holy Spirit to the Apostles, and hands it on to their successors in its full purity, so that led by the light of the Spirit of truth, they may in proclaiming it preserve this word of God faithfully, explain it, and make it more widely known. Consequently it is not from Sacred Scripture alone that the Church draws her certainty about everything which has been revealed. Therefore both sacred tradition and Sacred Scripture are to be accepted and venerated with the same sense of loyalty and reverence.

10. Sacred tradition and Sacred Scripture form one sacred deposit of the word of God, committed to the Church. Holding fast to this deposit the entire holy people united with their shepherds remain always steadfast in the teaching of the Apostles, in the common life, in the breaking of the bread and in prayers (see Acts 2, 42, Greek text), so that holding to, practicing and professing the heritage of the faith, it becomes on the part of the bishops and faithful a single common effort.

    But the task of authentically interpreting the word of God, whether written or handed on, has been entrusted exclusively to the living teaching office of the Church, whose authority is exercised in the name of Jesus Christ. This teaching office is not above the word of God, but serves it, teaching only what has been handed on, listening to it devoutly, guarding it scrupulously and explaining it faithfully in accord with a divine commission and with the help of the Holy Spirit, it draws from this one deposit of faith everything which it presents for belief as divinely revealed.

    It is clear, therefore, that sacred tradition, Sacred Scripture and the teaching authority of the Church, in accord with God's most wise design, are so linked and joined together that one cannot stand without the others, and that all together and each in its own way under the action of the one Holy Spirit contribute effectively to the salvation of souls.

# Straight to the Source

ADDITIONAL READINGS FROM PRIMARY SOURCES

## Focus Questions

1. Who did Jesus commission and what did He commission them to hand on? How did they accomplish this task?
2. Who else fulfilled Christ's commission?
3. What was done in order for the Gospel to be kept whole and alive forever?
4. How long is this apostolic preaching to be preserved?
5. What does everything handed on by the Apostles include?
6. What three things are the Apostles and their successors to do in the "light of the Spirit of truth"?
7. What two things form the one sacred deposit of the Word of God?
8. Who has the task of authentically interpreting the Word of God? Where did this authority come from?
9. Why is the Magisterium not above the Word of God?

UNIT 2

# What Is Sacred Scripture?

We can know God because he revealed Himself to us. Alongside Sacred Tradition, Sacred Scripture is one of the primary accounts of this divine revelation. More than just human accounts of divine action, the books of Sacred Scripture were inspired by the Holy Spirit. Sacred Scripture, therefore, is God Himself telling us about His direct actions in history and explaining what those actions mean. In addition to these historical accounts, the Scriptures also contain inspired theological and moral writings, through which God tells us about Himself and about His relationship with us.

Christians divide Sacred Scripture into two sections: The Old Testament and the New Testament. The Old Testament is the inspired record of God's covenant with Israel and is sacred for both Jews and Christians. The New Testament is the inspired record of the life and ministry of Jesus Christ and His early followers. It is considered Sacred Scripture only by Christians. Christians venerate both the Old and the New Testaments as the true Word of God, because we recognize that God's relationship with Israel culminates with the Incarnation of the Word of God in Jesus Christ (CCC 123). Thus, the Old Testament is fulfilled by the New Testament; it is not made void.

Sacred Scripture is one of God's greatest gifts to us. It also is an encounter with Jesus. If we want to know Jesus and know who we are in His eyes, there is no greater help than Sacred Scripture. Before we delve into the texts themselves, though, we need to look a little more closely at the question, "What is Sacred Scripture?"

## In This Unit

- **Chapter 5:** Divine Inspiration
- **Chapter 6:** How Was the Bible Put Together?
- **Chapter 7:** Sacred Scripture in the Life of the Church

Chapter 5

# Divine Inspiration

# Chapter Overview

Scripture is God's written Word. While He used human authors to write the books of Scripture, God divinely inspired them. If we want to understand God's inspired Word we need to know how to approach and read Scripture. It is important to understand the historical context as well as know the literary form of what we are reading in order to grasp it fully. Are you willing to dig deeper into what Scripture is saying to you so you can encounter God's love in transformative ways through this beautiful love letter He has prepared for you?

## In this chapter you will learn that ...

- Scripture is divinely inspired.
- We must understand the historical context of passages in Scripture in order to properly understand them.
- We must know what literary form is being used in the passage of Scripture we are reading.
- Scripture is inerrant.
- We cannot read Scripture with a fundamentalist approach.

### Bible Basics

All scripture is inspired by God and is useful for teaching, for refutation, for correction, and for training in righteousness.

2 TIMOTHY 3:16

### Connections to the *Catechism*

CCC 104 (page 70)
CCC 110 (page 63)

## Divine Inspiration

God is the author of Sacred Scripture (CCC 105), but this does not mean God dropped the Bible, fully written, from the sky. Nor did He dictate to the human authors the exact words He wanted them to write down. Rather, He gave human beings the gift of **divine inspiration**. This, the Church teaches, allowed the human authors of the Bible to be true authors of God's Word: God "made full use of their own faculties and power so that, though he acted in them and by them, it was as true authors that they consigned to writing whatever he wanted written, and no more" (DV 11).

This understanding of inspiration is found in the Bible itself. In 2 Timothy 3:16, St. Paul writes, **"All scripture is inspired by God and is useful for teaching, for refutation, for correction, and for training in righteousness."** In the original Greek of that passage, the word we translate as inspire is **theopneustos**, which literally means "God-breathed" and emphasizes the divine authorship of Sacred Scripture.

Nevertheless, this can be a bit confusing. How can a book have two authors—one divine, the other human? Pope Benedict XVI answered that question by comparing the inspiration of Scripture to the Incarnation of

### Vocabulary

**Divine Inspiration (n.):** The gift of the Holy Spirit that God gave to the human authors of the Bible which enabled them to write that which He wanted committed to writing for the sake of our salvation.

**Theopneustos (adj.):** Greek for "God-breathed."

The four Evangelists Matthew, Mark, Luke, and John were guided by the divine inspiration of the Holy Spirit when writing their Gospel accounts.

*The Four Evangelists* by Jacob Jordaens (ca. 1630).

God: "[A]s the word of God became flesh by the power of the Holy Spirit in the womb of the Virgin Mary, so sacred Scripture is born from the womb of the Church by the power of the same Spirit" (*Verbum Domini* 19).

In other words, even though Jesus was conceived through the power of the Holy Spirit, Mary was completely his mother. The Apostle's Creed states: "He was conceived by the power of the Holy Spirit and born of the Virgin Mary." In the same way, "Sacred Scripture is born from the womb of the Church by the power of the same Spirit" (VD 19).

The writings of Sacred Scripture were written by their human authors through the power of the Holy Spirit. This means that what they wrote is exactly what he intended them to write—no more, no less. In this way, God is the true author of Sacred Scripture, so we can trust that the Bible is both sacred and true. It also means, however, that the human authors used their concepts and understanding, their literary abilities, and their language in composing the Scripture. They weren't robots; they were men, who brought their own gifts, talents, and experiences to the sacred text. This is what "inspiration" means.

**The writings of Sacred Scripture were written by their human authors through the power of the Holy Spirit.**

## Understanding Context

Not only did the Scriptures have real human authors, but those human authors wrote their work to be read by people who lived in a certain time and place. Since we do not live in that time and place, the meaning of Scripture is not always obvious to us. However, if we look at the historical, political, social, and cultural contexts of the biblical books' production, what is difficult to understand can become much clearer. The *Catechism* explains:

> **"In order to discover the sacred authors' intention, the reader must take into account the conditions of their time and culture, the literary genres in use at that time, and the modes of feeling, speaking, and narrating then current. 'For the fact is that truth is differently presented and expressed in the various types of historical writing, in prophetical and poetical texts, and in other forms of literary expression.'" (CCC 110).**

### *Historical Context*

For the average modern reader who does not have an extensive background in ancient Jewish history or culture, the footnotes of the Bible provide a valuable resource to learn more about the historical context of a particular story. Without this context provided by these notes, we can often grasp only part of the meaning of a passage. Therefore, when we read the Scripture within its historical context, layers of meaning open up to us and we can begin to understand what the author intended to communicate.

### *Literary Context*

**The Bible is a mixture of different types of texts: history, poetry, parables, prophecies, and more.**

In addition to the historical context, we also need to consider the literary form of the passage we are reading. Remember, the Bible is a mixture of different types of texts: history, poetry, parables, prophecies, and more. If we do not take into consideration what kind of writing we are reading, the author's intent can be easy to miss. For example, let us read the first part of Psalm 23:

> **"The LORD is my shepherd;**
> **there is nothing I lack.**
> **In green pastures he makes me lie down;**
> **to still waters he leads me;**
> **he restores my soul.**
> **He guides me along right paths**
> **for the sake of his name.**
> **Even though I walk through the valley of the shadow of death,**
> **I will fear no evil, for you are with me;**
> **your rod and your staff comfort me" (Psalm 23:1–4).**

If we read that Psalm not as poetry, but as history, we could walk away thinking the author actually believes God is a shepherd, who carried a rod and a staff and who literally leads us down some road called "righteousness".

## Is the Bible always literally true?

When we read the Bible, we must keep in mind that it must be interpreted within the context of the literary type of each book, the historical and cultural context, and in continuity with the rest of Scripture, as you will learn more about in chapter 8. When we take this context into account, we discover the meaning that comes directly from the text and the intention of the inspired author, which is called the "literal sense" of Scripture. The literal sense is the basis for all other senses of Scripture, so the Scriptures can be understood as always having a true "literal" meaning. However, the Church does not propose a **fundamentalist** approach to Scripture in which Scripture is understood as always being "literally" true (in the sense of being simply true without the need of analysis or interpretation of context).

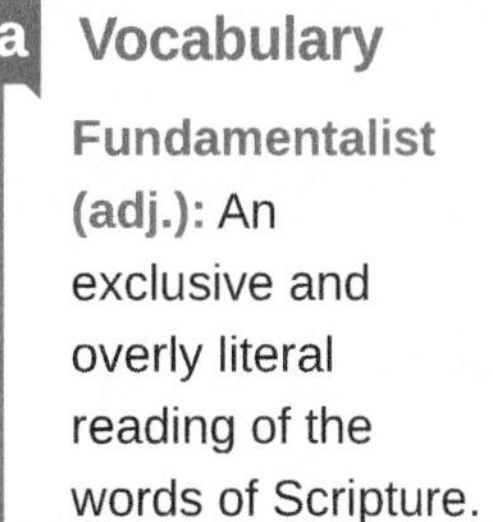

**Vocabulary**

**Fundamentalist (adj.):** An exclusive and overly literal reading of the words of Scripture.

In short, the Church does not claim that the Bible always presents scientific or historical facts. The Bible's purpose is to present truths about God and humanity. Many portions of the Bible are historically and factually true, such as the Incarnation, Crucifixion, and Resurrection of Jesus. The contextual approach to interpreting Scripture will always give you the right perspective. The Church is aware of the difficulties attached to the interpretation of Scripture and has given guidelines for how it should be approached, as will be discussed in greater detail in Unit 3..

The idea would, quite rightly, strike us as absurd. If we recognize that the Psalm is a work of poetry that makes use of metaphor to express a deeper truth about our relationship with the Lord, it makes much more sense.

The example above is a simple one. The average reader can quickly infer that the passage should not be interpreted literally. It is not always that easy, though. Consider the opening chapter of Genesis. Is the author of that book really saying God created the world in six twenty-four hour days or was he using a literary device to express some kind of deeper truth about creation?

In cases like this one, the guidance of the Magisterium of the Church becomes particularly important. God has not left us to our own devices when it comes to making sense of Scripture. Rather, we have the Tradition and living Magisterium of the Church as our guide.

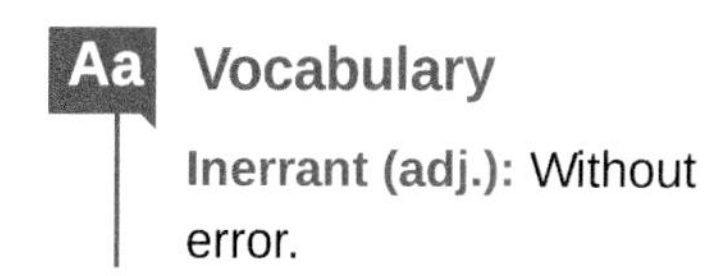

**Vocabulary**

**Inerrant (adj.):** Without error.

## Free from All Error

Although the Scriptures can be difficult to understand, Catholics still believe they are **inerrant**, or without error. It is tempting to dismiss this notion, since in our own experience nearly everything contains at least some errors. However, most books are not written by God. God is the author of Sacred Scripture, and He gave it to us to teach us truths about Himself and

God is the author of Sacred Scripture. Therefore the truths it contains are free from error.

*God the Son* by Viktor Mikhailovich Vasnetsov (between 1885 and 1896).

### Lives of Faith

## St. Matthew

How often today do you hear something referred to as "life-changing"? It is a phrase thrown around pretty loosely in our culture.

*This new pair of shoes is life-changing!*
*This new movie will change your life!*
*This new smartphone is life-changing!*
*This new band will change your life!*

The truth is that changing your life in even the smallest way is incredibly difficult. Those who have tried to establish new (good) habits or build new routines know just how hard it is to actually *live* differently.

But all it took to change St. Matthew's life was two words: Follow me.

Matthew was a tax collector and sinner. Tax collectors at the time of Jesus were considered traitors to the Jews. The Romans were the foreign occupiers of their land, and the tax collectors worked for the Romans by collecting money from their fellow Jews. Even worse, they often collected more than they had to because that is how tax collectors made their own living. Suffice it to say Matthew was not the most popular man in his village.

However, everything changed one day when Jesus walked by Matthew's booth. Matthew was sitting there, doing his work, minding his own business when Jesus stopped, looked at him, and said, "Follow me." Two simple words.

At Jesus' invitation, Matthew immediately got up, left his booth, and followed Him. He became one of the Twelve Apostles. His reputation was so bad in the town that when he invited Jesus to his home that night for dinner, the Pharisees asked Jesus why He was spending His time with tax collectors and sinners. It is from that party we get one of Jesus' well-known sayings: **"Those who are well do not need a physician, but the sick do. I did not come to call the righteous but sinners,"** (Mark 2: 17).

St. Matthew would spend the next few years traveling with Jesus, watching and learning from Him and being sent out by Him to proclaim the Good News. He was at the Last Supper. He was in the garden when Jesus was taken by the soldiers. He was hiding with the other Apostles when Jesus was crucified. He was in the upper room when Jesus appeared to them after His resurrection. He was sent by Jesus on mission to evangelize the world. He received the Holy Spirit at Pentecost. And he helped build the early Church, spreading the message of God's love.

St. Matthew is the attributed writer of the Gospel of Matthew, the first of the four Gospels in the Bible. Each of the Gospels possesses a unique flair, and for Matthew it was important to emphasize to the Jewish people how Jesus was the fulfillment of the prophecies in the Old Testament.

His Gospel starts with the lineage of Jesus, showing how He descended from Abraham and King David. His Gospel is filled with references to Old Testament passages to show how they came to be fulfilled in Jesus. His Gospel also emphasizes Jesus' Jewish heritage and practices. To the people Matthew was writing to, it was important to emphasize that Jesus was the promised Messiah.

St. Matthew gave his entire life to Jesus. And he did it because of two simple words. *Follow me*. How will you respond to Jesus' same invitation to you?

our salvation. By nature, God is incapable of deception. He also knows all and is the source of all perfection. This means God does not make errors, let alone allow any into His book of self-revelation.

The Church's teaching about Scriptural inerrancy, however, does not mean every statement in the Bible is literally true without consideration for historical context and literary form. Again, using the previous example, God does not earn a salary as a shepherd. That is not literally true, but it is metaphorically true and the author was not intending to assert otherwise.

The teaching about inerrancy also does not deny that the Bible sometimes seems to assert things most people today believe are false (for example, that the sun rotates around the earth; see Josh. 10:12–13; Ps. 19:4–7, 93:1, 104:5). Instead, it means everything written in the Bible is supposed to be there as part of God's plan for our salvation. We may not immediately understand why God wants something there in some particular way or what point He is trying to make. Nevertheless, we can trust that everything in the Bible is just as God wants it, and God does not deceive. He is good and loving; He does not lead us astray. To do so would be inconsistent with His nature. At the same time, we need to put real effort into understanding this revelation. Even the Doctors of the Church, including people such as St. Augustine, faced difficulties in their understanding of what seemed to be inconsistencies or mistakes in Scripture. In a letter to St. Jerome, St. Augustine wrote: "And if in these writings [Scripture] I am perplexed by anything which appears to me opposed to truth, I do not hesitate to suppose that either the manuscript is faulty, or the translator has not caught the meaning of what was said, or I myself have failed to understand it."

In sum, our knowledge of the Bible's meaning is not simple or completely unchanging. We cannot just pick up the Bible and read it like a science book or a book of modern history and expect to understand everything that it says without effort or difficulties. Moreover, as our knowledge of the world around us grows—as our knowledge of biology, geology, history, archeology, linguistics, and any number of other fields broadens—our understanding of Scripture should deepen. Guided by the Magisterium, we can bring the fruits of our study to bear on the inerrant and inspired Word of God and discover more truth about God. What might seem like a contradiction today can become an opportunity for new insights into God and ourselves tomorrow.

**Our knowledge of the Bible's meaning is not simple or completely unchanging.**

# The Truth Is...

Scripture is difficult to understand. There are a lot of passages that can cause us to pause and truly wonder what is going on. There are passages that make God seem vengeful. There are passages that seem to contradict other passages. There are passages that seem barbaric and uncharitable. There are passages that can seem downright boring and completely irrelevant to our situation in life. Some of it can seem outdated and not applicable in today's culture. Every one of us has felt this regarding Scripture at some point in our lives.

The reality is, this is why we need the Church to help us understand and interpret the Scriptures. A book that is this important needs to be read carefully and understood well. We also need to ask ourselves if we really trust the author, if we really trust God. If the answer to that question is yes, then in faith, we can trust there is a good explanation for the things we struggle to understand. Will we walk away in frustration, or are we willing to do the work and seek out the answers we are looking for?

Chapter 5

# Focus and Reflection Questions

1. What do we mean when we say God is the author of Sacred Scripture?
2. What does the Greek word for inspiration, theopneustos literally mean?
3. How does Pope Benedict XVI help us understand the concept of divine inspiration?
4. What sort of context is important to understand when reading Scripture? Why?
5. Why is considering the literary form of the passage we are reading important? What example does the author use to illustrate this?
6. What does it mean that Scripture is inerrant?
7. Why do we believe Scripture is inerrant?
8. How would you respond to someone that claimed Scripture is not inerrant because it asserts things most people today believe are false, like the sun rotates around the earth?
9. How does St. Augustine reconcile apparent contradictions that are found in Scripture?
10. How could you answer the question: Is the Bible always literally true?
11. How was St. Matthew's life changed when he answered Jesus' call to follow Him?

# Straight to the Source

ADDITIONAL READINGS FROM PRIMARY SOURCES

## *Catechism of the Catholic Church* no. 104

In Sacred Scripture, the Church constantly finds her nourishment and her strength, for she welcomes it not as a human word, "but as what it really is, the word of God." "In the sacred books, the Father who is in heaven comes lovingly to meet his children, and talks with them."

1. How would understanding the "human words" of Scripture help lead us to see the "word of God" more clearly?
2. How does this passage shed light on how you are called to approach Scripture?

## *Dei Verbum* 11–12—The Dogmatic Constitution on Divine Revelation from the Second Vatican Council, November 18, 1968

11. Those divinely revealed realities which are contained and presented in Sacred Scripture have been committed to writing under the inspiration of the Holy Spirit. For holy mother Church, relying on the belief of the Apostles (see John 20:31; 2 Tim. 3:16; 2 Peter 1:19–20, 3:15–16), holds that the books of both the Old and New Testaments in their entirety, with all their parts, are sacred and canonical because written under the inspiration of the Holy Spirit, they have God as their author and have been handed on as such to the Church herself. In composing the sacred books, God chose men and while employed by Him they made use of their powers and abilities, so that with Him acting in them and through them, they, as true authors, consigned to writing everything and only those things which He wanted.

    Therefore, since everything asserted by the inspired authors or sacred writers must be held to be asserted by the Holy Spirit, it follows that the books of Scripture must be acknowledged as teaching solidly, faithfully and without error that truth which God wanted put into sacred writings for the sake of salvation. Therefore "all Scripture is divinely inspired and has its use for teaching the truth and refuting error, for reformation of manners and discipline in right living, so that the man who belongs to God may be efficient and equipped for good work of every kind" (2 Tim. 3:16–17, Greek text).

12. However, since God speaks in Sacred Scripture through men in human fashion, the interpreter of Sacred Scripture, in order to see clearly what God wanted to communicate to us, should carefully investigate what meaning the sacred writers really intended, and what God wanted to manifest by means of their words.

1. Paragraph 11 tells us that, in composing the sacred books, "God chose men," and employed them to write "those things which He wanted." Why do you think God chose to reveal Himself in this way, that is, in written word, using the powers and abilities of human beings?
2. Because we can be confident in the truth of Scripture, what are some of the ways that we can use Scripture in our lives?

# Straight to the Source

ADDITIONAL READINGS FROM PRIMARY SOURCES

## *Verbum Domini* 44—Post-Synodal Apostolic Exhortation of Pope Benedict XVI, September 30, 2010

The fundamentalist interpretation of sacred Scripture

44. The attention we have been paying to different aspects of the theme of biblical hermeneutics now enables us to consider a subject which came up a number of times during the Synod: that of the fundamentalist interpretation of sacred Scripture. The Pontifical Biblical Commission, in its document The Interpretation of the Bible in the Church, has laid down some important guidelines. Here I would like especially to deal with approaches which fail to respect the authenticity of the sacred text, but promote subjective and arbitrary interpretations. The "literalism" championed by the fundamentalist approach actually represents a betrayal of both the literal and the spiritual sense, and opens the way to various forms of manipulation, as, for example, by disseminating anti-ecclesial interpretations of the Scriptures. "The basic problem with fundamentalist interpretation is that, refusing to take into account the historical character of biblical revelation, it makes itself incapable of accepting the full truth of the incarnation itself. As regards relationships with God, fundamentalism seeks to escape any closeness of the divine and the human … for this reason, it tends to treat the biblical text as if it had been dictated word for word by the Spirit. It fails to recognize that the word of God has been formulated in language and expression conditioned by various periods". Christianity, on the other hand, perceives in the words the Word himself, the Logos who displays his mystery through this complexity and the reality of human history. The true response to a fundamentalist approach is "the faith-filled interpretation of sacred Scripture". This manner of interpretation, "practiced from antiquity within the Church's Tradition, seeks saving truth for the life of the individual Christian and for the Church. It recognizes the historical value of the biblical tradition. Precisely because of the tradition's value as an historical witness, this reading seeks to discover the living meaning of the sacred Scriptures for the lives of believers today", while not ignoring the human mediation of the inspired text and its literary genres.

1. What is the problem with the fundamentalist interpretation of Scripture?
2. Why is a "faith-filled interpretation of Scripture" better?

Chapter 6

# How Was the Bible Put Together?

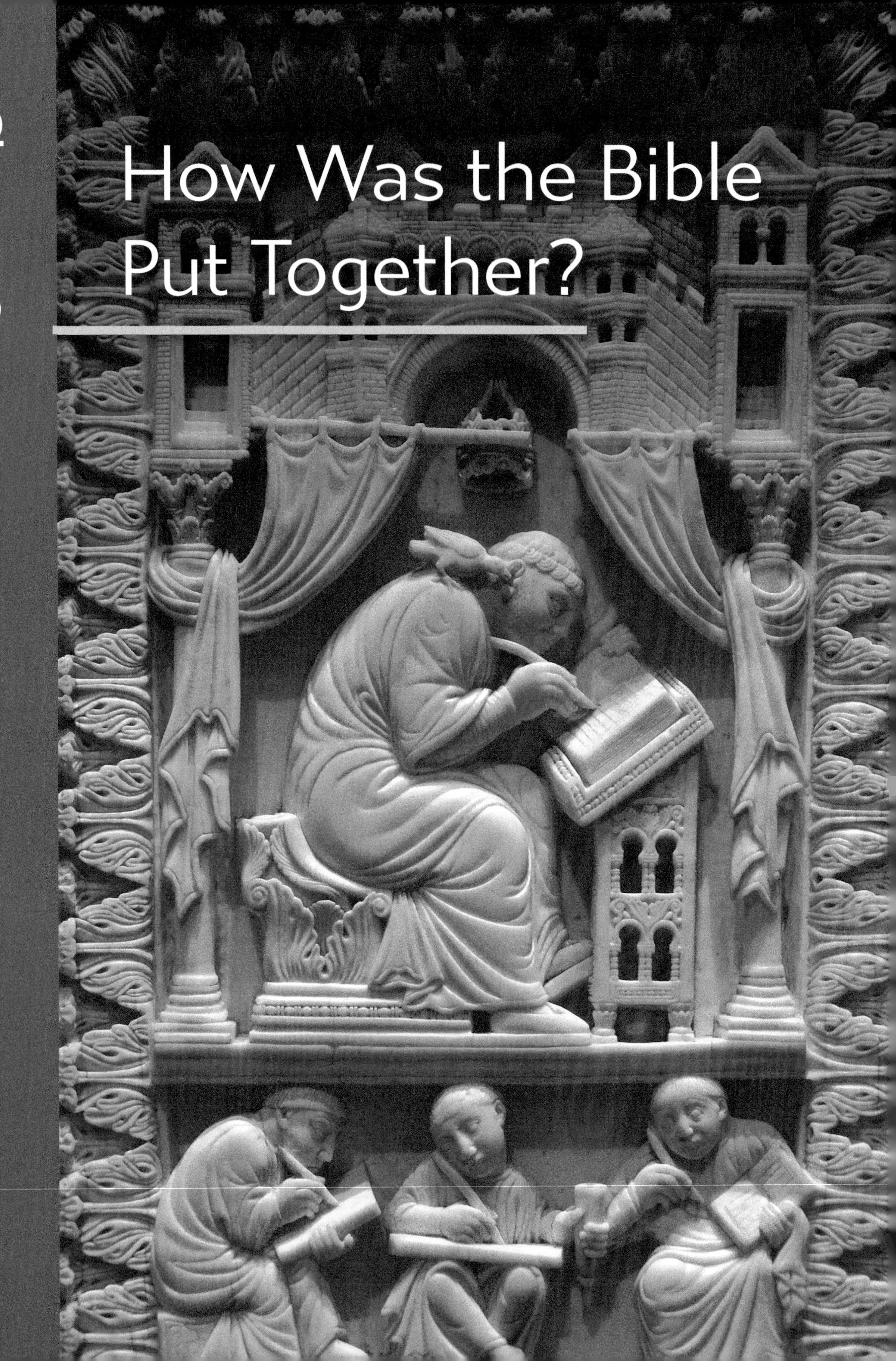

# Chapter Overview

These days, you can find a Bible as easily as you can find a bookstore, website, or smartphone. But where did it come from? The writings we call the Bible did not just drop magically from Heaven as some assume. During the time of the early Church, different Jewish communities recognized different lists of Scripture as inspired, while Christians read writings among their communities. Within a few centuries after Christ's death, the Church's bishops, guided by the Holy Spirit, made clear which books were divinely inspired and, therefore, worthy of inclusion in the Bible.

Some people think that since the writings that would later become the Bible were written down by human beings, and since other people then determined the official list of divinely inspired books, the Bible is a purely human invention. On the contrary, the beautiful way in which God invites human beings to cooperate with Him in His salvific mission is a powerful sign of His love for us!

## In this chapter you will learn that …

- The question of which books were the inspired Word of God was a pressing controversy for the early Christians.
- The controversy over which books were truly inspired ultimately led to the formation of the Biblical canon, or list of inspired books.
- As important as the Scriptures are, they are just one part of the revelation of God; not its entirety.
- The Bible is translated into different languages because the Bible is the living Word of God meant for everyone.

**Bible Basics**

"Go, therefore, and make disciples of all nations, baptizing them in the name of the Father, and of the Son, and of the holy Spirit, teaching them to observe all that I have commanded you. And behold, I am with you always, until the end of the age."

MATTHEW 28:19–20

## How Was the Bible Put Together?

The Bible is by far the most well-known book in history. Bibles are everywhere. There are millions of copies in nearly every language, and the Bible is posted on thousands of websites. Because of the availability of the Scriptures, it is tempting to take its existence for granted. But it has not always been that way. It actually took centuries for the Bible as we know it to come together.

First, came the books of the Old Testament. They were written by the Jewish people during the thousands of years before the birth of Christ, over 2,000 years ago. Then came the New Testament books. They were written over the course of the first century after the Death of Christ. In addition to those books, there were other books written about God by Jews and Christians during those same time periods, and they too seemed like they might be inspired. But were they?

That question—which books were the inspired Word of God and which books were just the writings of men—became a pressing controversy for the early Christians. They needed to know which books were inspired by God and worthy of being read in the Christian liturgy (the Mass). That controversy ultimately led to the formation of the Biblical canon, or list of inspired books. After several hundred years and a great deal of discussion, the Holy Spirit guided the Church to determine which books belonged in the Bible and which books did not. Over a thousand years later, the Church defined that canon dogmatically, meaning to deny that list was to deny the fullness of the Faith.

**After several hundred years and a great deal of discussion, the Church settled which books belonged in the Bible and which books did not.**

The history of how the Bible came together can seem complicated, but it helps to remember that as important as the Scriptures are, they are just one part of the revelation of God; not its entirety. Jesus himself is the fullness of God's revelation, and divine revelation is transmitted through both Scripture and Sacred Tradition. Therefore, to better understand how Scripture came to be, we need to begin by situating it within history and Tradition.

## Oral Tradition

The most effective way to communicate a message is not to write a book; it is to go and speak with someone face-to-face. This is true now, and it was especially true in ancient times before the printing press and widespread literacy. Just think of how often what we say is misconstrued in texts and when we use social media. It is much easier to understand someone when we talk with them in person. This is why Jesus commanded his Apostles, **"Go, therefore, and make disciples of all nations, baptizing them in the name of the Father, and of the Son, and of the holy Spirit, teaching them to observe all that I have commanded you. And behold, I am**

*Illuminated Bible* Photo Credit: Adrian Pingstone (February 19, 2005).

▲ Sacred Scripture is composed of two collections of divinely inspired books: the Old Testament and the New Testament.

**with you always, until the end of the age" (Mt. 28:19–20)**. Note: Jesus tells them to "go," teach, and baptize, not to "stop and write." Jesus Himself shared the Gospel this way (Acts 1:1), and he called the Apostles to follow His example.

The Apostles were equipped to do this because of the time they had spent with Jesus listening to His teachings and observing the witness of His life. Then, after His Death and Resurrection, the Holy Spirit descended upon the Apostles at Pentecost and granted them an even fuller understanding of Jesus and His mission. When the Apostles went out, first into Jerusalem and then across the known world, they preached this knowledge, understanding, and way of life. We call this preaching phase in the spreading of the Gospel oral tradition (CCC 126).

Eventually, some of the Apostles and their closest followers wrote down some of this tradition. Their writings then became the New Testament. This apostolic preaching, both the books and the unwritten oral tradition, was added to the written books and the oral tradition of the Jews. Through this process the Church received both her Tradition and her Scripture.

## Written Tradition

As we have already mentioned, Sacred Scripture is really two collections of books: the Old Testament and the New Testament. Long before the coming of Jesus and the writing of the New Testament, the Old Testament had largely taken shape. The Old Testament came into being when the people of Israel settled in the Promised Land, and scholars and scribes began the work of writing down and editing their tradition. During this centuries-long process, Jewish oral tradition and many different text traditions were brought together to form a single body of sacred texts: the Old Testament. Jesus and the early Christians knew the Old Testament writings well, and whenever we read the New Testament authors referencing the Scriptures, we should remember they are referencing these books.

Unlike the Old Testament, the books of the New Testament were written either by eyewitnesses to the events of Jesus' life or by close companions of the Apostles. The work that Jesus had mandated to His followers was well underway and the Christian community was rapidly spreading by the time the New Testament books were written. These new inspired writings recorded and preserved some of the apostolic preaching that animated early Christian communities.

For as much as the writings of the New Testament tell us about Jesus and the Church He established, however, they are not exhaustive. They do not tell us everything that we know about Jesus and God's plan for our salvation. Rather, the inspired authors wrote by: "selecting some things from the many which had been handed on by word of mouth or in writing, reducing some of them to a synthesis, explaining some things in view of the situation of their churches and preserving the form of proclamation but always in such fashion that they told us the honest truth about Jesus" (DV 19).

The books of the New Testament were written by eyewitness and close companions of Jesus.

*Communion of the Apostles* by Luca Signorelli (1512).

These writings did not compete with or replace the preaching of the Apostles or their successors, the bishops. Rather, the written tradition complemented the oral tradition, and together they conveyed the full truth about Jesus to the faithful.

## Setting the Canon of Scripture

The Catholic Church accepts as inspired forty-six books in the Old Testament and twenty-seven books in the New Testament (CCC 120). These seventy-three books form the **canon of Scripture**. But how do we know these books are the inspired books and not others? Could the Church have missed one? Protestants have only 66 books in their canon—why? In short, why is our Bible the way it is, and how did it get to be that way?

The first thing we need to recognize is that the very idea of a Scriptural canon took several centuries to develop. It is probably a mistake to talk about a "canon" before the late fifth century (AD 400–500). This is not to say there was no Scripture before the canon—there certainly was! Jesus himself quotes the Old Testament. Rather, it was not clear that some sort of definite list of inspired works ought to be put together. It was not clear there were important distinctions between "important" or "sacred" books and "inspired" books, nor what those distinctions would be. The Jews themselves did not have a definite list of "canonical" books for the Old Testament. Rather, there were several traditions, each of which considered a different set of books to be sacred.

Furthermore, it was not at first clear that Christians would make additions to the sacred writings. Initially, the Church only learned about Jesus through the preaching of the Apostles, and Jesus did not order the Apostles to write anything down. The first community of Christians was not thinking about writing about Jesus; they were still processing what they were hearing from the Apostles. However, in time God inspired some men to write letters and Gospels that preserved much of the oral tradition for future generations. He also helped others to recognize the necessity of including these writings in Sacred Scripture.

Christianity is a religion that understands history as integral to salvation. The unfolding of our understanding of Scripture over time is a part of this salvation history. Far from calling into question the validity of Scripture, the recognition that it came together over centuries verifies that God works out our salvation through our history and not in opposition to it. God did not make the Bible appear in a puff of smoke and then order us to follow its teachings. Rather, He helped the Bible grow and develop as the people of God grew and developed. In this way, it is complementary to both our nature and our tradition.

**Aa Vocabulary**

**Canon of Scripture (n.):** The official list of inspired books that make up the Bible.

**God inspired some men to write letters and Gospels that preserved much of the oral tradition for future generations.**

*Saint Jerome Writing* by Caravaggio (ca. 1606).

▲ St. Jerome translated the Bible into Latin. This translation is known as the Vulgate.

Again, why did it take so long or the Church to definitively declare which books belonged in the Bible? If the question of the canon was settled in the fifth century, why did the canon not become an official dogma of the Church until the sixteenth century?

This is not unusual. Often in the history of the Church, the pope and bishops make definitive statements of doctrine only in response to problems. This is what happened with Sacred Scripture.

**Aa Vocabulary**

**Septuagint (n.):** The pre-Christian Greek translation of the Old Testament books made by Jewish scholars and later adopted by Greek speaking Christians.

### *First Magisterial Statements*

Early on, out of necessity the Church had to decide which books could be read at Mass. From the beginning, the Christian communities read from the Jewish Scriptures and from important writings of either the Apostles themselves or their close collaborators (CCC 1345). However, different communities sometimes read from different books, and settling which books should be read was not easy. In large part this was because as Christianity spread throughout the Roman Empire, communication between Christian communities was often difficult. Christianity was illegal in the Roman Empire, and starting in the first century, Christians were subject to multiple persecutions. During this period of persecution, many Christians were put to death and became martyrs.

Despite the challenges, the early Church generally agreed on which books qualified. As the early Christians worshipped in the liturgy, a certain consensus emerged concerning which books were sacred. There were still disagreements, but they were minor. Most Christians read from the **Septuagint** version of the Old Testament. This version includes all the books now in the Catholic Old Testament. It also was the version most often cited in the texts of the New Testament. As for the books of the New Testament, the 27 books we now hold to be inspired were widely regarded as inspired.

### *Early Councils*

In AD 313 the emperor Constantine made Christianity legal in the Roman Empire. This freed the bishops to organize the Church, sort out its inconsistencies, and deal with its problems. The primary mechanism for this work was the council. A council was a gathering of bishops convened to assert a consistent teaching and heal discord. Different types of councils existed: there were large councils with significance across the Christian world, which came to be known as ecumenical councils, and smaller regional councils, sometimes called synods. Various councils and **synods** were held over the centuries, such as the Council of Hippo (AD 393) and the Councils of Carthage in AD 397 and 419. Various pronouncements were made at these meetings of bishops affirming and reaffirming the list of canonical books—the exact same list of inspired books the Catholic Church holds today.

In declaring these seventy-three books to be canonical, the bishops and popes rejected such pseudo-Biblical writings as the **Gnostic gospels** falsely attributed to St. Thomas and St. Mary Magdalene which were circulating widely in the period.

**Gnosticism** was a Christian heresy that denied the true humanity of Christ and also His redemptive suffering and Death on the Cross. Many of the Church Fathers wrote against Gnosticism along with other heresies such as **Arianism**, and in doing so they helped define the boundaries of Christian orthodoxy. This helped clarify which books were inspired.

The canonical books of the New Testament, as generally agreed upon in the fourth century, share three characteristics:

| I | II | III |
|---|---|---|
| **Apostolic Origin** | **Universal Acceptance** | **Liturgical Use** |
| A book coming from an eyewitness of Jesus or a close companion of an apostle. | The book had to be known and accepted by the wider Christian community. | The book had to be used within the context of worship. |

The canonical books of the Old Testament share these same characteristics with the exception that rather than having been written by the apostolic Church, they were accepted by the Apostles as Scripture. These multiple characteristics boil down to one: that the book in question was accepted as Scripture in the apostolic Tradition of the Church. This was the ultimate criterion for canonical status.

### Aa Vocabulary

**Synod (n.):** A meeting of bishops of a particular region, of the whole world, or of bishops and priests and other members of the faithful within a particular diocese to address the doctrinal and pastoral needs of the Church.

**Gnostic Gospels (n.):** Ancient books about the life of Christ that are infused with theology that reflects the Gnostic heresy rampant at the time. Two are falsely attributed to St. Thomas the Apostle and St. Mary Magdalene

**Gnosticism (n.):** The name given to a heresy of the early Church that taught, among other things, that Jesus was not fully human, the material world was evil, and salvation was achieved through secret knowledge, or gnosis.

**Arianism (n.):** An influential heresy of the early Church that taught that Jesus, the Son of God, was created by God the Father, and therefore not truly equal to Him or of the same substance.

## Vocabulary

**Apocryphal Books (n.):** Those seven books of the Old Testament and parts of the books of Esther and Daniel that are not considered by most Protestants to be inspired writings but are still considered valuable for their historical, spiritual, and theological significance. Also called the "apocrypha."

**Council of Trent (n.):** An ecumenical council held from 1545–1563 in Trent, Italy that sought to affirm Church teaching, answer Protestant heresies, and end abusive practices within the Church.

### *The Council of Trent*

Due to the challenges presented by the Protestant Reformation, it was not until the 16th century that it became necessary for the Church to formally and dogmatically declare the official canon of Scripture. Some Protestant groups removed certain books from the Old Testament, arguing they were **apocryphal**, or not authentic. They argued that only those Old Testament books written originally in Hebrew, not Greek, were inspired by God. Faced with this dissent from accepted teaching, the bishops at the **Council of Trent** (1543–1563) definitively confirmed the traditional canon as it had been established in the early Church and as it had been accepted for over a thousand years. The Biblical canon was now a matter of Catholic dogma.

## Translating the Scriptures

Over the past two millennia, the Bible has been translated into more than 500 languages, and many of these have multiple versions. There are over 100 well-known English translations. This wide variety of translations and versions can raise more than a few questions. After all, if the Holy Spirit is the author of the Bible, which version is the actual Word of God? Which version does He endorse? When translators disagree, how can we know who is right about what the Bible actually says? Is the Scripture in the original languages the only true Bible?

The answers to these questions go to the heart of our understanding of Sacred Scripture.

First, it is helpful to know that the books of the Old Testament were written in Hebrew and Greek (and some Aramaic). The books of the New Testament were written in Greek. They were written in these languages

Sacred Scripture is fundamentally linked to the apostolic Tradition of the Church; it can only be understood properly in union with the teaching of the Apostles, handed down by Holy Mother Church.

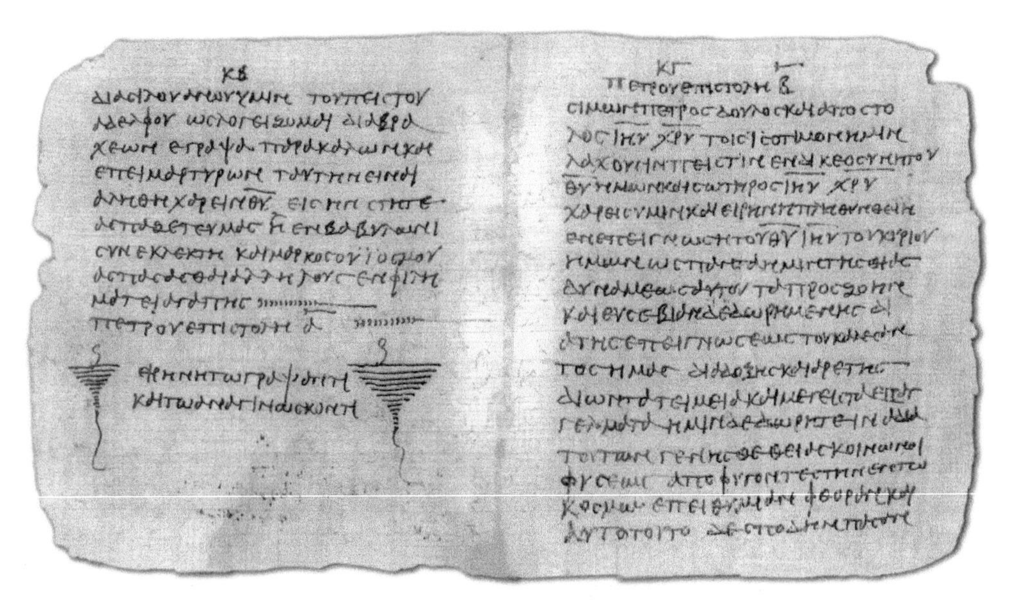

*Papyrus Bodmer* Author Unknown (copy of a 3rd century document).

## How Do We Deal with the Separation between Catholics and Protestants?

When discussing points of disagreement between Catholics and our Protestant brothers and sisters, it can be easy to become combative and place blame squarely on one side. The Catechism reminds us that the separation which exists between Christians is a painful wound to the unity of the Church (CCC 817). The blame for this rupture cannot be attributed to just one side or the other (CCC 817). Our separated brothers and sisters share our common Baptism and have many elements of grace and sanctification available to them (CCC 819). It is our responsibility as Catholics to work with, understand, and dialogue with those who are outside of the visible unity of the Church. We hope and pray that through our faithful witness and charity, all unity might be restored in Christ (CCC 820–821, 2 Cor. 5:18–21).

not because they are particularly holy languages but because they were the languages of the Jews and early Christians. Sacred Scripture is united fundamentally with the apostolic Tradition of the Church, and this Tradition has no "sacred" language.

Second, we need to remember that Scripture is a complement to and not a replacement for the preaching of the Apostles and their successors, the bishops. As we saw, Scripture was especially important for the worship of the early Church because it allowed the preaching of the Apostles to be preserved and repeated over and over again in the liturgy. Because of this, Scripture and the preaching of the Apostles cannot be separated.

However, the Apostles and bishops did not just preach in one language. From the very beginning, when the Apostles received the power of the Holy Spirit on Pentecost and started preaching in different tongues (Acts 2:1–13), the Word of God has been proclaimed in multiple languages. Because the Bible is always rightly read and understood within the context of the preaching, apostolic Church, translating the Bible into different languages is not a problem. The Word of God is not limited to a certain time, place, or culture; it is universal and meant for everyone.

### The Need for Translation

As the Church spread throughout the Roman world, translating the Bible into different languages became an important task. The Greek translation of the Hebrew Old Testament made the Bible accessible to the Gentiles. The entire Bible's early translation into **Latin**—the universal language of the Roman Empire—was an important step in Christianity's spread in the West. For centuries, everybody in the Western world who knew how to read, knew Latin, so the Latin (or **Vulgate**) Bible made the Scriptures as

**Aa Vocabulary**

**Latin (n.):** The universal language of the Roman Empire, which, until modern times, was read and understood by most educated people in the Western world. To this day, it is the official language of the Catholic Church.

**Vulgate (n.):** The 4th century Latin translation of the Bible that was mostly completed by St. Jerome. It became the official Latin translation of the Bible for the Catholic Church in the 16th century. The Latin word *vulgata* means "commonly used."

## Lives of Faith

# St. Jerome

His knuckles cracked as he flattened his fingers against the table top. He had done it again and spent too long writing without a break. This time the pain was particularly bad. The old man stood up and heard similar cracks in his knees and back.

It took a moment for his eyes to adjust to how dark the room was. The candle lit his table top well, but now that he was shuffling about, his eyes needed to adjust to the darkness of the rest of his cell. The old man thought about his friends. They were always trying to get him to stop. "You are too old," they told him. "Leave it for someone else." Because his eyes were bad, he had to hunch over his papers to get close enough to see, and it was no surprise that after all these years of writing his hands were cramped. But he was not going to stop.

He could feel the blood starting to return to his limbs. He had work to do. He might be sixty years old now, but he had time left, and he had to finish. The old man sat back down at his table and flexed his fingers again before picking up his quill and ink. He crouched down, his nose just a few centimeters from the parchment; he took a deep breath, and started writing again.

It is AD 402, and you have just glimpsed an evening in the life of St. Jerome. Born in 342 in present day Eastern Europe, Saint Jerome studied grammar, rhetoric, philosophy, theology and—perhaps most importantly—Latin and Greek. He was a gifted student, and after growing out of a slightly rebellious youth and converting to Christianity, desired a life of solitude and simplicity.

He so badly wished to live life as a hermit or monk and did not want to be ordained a priest, but gave in after the pope himself promised Jerome the freedom to pursue the life of solitude he desired. After his ordination he served as the personal secretary to Pope Damasus, who set him on the work that would consume the rest of his life.

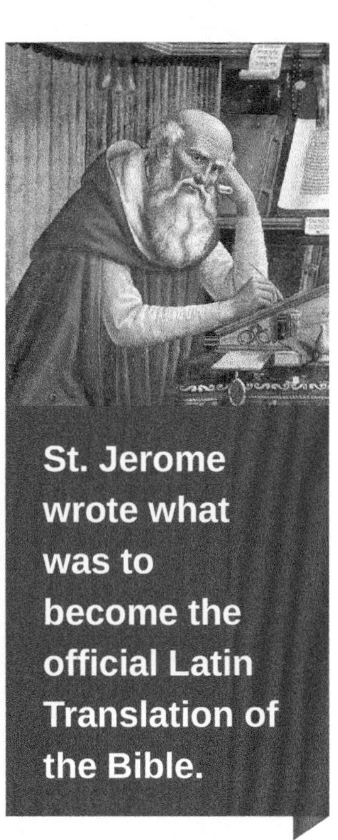

**St. Jerome wrote what was to become the official Latin Translation of the Bible.**

Pope Damasus asked Jerome to correct a Latin translation of the New Testament. But Jerome did not stop when he was done with the pope's request. He continued on—learning Hebrew in the process—and in the end translated the entire Bible into Latin! It took him more than twenty years to complete, but it was a project well worth the time.

At the Council of Trent, nearly 1200 years after he died, Jerome's translation of the Bible—known as the Vulgate—was affirmed by the Catholic Church as the official Latin translation of the Bible.

St. Jerome devoted his life to translating the Bible. But it was really much more than that; St. Jerome devoted himself to Jesus. It is from the words of St. Jerome that we get one of the most powerful reminders about the Bible: "Ignorance of Scripture is ignorance of Christ."

available as possible to them. As knowledge of Latin waned in modern times and more and more people learned how to read their vernacular languages, we have experienced an explosion in the number of Bible translations with the full support of the Church. This, along with printing technologies, has made the Bible extremely accessible. However, it has also introduced some problems.

Translating from one language to another is difficult. Translators have to make countless decisions concerning the real meaning of the original text so that text can be accurately expressed in the second language.

Generally, translators choose between two approaches: either a **literal translation** or a **dynamically equivalent translation**. Literal translations attempt to replace the words of the original language with words in the secondary language that have the same simple meaning: cows are cows, men are men, to run is to run, etc. This is straightforward. The challenge, though,

*Saint Jerome in His Study* by Antonio da Fabriano II (1451).

**Aa Vocabulary**

**Literal Translation (n.):** A straightforward translation of the Bible that replaces words in the original language with words in the secondary language that have the same simple meaning and without regard for figures of speech of nuances in meaning.

**Dynamically Equivalent Translation (n.):** A translation of the Bible that uses different words or different figures of speech from those in the original in the attempt to preserve the actual, deep meaning of the original.

Bible translators have to make countless decisions concerning the real meaning of the original text so it can be accurately expressed in the second language.

is that languages have all sorts of figures of speech and words have all sorts of secondary levels of meaning that can be lost in literal translations.

Dynamic equivalency is when the translator uses different words or different figures of speech in the attempt to preserve the actual, deep meaning of the original.

Biblical scholars constantly debate questions of translation, and the many English translations they have made are a testament to the level of disagreement. This is why it matters that the Scriptures remain imbedded in the apostolic Tradition of the Church. Tradition helps guide the translators. It also helps the Church determine when translators have gone too far or when they have not gone far enough. The Church's Magisterium has approved certain translations as reliable and has made sure those translations have notes that help explain the most difficult passages.

**The Scripture was written as a complement to the preaching of the Apostles and developed in the context of the Christian liturgy.**

Perhaps most importantly, it helps that the Bible is integrated into the Church's liturgy, which is where many Catholics primarily engage it. In the Mass, the Bible is explained by the priest or deacon in his homily, and the words of the translation are always understood in connection with the Eucharist, which serves as a type of anchor that will not let the meaning of the Bible drift too far. The Scripture was written as a complement to the preaching of the Apostles and developed in the context of the Christian liturgy. This remains where it is most at home, in all its hundreds of translations.

In the Church's liturgy, the priest or deacon explains the Bible during the homily.

*St. Peter Preaching in the Presence of St. Mark* by Fra Angelico (ca. 1433).

# The Truth Is...

The Bible did not fall out of the sky in its present form. And neither did Jesus write a book which He then gave to the Apostles and asked them to share it with people. No, like most things in our human experience, the Church had to gradually come to recognize those books which were inspired and those which were not. Of course this does not mean the Church simply made up the canon of Scripture. Rather, she listened to the prompting of the Holy Spirit, she observed the sense of the faithful, and through the wisdom of the Apostles and their successors, she recognized which books were divinely inspired—which books spoke truthfully, faithfully and with consistency and which books did not.

This process and the remarkable consistency which the Church has always proclaimed the authentic canon of inspired books of the Bible should give us confidence in the Church and in the working of the Holy Spirit. While all human beings are fallible, God is not. He sends His Holy Spirit to guide the Church and to ensure the Word of God remains complete throughout the centuries. This great gift to the Church helps us put our faith in the Church and her teachings even when it may otherwise seem hard to do so.

Chapter 6

# Focus and Reflection Questions

1. When was the Old Testament written?

2. When was the New Testament written?

3. What do we call the official list of inspired books of the Bible?

4. How were the Apostles especially equipped to share the Gospel?

5. What is the period when the Apostles went out, first into Jerusalem and then across the known world, preaching their Christian knowledge, understanding, and way of life?

6. When New Testament authors mention the Scriptures, what are they referring to?

7. Who wrote the books of the New Testament?

8. The canonical books of the New Testament, as generally agreed upon in the fourth century, share three characteristics. What are they?

9. What do you think the author means by saying "Christianity is a religion that understands history as integral to salvation"?

10. What Church Council dogmatically declared the canon of Scripture was the same as it had been since the early Church?

11. Why is the translation of the Bible into different languages not a problem?

12. Why is Scripture most "at home" within the liturgy?

13. Why do you think an accurate translation of Scripture was so important to St. Jerome?

# Straight to the Source

ADDITIONAL READINGS FROM PRIMARY SOURCES

## Quote from St. Irenaeus, *Against Heresies* (Book III, Chapter 5), approx. AD 180

Therefore, since the tradition from the Apostles does exist in the Church and is permanent among us, let us revert to the Scriptural proof furnished by those Apostles who did also write the Gospel, in which they recorded the doctrine regarding God, pointing out that our Lord Jesus Christ is the Truth, and that no lie is in Him.

1. According to St. Irenaeus, from whom do we know the Truth of Jesus Christ? Where is this truth found?
2. St. Irenaeus wrote the book from which the quote comes in AD 180. That is approximately 150 years after Jesus's Death, Resurrection, and Ascension. On one hand, that may seem as though a lot of time had passed between when Irenaeus wrote and when Jesus lived on the earth. But, let us put that time into perspective: 150 years is almost 100 years less time than has passed between the signing of the Declaration of Independence in 1776 and today. 150 years ago, Mark Twain published his first book. The first transcontinental railroad was also completed 150 years ago. The Indian civil rights leader, Mohandas Gandhi was born 150 years ago. In our modern memory, these are all relatively recent events. Irenaeus' lifetime was not that far removed from that of Christ and the Apostles and his understanding of the Truth of Christ, which is virtually identical to the way we understand it today, was contemporary knowledge to him.

   How does this perspective and context change your appreciation for how the Church has come to preserve and hand on the Word of God?

## *Dei Verbum* 8—The Dogmatic Constitution on Divine Revelation from the Second Vatican Council, November 18, 1968

This tradition which comes from the Apostles develop in the Church with the help of the Holy Spirit. For there is a growth in the understanding of the realities and the words which have been handed down. This happens through the contemplation and study made by believers, who treasure these things in their hearts (see Luke, 2:19, 51) through a penetrating understanding of the spiritual realities which they experience, and through the preaching of those who have received through Episcopal succession the sure gift of truth. For as the centuries succeed one another, the Church constantly moves forward toward the fullness of divine truth until the words of God reach their complete fulfillment in her.

The words of the holy fathers witness to the presence of this living tradition, whose wealth is poured into the practice and life of the believing and praying Church. Through the same tradition the Church's full canon of the sacred books is known, and the sacred writings themselves are more profoundly understood

# Straight to the Source

ADDITIONAL READINGS FROM PRIMARY SOURCES

and unceasingly made active in her; and thus God, who spoke of old, uninterruptedly converses with the bride of His beloved Son; and the Holy Spirit, through whom the living voice of the Gospel resounds in the Church, and through her, in the world, leads unto all truth those who believe and makes the word of Christ dwell abundantly in them (see Col. 3:16).

1. Where and by whose help does the Tradition develop?
2. How does the growth and understanding of the content of the apostolic preaching occur?
3. What has occurred through the Tradition of the Church?
4. The quote from *Dei Verbum* describes the relationship between the Word of God and His Church as a conversation between Him and His Son, Jesus' bride, which is the Church. Do you think this is a good way to describe the way God speaks to us in Scripture (and Tradition), as a loving conversation? Why or why not?

### Decree Concerning the Canonical Scriptures, Fourth Session of the Council of Trent, April 8, 1546

The holy, ecumenical and general Council of Trent, lawfully assembled in the Holy Ghost, the same three legates of the Apostolic See presiding, keeps this constantly in view, namely, that the purity of the Gospel may be preserved in the Church after the errors have been removed. This [Gospel], of old promised through the Prophets in the Holy Scriptures, our Lord Jesus Christ, the Son of God, promulgated first with His own mouth, and then commanded it to be preached by His Apostles to every creature as the source at once of all saving truth and rules of conduct. It also clearly perceives that these truths and rules are contained in the written books and in the unwritten traditions, which, received by the Apostles from the mouth of Christ Himself, or from the Apostles themselves, the Holy Ghost dictating, have come down to us, transmitted as it were from hand to hand. Following, then, the examples of the orthodox Fathers, it receives and venerates with a feeling of piety and reverence all the books both of the Old and New Testaments, since one God is the author of both; also the traditions, whether they relate to faith or to morals, as having been dictated either orally by Christ or by the Holy Ghost, and preserved in the Catholic Church in unbroken succession. It has thought it proper, moreover, to insert in this decree a list of the sacred books, lest a doubt might arise in the mind of someone as to which are the books received by this council. They are the following: of the Old Testament, the five books of Moses, namely, Genesis, Exodus, Leviticus, Numbers, Deuteronomy; Josue, Judges, Ruth, the four books of Kings, two of Paralipomenon, the first and second of Esdras, the latter of which is called Nehemias, Tobias, Judith, Esther, Job, the Davidic Psalter of 150 Psalms, Proverbs, Ecclesiastes, the Canticle of Canticles, Wisdom, Ecclesiasticus, Isaias, Jeremias, with

# Straight to the Source

ADDITIONAL READINGS FROM PRIMARY SOURCES

> Baruch, Ezechiel, Daniel, the twelve minor Prophets, namely, Osee, Joel, Amos, Abdias, Jonas, Micheas, Nahum, Habacuc, Sophonias, Aggeus, Zacharias, Malachias; two books of Machabees, the first and second. Of the New Testament, the four Gospels, according to Matthew, Mark, Luke and John; the Acts of the Apostles written by Luke the Evangelist; fourteen Epistles of Paul the Apostle, to the Romans, two to the Corinthians, to the Galatians, to the Ephesians, to the Philippians, to the Colossians, two to the Thessalonians, two to Timothy, to Titus, to Philemon, to the Hebrews; two of Peter the Apostle, three of John the Apostle, one of James the Apostle, one of Jude the Apostle, and the Apocalypse of John the Apostle. If anyone does not accept as sacred and canonical the aforesaid books in their entirety and with all their parts, as they have been accustomed to be read in the Catholic Church and as they are contained in the old Latin Vulgate Edition, and knowingly and deliberately rejects the aforesaid traditions, let him be anathema. Let all understand, therefore, in what order and manner the council, after having laid the foundation of the confession of faith, will proceed, and who are the chief witnesses and supports to whom it will appeal in conforming dogmas and in restoring morals in the Church.

1. While this declaration from the Council of Trent may be challenging to read because it was written over 500 years ago, what is not challenging to see is that the canon of Scripture it declares is the exact same canon of Scripture we find in Catholic Bibles today. And the Council Fathers also note that this canon is the same that Church has always adhered to from the very beginning. How does the consistency of the canon of Scripture over 2,000 years help to support that authority of the Word of God and of the Church?

2. The Council of Trent was held in part as a response to the Protestant Reformation when Protestant reformers challenged the authority of the Church and even the traditional canon of Scripture. Why do you think it was necessary for the Church to formally declare the canon here and to declare that anyone who taught otherwise would be anathema, or excommunicated, from the Church?

Chapter 7

# Sacred Scripture In the Life of the Church

# Chapter Overview

The Church eagerly invites everyone to read and know Scripture. She wants each of us to incorporate Scripture into our prayer lives and she guides us in how to interpret the Word of God properly. There are many ways to do this, from the theological study of Scripture, to praying with Scripture in the Liturgy of the Hours, at Mass, in the Rosary, and by using the steps of *Lectio Divina*. The written Word of God is spoken to each one of us in these devotions. Reading the Bible is an essential part of anyone's spiritual life, and as St. Jerome said, "ignorance of Scripture is ignorance of Christ." Therefore, in order for us to know Christ, we must know Scripture.

## In this chapter you will learn that ...

- Catholics are called to know Christ in Scripture through the Mass and various forms of prayer such as the Liturgy of the Hours, the Rosary and *Lectio Divina*.
- Praying with Scripture connects the faithful today with all those who have prayed with Scripture throughout history, to the days when Christ walked the earth.
- The Mass is divided into two major sections, both saturated with Scripture in nearly every word spoken and prayed.
- All Catholics are called to read and understand the Bible with the guidance and teaching of the Magisterium and in the context of Sacred Tradition.

### Bible Basics

"Lord, I am not worthy to have you enter under my roof; only say the word and my servant will be healed."
MATTHEW 8:8

"Hail, full of grace, the Lord is with thee: blessed art thou among women."
LUKE 1:28 (DOUAY-RHEIMS)

## Aa Vocabulary

**Second Vatican Council (n.):** The most recent ecumenical council of the Church held at the Vatican between 1963 and 1965. Also called Vatican II.

## The Importance of Sacred Scripture

Scripture has always been important to the Church. Even before the New Testament was written, the Christian community revered the Jewish sacred books that would come to make up the Old Testament. The Scriptures are an indispensable part of divine revelation, and through reading the Bible frequently, we can come to know Jesus Christ better. If the Bible is truly God Himself speaking, it is hard to imagine a better use of our time than listening to Him speaking through it.

It is sometimes said the Catholic Church does not support the faithful's reading of Scripture. This is not true. In fact, the **Second Vatican Council**, mandated that "Easy access to Sacred Scripture should be provided for all the Christian faithful" (*DV* 22). The Church does teach, though, that while we ought to read and study the Bible, we must always do so within the context of Sacred Tradition. When understood in this way, reading the Bible should be a part of every Christian's devotional life.

Sacred Scripture is one of our surest ways of getting to know Jesus Christ. St. Jerome even claimed that "ignorance of Scripture is ignorance of Christ."

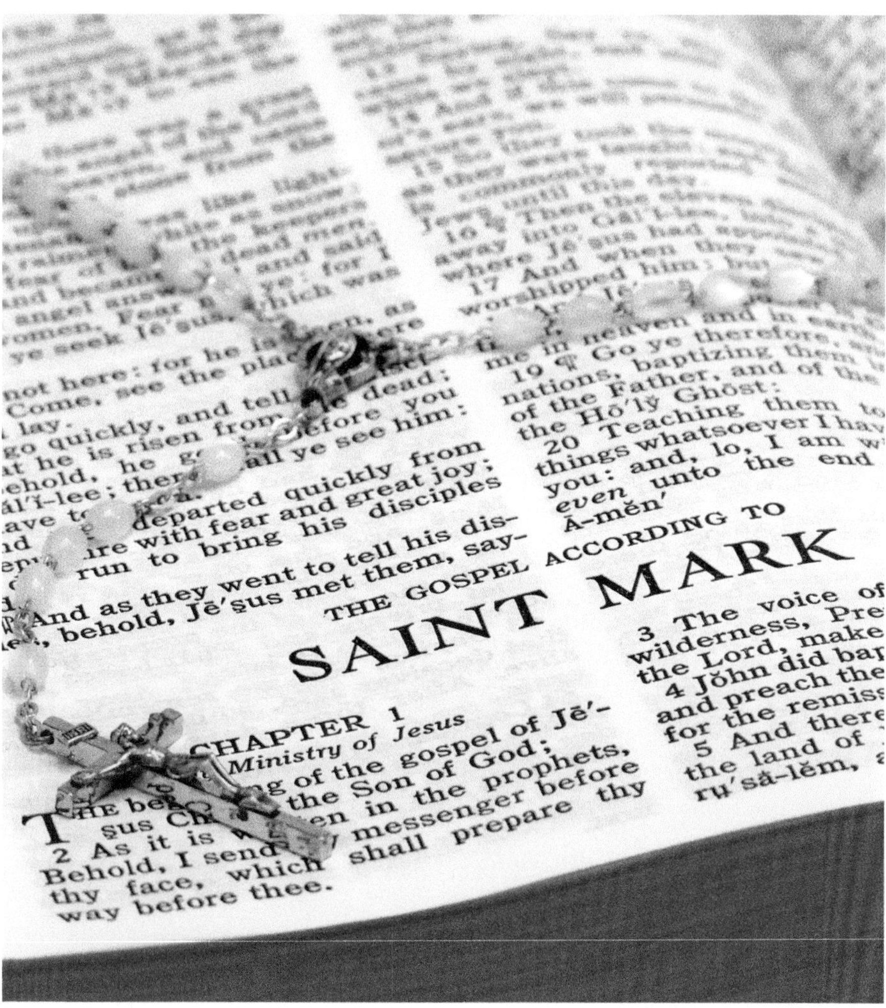


*Close Up of Saint Mark Bible Page with Rosary*
Photo Credit Joe Fallico / Shutterstock.

One way Catholics engage with Scripture is to think deeply about it. We try to understand what it says and then piece this information together with other things we know in order to arrive at new knowledge. This practice is called **theology**. Theology is the study of God. It is humanity's thinking through revealed truth. Theologians ask this question: Based on the things that God has shown us about Himself and based on what we know about ourselves and the world, what can we determine to be true?

Because God is the author of Scripture, the Bible is central to the project of theology; it provides theologians with a great deal of information about both God and us. If we are trying to learn more about God, it makes sense to start with His Word. For this reason, Vatican II calls Scripture "the soul of sacred theology" (*DV* 24).

However, theology is not just the study of the Bible. Rather, it is the study of God through the study of the Bible, Sacred Tradition, and natural revelation (experience). This means theology is not an end in and of itself. We do not practice it just to practice it or because we think it is fun to theorize about God. Instead, we study it to know God and ourselves better. Theology should deepen our relationship with God; it should help us love him more and do His will in the world. That is why God inspired the Scriptures: so we could learn about Him, think about Him, and follow Him.

## Scripture and Prayer

### *The Liturgy of the Hours*

The Bible is not just a book for personal devotion or for theological study. As we have seen, from the very beginning the Scriptures had a prominent place in the **liturgy** of the Church (CCC 1345). When we think of Catholic liturgy, our first thought is of Holy Mass. In addition to Mass, the Church daily celebrates the **Liturgy of the Hours**, also known as the Divine Office. The Bible is an integral part of this liturgy as well.

The Liturgy of the Hours gets its name because it is broken up into seven "hours" or periods of prayer throughout the day (*Matins, Lauds, Terce, Sext, None, Vespers, and Compline*). These small "liturgies" form the one Liturgy of the Hours. Each hour integrates the singing of the Psalms with readings from the Bible, prayers, hymns, and readings from the Fathers and Doctors of the Church. In this liturgy, Scripture is integrated fully into the Tradition of the Church, and this whole body of revelation—Scripture and Tradition—is integrated into the rhythm of the daily life of the praying Church.

Likewise, because the Liturgy of the Hours has its roots in Jewish temple worship, it unites the Church with its ancestors in Israel. When we pray the Hours, we participate in the full scope of Salvation History. The Vatican II

**Aa Vocabulary**

**Theology (n.):** The study of God based on divine revelation.

**Liturgy (n.):** The public work or worship of the Church. It is the participation of the people of God in the "work of God," which is our salvation from sin.

**Liturgy of the Hours (n.):** The public prayer of the Church which sanctifies the whole course of the day and night. It consists of a variety of prayers, Scripture readings, most especially the Psalms, and writings of the saints, divided into "hours," which are prescribed to be prayed at specific times of day.

**Aa Vocabulary**

**Ambo (n.):** A raised podium or lectern in a Church sanctuary from which the Scripture readings are proclaimed during Mass.

**Lectionary (n.):** The official liturgical book from which the reader proclaims the Scripture readings during Mass.

**Immaculate Conception (n.):** The dogma that from the first moment of her conception, by the grace of God, Mary was preserved from Original Sin.

document *Sacrosanctum Concilium* taught that the Liturgy of the Hours is nothing less than the prayer that Jesus Himself, united with His body, the Church, addresses to the Father. Therefore, praying the Hours unites Christians with each other throughout history and with Christ.

Given the understanding of Scripture that we have discussed so far, it should be clear how perfectly the Bible fits into this prayer. When we sing the Psalms of the Bible in the Liturgy of the Hours, we are not reciting texts from some distant past. Rather, we enter into the timeless prayer of the Church; the text of the Bible is pulled up off the page and made as real as it was when the Jews of the Old Testament first sang the hymns of praise, supplication, contrition, and thanksgiving. Likewise, as we move through the day and the seasons of the year, we read the Scripture guided by the prayers of the Church and the writings of her greatest saints. The Liturgy of the Hours is prayed daily by monks, nuns, and clergy, and the Church encourages the laity to pray it as well.

### *Scripture in the Mass*

In the life of the Church, Scripture is truly alive. Perhaps nowhere is this more powerfully the case than in the Mass. The first part of every Mass is called the Liturgy of the Word. During the Liturgy of the Word, we normally read from the Old Testament, sing Psalms, read from the epistles of the New Testament, and read from one of the Gospels. These readings are proclaimed from the **ambo**, which is a raised lectern in the sanctuary. This draws the congregation's attention to the proclamation of the Word. The readings are read out of the **lectionary**, which is essentially a Scriptural calendar, with specific readings for every liturgical day. These readings have been chosen by the Church because they have some connection with each other and with the liturgical day. Consider the Feast of the **Immaculate Conception**.

The Immaculate Conception is the celebration of the conception of Mary without the stain of original sin. The Church teaches that Mary was born "full of grace" and so without the sin everyone else has inherited through the Fall of Adam and Eve. Through Mary, Christ entered the world and defeated sin completely. The readings proclaimed on this feast tell this story.

The first reading concerns sin entering the world through Adam and Eve (Gen. 3:9–15, 20). The Psalm then praises God for the victory over evil that He brings to His people, setting the stage for the defeat of sin in the New Testament (Ps. 98:1–4). In the second reading, we hear St. Paul explaining that it is through Christ that the grace of God, given for the forgiveness of our sins, enters the world (Eph. 1:3–6, 11–12). The Gospel reading

*The Last Supper* by Juan de Juanes (ca. 1562).

▲ Sacred Scripture reveals to us that Our Lord instituted the Sacrament of the Eucharist at the Last Supper.

recounts how Christ came into the world through the humble statement, **"May it be done to me according to your word" (Luke 1:38)**, spoken by Mary, whom the angel declares to be **"full of grace" (Luke 1:28, Douay-Rheims version)**. The Church has long understood Mary to be the new Eve, through whom the victory that God promised in our first reading (Gen. 3:15) came into the world. This is the reason so many statues of Mary depict her standing on the serpent. Where Eve's "no" to God brought sin, Mary's "yes" brought salvation.

The readings on the Feast of the Immaculate Conception illuminate Mary's role as the new Eve in the story of our salvation. But in the Mass, these readings do not stand alone. As soon as they are completed, the bishop, priest, or deacon gives a **homily** in which he explains their connections, their meaning, and the way of life to which they call us. The Mass for the Immaculate Conception also has special prayers that further articulate the Church's understanding of Mary's place in Salvation History and praise the Lord for the gift of her grace-filled conception.

In the Mass, Sacred Scripture is interpreted by the Church through the organization of the readings, through the homily, and through the association of the readings with certain liturgical days and prayers. But the Mass is not biblical just because we read the Bible at Mass. The Mass is biblical because almost every prayer or action in Mass has a connection with Scripture.

For example, before we receive the Eucharist, we pray: "Lord, I am not worthy that you should enter under my roof, but only say the word and my soul shall be healed." This is a quotation and re-interpretation of the

**Aa Vocabulary**

**Homily (n.):** A preaching by an ordained minister to explain the Scriptures proclaimed at Mass.

### Lives of Faith

## St. Benedict

They knew they had made a terrible mistake, but the poison would fix it.

When the abbot had died, the group of monks thought they were being smart to ask this simple local man to be their new leader. He was just a hermit who lived in a cave! He would be a pushover, a placeholder. He would be leader in name, but really this group of monks would be able to do whatever they wanted.

However, they had gotten it all wrong. He was far from a pushover and not a placeholder. He lived the strict rule of life he wanted enforced, and it clashed with everything the monks had intended.

So, they had devised a simple plot. Poison him at dinner, be rid of him, and try again with a new abbot. The cup had been poured, poisoned, and served. Now it was only a matter of moments until their mistake would be undone.

The abbot sat and began to pray the blessing over their meal. And then it happened.

First, they heard the rattling. Then, they opened their eyes. The cup was vibrating on the table, wine splashing out. It vibrated faster and faster until it shattered, spilling the wine all over the table. The monks looked from the shattered clay and puddle of wine that was once the poisoned cup, up into the eyes of the abbot. He was staring at them. But he did not look angry. Rather, he looked sad.

After that the abbot went back to his cave and his simple way of life. That might have been the first community he led, but even though they had tried to poison him, it would not be his last. God had much more in store for the life of St. Benedict.

Benedict was passionate about his faith from a very young age. While studying in Rome he became disgusted by the sinfulness of the city. He fled to the countryside, choosing to live simply in silence, work, and prayer.

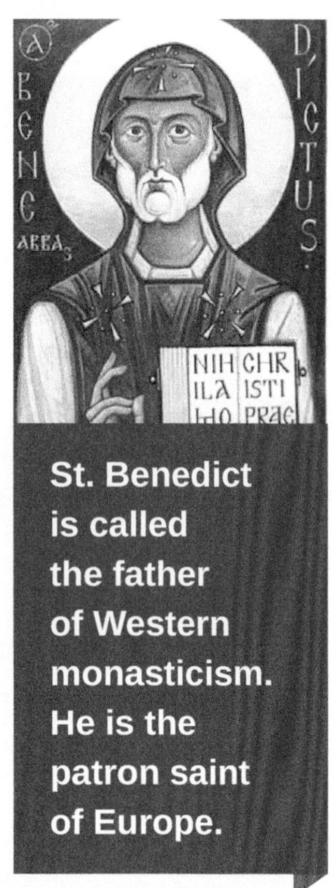

**St. Benedict is called the father of Western monasticism. He is the patron saint of Europe.**

Word spread about this holy man and his way of life. Hundreds of men came to him in the wilderness asking him to lead them. Benedict established twelve communities with twelve monks in each and gave them a rule of life.

The rule of St. Benedict is a guide for living for a Christian community of monks. It includes directions on what they should wear, how they should talk to each other, what they should read and eat, how they should work, and more. It became favorable for how it walked the tightrope between being strict and reasonable.

Among the many regulations and prescriptions of the rule, it emphasized Scripture as the primary reading and prayer for a monk. Benedict said, “For what page or word of the Bible is not a perfect rule for temporal life?” He prescribed Scripture to be used as a part of their schedule of daily prayers, often had Scripture read at meal times, and encouraged the monks to memorize Scripture as much as they could. Benedict was also one of the early proponents of *Lectio Divina.*

St. Benedict died in AD 543, but his rule lives on and is still used by men and women around the world today.

centurion's response to Jesus when He offered to come heal his servant: **"Lord, I am not worthy to have you enter under my roof; only say the word and my servant will be healed" (Mt. 8:8)**. Likewise, almost all the major prayers of the Mass, from the Gloria in the beginning, to the Eucharistic Prayers, find parallels in Scripture.

This does not always mean we simply quote Scripture in the Mass. For example, when we pray the Our Father at Mass, we are not just reciting a Scripture passage. Rather, we are obeying Christ's command to pray in a certain manner (Mt. 6:9–14). The Bible records the reason we pray the Our Father: Jesus told us to do so. But, this command of Christ's came before it was recorded in the Bible. It is certainly the case that the early Christians prayed the Our Father before it was written down in the Gospels. So our prayer is not just a recitation of Scripture passages. Instead, it is rooted in the early Church's actual encounter with Christ.

The Bible and liturgy grew up together and belong together. In the Mass, from the **Liturgy of the Word** to the **Liturgy of the Eucharist**, Sacred Scripture finds its most appropriate home. It is fundamentally united with the tradition of the Church, the preaching of her priests, and the worship of the faithful.

## Scripture in Personal Prayer

In the Church's liturgy, Scripture comes alive in a social way. Together, we read Scriptures and pray Scriptures. The Scriptures are also appropriately read in a devotional way by individuals or small groups in parishes, schools, and other prayerful gatherings. Classes or small groups often come together to read, pray, and discuss the readings from Sunday Mass. In this way, they extend their celebration of Sunday Mass through the week and engage prayerfully with all the different parts of Scripture from which the lectionary draws.

Another method of prayerful reading of Scripture is called ***Lectio Divina***, or divine reading. *Lectio Divina* grew out of the spiritual reading practiced by monks for centuries during the Middle Ages. Rather than just reading or studying the Bible, when we practice *Lectio Divina*, we actually pray it, inviting the Holy Spirit to guide us through the Bible. *Lectio Divina* is often broken down into four steps: *Lectio*, or reading, in which we read a passage of Scripture (or better yet, have it read to us) and listen to God's Word as if He is speaking directly to us; *Meditatio*, or meditation, in which we meditate upon the passage to discern what the text–and God–says to us; *Oratio*, or prayer, in which we respond to the Lord by praying to Him about what we have read; and *Contemplatio*, or contemplation, in which we contemplate what we have read and meditated upon by resting

### Aa Vocabulary

**Liturgy of the Word (n.):** The first part of the Mass in which we receive the written word of God. Here, the Scriptures are proclaimed and the priest teaches in a homily. We also join together in prayer for others and profess our faith.

**Liturgy of the Eucharist (n.):** The second part of the Mass in which we receive the Body and Blood, Soul and Divinity of Jesus Christ in the Eucharist. Here, the priest prays the words of consecration and changes the bread and wine into the Body and Blood of Christ. Those well-disposed also come to the altar to receive Holy Communion.

***Lectio Divina* (n.):** An ancient form of praying with Scripture that is a slow and thoughtful encounter with the Word of God. Latin for "divine reading."

in the Lord's presence and allowing Him to move within us and speak to us. It is not necessary, however, to follow a strict method. We can pray the Scriptures just by reading them prayerfully and with care, placing ourselves in the scene or reflecting on how the words apply to our life and letting these thoughts move us to pray to God and give him thanks.

In many other forms of personal or communal prayer, we often engage Scripture without realizing it. Consider the **Rosary**. The central prayers of the Rosary are the Our Father and the Hail Mary. We already discussed the Our Father. It is directly biblical, taken right from the mouth of Christ. The Hail Mary is also biblical. **"Hail, full of grace, the Lord is with thee" (Luke 1:28, Douay-Rheims version)** is the angel's greeting to Mary at the Annunciation. **"Most blessed are you among women, and blessed is the fruit of your womb" (Luke 1:42)** is the greeting offered to Mary by Elizabeth at the Visitation. Both of these greetings point to Mary as the mother of God, so the prayer continues with the Church making this assertion: "Holy Mary, Mother of God." Finally, we ask for her intercession "Pray for us sinners, now and at the hour of our death."

The Rosary is biblical on another level as well. During each decade of the Rosary, we contemplate a different mystery in the life of Jesus and His mother. There are twenty mysteries in total. When we pray them, we contemplate the major events in Jesus and His mother's life. Most of these events are found in the Bible. Likewise, the Rosary parallels the liturgical calendar, so in praying it, we experience not only biblical history, but also the liturgical life of the Church in miniature.

### Vocabulary

**Rosary (n.):** A prayer in honor of the Blessed Virgin Mary, which repeats the "Hail Mary" prayer in "decades" of ten prayers, each preceded by an "Our Father" and concluded by a "Glory Be," accompanied by meditation on the mysteries of Christ's life. It is typically prayed using a chain of beads.

The angel Gabriel greets Mary and bows in reverence. Each time we pray the Hail Mary we echo this angelic salutation found in Scripture.

*The Annunciation* by Leonardo da Vinci (ca. 1472).

**The Joyful Mysteries**

1. The Annunciation, Luke 1:30–33; John 1:14.
2. The Visitation, Luke 1:39–40.
3. The Nativity of the Lord, Luke 2:7.
4. The Presentation of the Lord in the Temple, Luke 2:22.
5. The Finding of the Lord in the Temple, Luke 2:46.

**The Luminous Mysteries**

1. The Baptism of the Lord, Matthew 3:16–17.
2. The Wedding at Cana, John 2:1–3.
3. The Proclamation of the Kingdom of God, Mark 1:14–15.
4. The Transfiguration of the Lord, Luke 9:28–31.
5. The Institution of the Holy Eucharist, Luke 22:19.

**The Sorrowful Mysteries**

1. The Agony in the Garden, Matthew 26:36–46; Mark 14:32–42; Luke 22:39–46.
2. The Scourging at the Pillar, John 19:1; Lamentations 1:12.
3. The Crowning with Thorns, John 19:1–5; Song of Solomon 3:11; Isaiah 1:6.
4. The Carrying of the Cross, John 19:16–17; Luke 23:27–28; Luke 9:23; Galatians 6:14.
5. The Crucifixion of the Lord, Luke 23:20–21; Matthew 27:26; John 19:17–18; John 19:30; Galatians 5:24; Galatians 2:19.

**The Glorious Mysteries**

1. The Resurrection of the Lord, Matthew 28:5–6; Mark 16:6; Luke 24:5–6; Colossians 2:12; Colossians 3:1.
2. The Ascension of the Lord, Luke 24:50–51.
3. The Descent of the Holy Spirit at Pentecost, John 14:16–17; John 16:7–13; Acts 2:1–4.
4. The Assumption of the Blessed Virgin, 1 Kings 2:19; Sirach 24:10–12.
5. The Coronation of the Blessed Virgin in Heaven, Song of Solomon 4:7–8; Revelation 12:1.

Through this "walk" through Scripture, the Rosary demonstrates that in the Catholic understanding, Scripture, tradition, liturgy, and devotions harmoniously co-exist, so the study and prayers of individual Christians are integrated with those of the entire Church, forming a single act of worship.

**[T]he Rosary demonstrates that in the Catholic understanding, Scripture, tradition, liturgy, and devotions harmoniously co-exist.**

## Do Catholics read the Bible?

Yes! As we have just seen, Catholicism is soaked in Scripture, and the central rite of Catholicism—the Mass—is profoundly Biblical. It is not only derived from the history of Israel, but it also uses Scripture throughout, bringing the Bible to life in a way not seen anywhere else. Likewise, Scripture is an encounter with Jesus, the Word of God, and the Eucharist is taking the Word of God into our very selves! In the Mass, our encounter with God is complete.

However, it is not just in the liturgy, that Catholics encounter the Bible. Catholics use the Scriptures for the study of theology, personal devotion and prayer, and public prayer. Moreover, many Catholic parishes offer Bible study groups and Vacation Bible School, so the faithful not only encounter the Word of God but also learn how to take their study of the Word deeper. As disciples of Christ, we are continually spurred on to a deeper knowledge of Scripture for as St. Jerome wrote, "Ignorance of the Scriptures is ignorance of Christ."

From where does the charge that Catholics do not read the Bible come? This criticism originates from a certain Protestant point of view, and it is based on various bits of half-truths or mistakes.

Prior to the advent of the printing press in the mid-1400s and widespread literacy, it was true that most Catholics never read the Bible. This was because most Catholics could not read *anything*; the majority of people were illiterate. For those few who could read, Bibles were hard to come by; each one had to be painstakingly copied by hand.

### Aa Vocabulary

**Protestant Reformation (n.):** A 16th century revolt began by Martin Luther that divided and eventually splintered Christianity. Many Christian churches formed as a result of this split, which are known as Protestant churches, or denominations. Though Jesus desires that His Church be one, all baptized Christians are brothers and sisters in Christ.

***Sola Scriptura* (n.):** The belief that the Bible is the only source of divine revelation held by most non-Catholic Christian churches. Latin for "by Scripture alone."

Printing technology, as well as more widespread literacy rates, developed at the same time as the **Protestant Reformation**. These developments aided the spread of the Protestant doctrine of ***sola scriptura***—the belief that the Bible is the only authoritative source of divine revelation—as well as their belief in the individual interpretation of the Bible—the idea that every Christian can interpret the Bible for himself.

However, the Church rejected this understanding of the Scriptures. The Bible, the Church believed, was not the only source of revelation about God. God also revealed Himself in nature and through Sacred Tradition. Catholic catechesis, then, included truths not drawn directly from the Bible. To those who held a *sola scriptura* point of view, this looked like the Church was prioritizing man-made traditions over biblical teaching. The Church's warning that the Bible was often hard to understand and its subsequent mandate that the faithful approach it with the guidance of the Magisterium, looked equally bad to Protestants. In their eyes, the Church was trying to keep the Bible from the faithful or prejudice their interpretation of it.

Likewise, unlike the Protestants, the Church maintained that biblical reading was not the only form of praiseworthy devotion. The Catholic faith also embraced (and still does) many devotional practices, from attending Mass, to making **the Way of the Cross**, to reciting the Rosary. As we have seen, none of these devotions are at odds with the Bible; in fact, they are profoundly Scriptural. However, they differ from the individual reading and interpretation of the Bible advocated by the Protestant reformers.

Aside from these doctrinal issues, the widespread belief that Catholics do not read the Bible does have some foundation in reality. For a long time, much of the laity did not engage Sacred Scripture as much as they should have. It was also true some clergy were hesitant to suggest that the faithful read the Bible more; to some it seemed a bit Protestant. However, what truth exists in these criticisms has been grossly over-blown. The Church, especially in the twentieth century, has never tired of encouraging the faithful to read the Bible.

Another truth that has contributed to the perception that Catholics do not read the Bible is the fact that the Catholic Church is far larger than any single Protestant community and has an inclusive understanding of its membership.

*Christ Carrying His Cross* by Titian (ca. 1560).

**Aa Vocabulary**

**The Way of the Cross (n.):** A traditional devotional prayer that focuses on the Passion of Jesus. It follows Jesus' path as He carried His Cross and was crucified.

As the Church sees it, anyone who is baptized and has not formally repudiated the Church is Catholic. Accordingly, the Church is like a nation, full of all kinds of people of varying degrees of education, piety, and enthusiasm. Many people who do not practice their faith will, when asked, identify themselves as Catholic. This is a wonderful characteristic of the Church. Catholicism has room for people in every stage of the spiritual journey—it is the universal Church, after all. But, one of the consequences is that people end up encountering Catholics who know very little about their faith and have perhaps never opened a Bible.

All these factors have come together to create the common misconception that Catholics do not read the Bible and the Church does not really want them to. Yet, while Catholics do not approach the Bible in the same way as Protestants, the Scriptures are of supreme importance in the life of the Church. All Catholics are encouraged to read and learn them.

# The Truth Is...

The only wrong way to read Scripture is to not read it at all. Maybe you have heard this saying before. It may be a little cheesy, but it is also very true. It does come with one caveat, however: there are right and wrong ways to interpret Scripture, which is why we need the guidance of the Magisterium of the Church to help us understand the Word of God. But, we will never know the Word of God if we never listen to it. In Scripture, God speaks to us directly in human language. How will we know what He is saying to us if we never open the Bible and start reading?

The Church invites us to incorporate Scripture into our daily lives in all sorts of ways: from the Mass, to the Liturgy of the Hours, from the theological study of Scripture to the spiritual contemplation of it in Lectio Divina. The Church wants us to know and interact with Scripture so that we might acquire our knowledge of Jesus and His Church and all His promises to us. But if you have never opened the Bible before (outside of religion class) or it has been a long time since you have done so, it can be a little intimidating to begin (or to begin again). So, start small. A good rule of thumb is to never let your head hit your pillow at night without having read something from the Bible. It does not have to be much; a passage or two will work. Even a single word from God has the power to change your life. After all, He made everything that exists in the entire universe using only four.

Chapter 7

# Focus and Reflection Questions

1. What does the Church teach about access to Sacred Scripture and the context within which it should be read?

2. What is theology?

3. Why does Vatican II call Scripture the "soul of sacred theology"?

4. How and by whom are the Liturgy of the Hours prayed?

5. What are the two main parts of the Mass?

6. What are some ways the Mass is rooted in Scripture?

7. What is *Lectio Divina* and what are its four parts?

8. How does praying the Rosary include Scripture?

9. What challenges did early Catholics face that kept them from being able to read the Bible themselves?

10. How does the Catholic belief in how to interpret Scripture differ from Protestants?

11. What factors add to the misconception that Catholics do not understand the Bible today?

12. Which Catholics are called to read and pray with the Scriptures?

13. What role did Scripture play in the rule of St. Benedict?

# Straight to the Source

ADDITIONAL READINGS FROM PRIMARY SOURCES

*For chapter 7, rather than the usual variety of selections from primary sources, we will look at in close detail the official and dogmatic teaching of the Catholic Church regarding divine revelation that is found in the Vatican II document Dei Verbum. You will read all of* Dei Verbum *in this course.*

## ***Dei Verbum 21–22, 26—The Dogmatic Constitution on Divine Revelation from the Second Vatican Council, November 18, 1968***

21. The Church has always venerated the divine Scriptures just as she venerates the body of the Lord, since, especially in the sacred liturgy, she unceasingly receives and offers to the faithful the bread of life from the table both of God's word and of Christ's body. She has always maintained them, and continues to do so, together with sacred tradition, as the supreme rule of faith, since, as inspired by God and committed once and for all to writing, they impart the word of God Himself without change, and make the voice of the Holy Spirit resound in the words of the prophets and Apostles. Therefore, like the Christian religion itself, all the preaching of the Church must be nourished and regulated by Sacred Scripture. For in the sacred books, the Father who is in Heaven meets His children with great love and speaks with them; and the force and power in the word of God is so great that it stands as the support and energy of the Church, the strength of faith for her sons, the food of the soul, the pure and everlasting source of spiritual life. Consequently these words are perfectly applicable to Sacred Scripture: "For the word of God is living and active" (Heb. 4:12) and "it has power to build you up and give you your heritage among all those who are sanctified" (Acts 20:32; see 1 Thess. 2:13).

22. Easy access to Sacred Scripture should be provided for all the Christian faithful. That is why the Church from the very beginning accepted as her own that very ancient Greek translation of the Old Testament which is called the septuagint; and she has always given a place of honor to other Eastern translations and Latin ones especially the Latin translation known as the vulgate. But since the word of God should be accessible at all times, the Church by her authority and with maternal concern sees to it that suitable and correct translations are made into different languages, especially from the original texts of the sacred books. And should the opportunity arise and the Church authorities approve, if these translations are produced in cooperation with the separated brethren as well, all Christians will be able to use them.

26. In this way, therefore, through the reading and study of the sacred books "the word of God may spread rapidly and be glorified" (2 Thess. 3:1) and the treasure of revelation, entrusted to the Church, may more and more fill the hearts of men. Just as the life of the Church is strengthened through more frequent celebration of the Eucharistic mystery, similar we may hope for a new stimulus for the life of the Spirit from a growing reverence for the word of God, which "lasts forever" (Is. 40:8; see 1 Peter 1:23–25).

# Straight to the Source

ADDITIONAL READINGS FROM PRIMARY SOURCES

## Focus Questions

1. The Church holds the Scriptures in high regard as she does the Eucharist. Why?
2. What should Sacred Scripture regulate and nourish?
3. What kind of access should the faithful have to the scriptures?
4. What is the Greek translation of the Old Testament called?
5. What is the Latin translation of the Bible called?
6. What does the Church say must happen in order for all people to have access to the Scriptures?
7. What should happen through the reading and study of the sacred books?

## Reflection Question

Given what you have learned about Scripture and Tradition and the authority of the Church in this chapter and in previous chapters, how would you explain to someone the Church's relationship to Scripture and Tradition and how the Church wants the faithful to interact with the Word of God?

UNIT 3

# Interpreting Scripture

The human authors of Scripture wrote using different writing styles and tried to communicate different ideas with their writing. Sometimes they wrote intending for every last detail to be as accurate as possible. Other times they intended to use poetic language full of metaphor. They also wrote using their own powers and abilities, which means that they did not have perfect knowledge about everything. This is especially important to remember because sometimes, when we read Scripture, especially today with our modern sensibilities and knowledge, we notice small details in Scripture that may not seem accurate.

For example, the book of Genesis tells us that the universe was created in six days. Through modern science we have come to discover that the universe is actually billions of years old and took much longer to be made. When we encounter a situation like this in the Bible, our first instinct should not be to question the accuracy of the Bible. Remember, God is the true author of Scripture and spoke through the human writers He inspired. We should always ask the basic question: "What is the truth that God wanted to communicate to us?" or, put another way, "What does God want us know from this story for the sake of our salvation?"

In the story of creation from Genesis, we can be certain that the human author was not trying to write a scientific account of how the universe came to be. Rather, he was writing in a style common in his time about certain fundamental truths about God, human beings, and our relationship with God. This does not mean that the story is untrue. Instead, it tells us different kinds of truths than we were initially looking for, deeper, more important truths. In order to understand more fully the things God wanted known through Scripture, we must consider how to interpret it authentically. Thankfully, in her wisdom, the Catholic Church has given guidance to ensure that our interpretation of Scripture does not stray from the truth.

## In This Unit

- **Chapter 8:** Authentic Interpretation of Scripture
- **Chapter 9:** The Bible in Relation to Science and History

Chapter 8

# Authentic Interpretation of Scripture

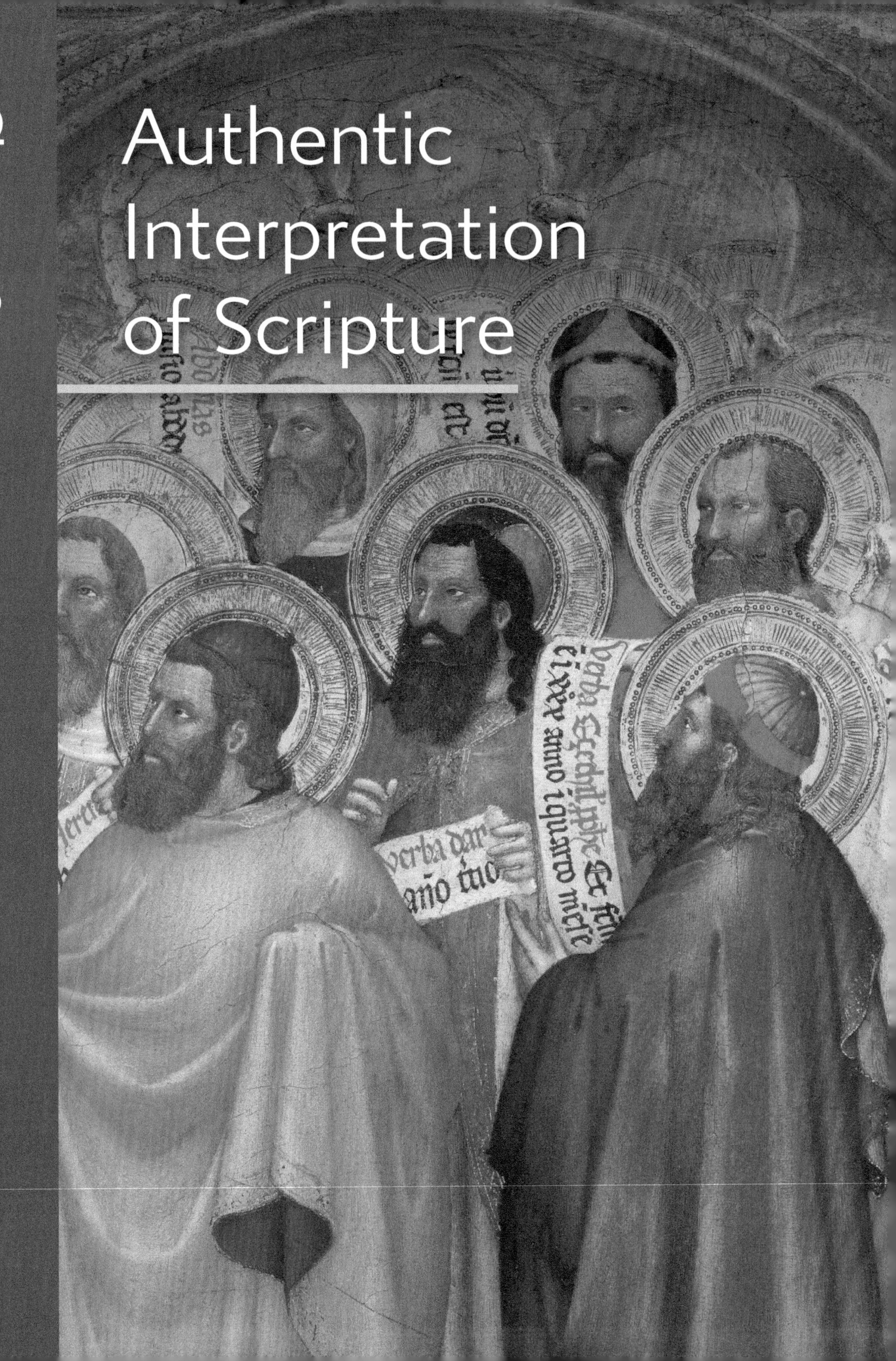

# Chapter Overview

To interpret Scripture is to determine what it means. Some believe this task (called *exegesis*) is entirely a personal matter: that Scripture means whatever you want it to mean. But this is not the correct way to understand Scripture. If this were the case, then two people might interpret the same Scripture passage to mean completely contradictory things. Sadly, this approach has led to a lot of division in the Church since the Protestant Reformation. Thankfully, the Catholic Church has given us a lot of direction on how to interpret Scripture correctly so we can grow in our relationship with the Lord.

## In this chapter you will learn that …

- Jesus entrusted to the Church the authority to interpret Scripture.
- The meaning of Scripture is not a matter of personal interpretation.
- The Scriptures belong to the Church as a whole, and you can rely on the wisdom of the Church when you read the Scriptures.
- Scripture has literal and spiritual senses; the spiritual sense is broken down into allegorical, moral, and anagogical senses.
- The desire to grow in a relationship with God should shape the way we read the Bible.

### Bible Basics

Know this first of all, that there is no prophecy of scripture that is a matter of personal interpretation, for no prophecy ever came through human will; but rather human beings moved by the holy Spirit spoke under the influence of God.
2 PETER 1:20–21

When the people saw the sign he had done, they said, "This is truly the Prophet, the one who is to come into the world."
JOHN 6:14

### Connections to the *Catechism*

CCC 85 (page 110)
CCC 86 (page 110)
CCC 116 (page 118)
CCC 117 (page 119)
CCC 1101 (page 119)

Aa **Vocabulary**

**Exegesis (n.):** An interpretation or analysis of scriptural text.

**The task of giving an authentic interpretation of the Word of God ... has been entrusted to the living, teaching office of the Church alone**

## The Role of the Magisterium

The Sacred Scriptures are a precious treasure to the Church, which means she takes the task of interpreting them (called **exegesis**) seriously. The Magisterium of the Church has the responsibility of ensuring that the sacred text is interpreted properly. This is part of the authority given by Jesus to the Apostles and their successors—the bishops together with the pope—that we learned about in Unit 1. The Scriptures bring us into communion with God through engaging His Word in prayerful dialogue, so it is an essential task of the Church to help us understand what God is communicating.

The *Catechism* explains this in the following way:

> **"The task of giving an authentic interpretation of the Word of God, whether in its written form or in the form of Tradition, has been entrusted to the living, teaching office of the Church alone. Its authority in this matter is exercised in the name of Jesus Christ. This means that the task of interpretation has been entrusted to the bishops in communion with the successor of Peter, the Bishop of Rome" (CCC 85).**

> **"Yet this Magisterium is not superior to the Word of God, but is its servant. It teaches only what has been handed on to it. At the divine command and with the help of the Holy Spirit, it listens to this devotedly, guards it with dedication, and expounds it faithfully. All that it proposes for belief as being divinely revealed is drawn from this single deposit of faith" (CCC 86).**

Why, is any of this necessary? Why cannot individual Christians just interpret the Bible on our own? Why do we need the Church to tell us what the text means?

It is true that every Christian can and should study the Scriptures, and strive to understand them. At the same time, we cannot do this in isolation from the Church. As we learned in Unit 2, Scripture plays a central role in the life of the Church through liturgy and personal prayer, the ministry of preaching and teaching, and in the study of theology. The Scriptures also "grew up" within the Church: the New Testament authors wrote their Gospels and letters for the Church; they intended them to be read in the Church; and it was the Church who recognized which books were divinely inspired.

The Scriptures belong to the Church as a whole. Like the first Christians, we receive them in and through the Church, which has handed them on and taught them through the ages. For these reasons, you cannot accurately interpret the Scriptures apart from the context of the Church's life and tradition.

*Passion Altar, Left Wing: Foot Washing* by Unknown Artist (ca. 1480).

Christ washes His disciples' feet at the Last Supper. He gave the disciples authority to teach and interpret Scriptures, and charged them to follow His example as leaders of His Church.

Moreover, as we learned in Unit 2, the inspired authors of the Scriptures wrote according to the customs of their time and culture. Therefore, the meaning of the Scriptures is not always obvious, and people can easily misunderstand the meaning of a particular passage or disagree on how a certain statement should be understood. These misunderstandings and disagreements can have serious consequences, causing division in the Church and creating confusion about who God is, what we must do to be saved, or what is right and wrong.

To protect the Church against this division and confusion, Jesus gave the Apostles and their successors the authority and responsibility to ensure the Scriptures are interpreted properly. Interpreting the Scriptures can be a challenge, but just as you might rely on the experience of a teacher to help you prepare for an important test or carry out a tricky science experiment, you can rely on the wisdom of the Church when you read the Scriptures. When we read the Bible in light of the tradition, we are drawing on the experience of the Church's greatest saints and teachers.

**When we read the Bible in light of the tradition, we are drawing on the experience of the Church's greatest saints and teachers.**

Aa **Vocabulary**

**Historical-critical Method (n.):** The name given to the method of Scripture analysis that considers the historical context of Scripture.

## Modern Biblical Interpretation and Recent Church Teaching

In the modern era, important developments occurred in the way we interpret the Scriptures. Scholars developed a form of research called the **historical-critical method**. This method originated in seventeenth-century Europe, with scholars who believed certain research techniques could help them understand past events better, learn more about the writers of certain texts, and discern fact from fiction in historical narratives.

Beginning in the eighteenth and nineteenth centuries, biblical scholars sought to apply these methods to the study of Sacred Scripture. They wanted to use them to determine how and why the texts of the Bible were composed. At first the Church responded to these new methods with great caution. It rightly suspected some people might use these methods to treat the Scriptures as a collection of merely human texts. The Church recognized that this would break with the tradition of Catholic exegesis stretching back to the Fathers of the Church, undermining the reverence due to Sacred Scripture and belief in the Bible's reliability and unity.

However, the Church also recognized that because the Scriptures developed in history, these methods, when used rightly, did have a legitimate place. In the twentieth century, the Magisterium of the Church sought to better formulate the principles of authentic interpretation and determine their proper role in Catholic exegesis. By doing this, they hoped to bring about a renewal of the study and appreciation of Scripture in the life of the whole Church.

Pope St. Paul VI presiding over the commencement of the Second Vatican Council.

*Pope Paul VI during the Second Vatican Council*
Photo Credit: Lothar Wolleh (between 1963 and 1965).

## The Bible is old, so why do people think it applies to them today?

Condemning books based on their age is really a form of "historical snobbery." Whether or not something is true has nothing to do with whether or not that thing is old. A work or idea that is thousands of years old and still around is more worthy of consideration, not less.

Even though the Bible was written in a certain time and place, the "Good News" of the Bible remains timeless and universal. It speaks to us as human beings in our lives today. In fact, the Church does not believe the Word of God is "old," even if the Bible itself is. Rather, the Church teaches that the Word of God is alive. First, this is because of its relationship to Jesus, the living Word of God. Second, this is because the Bible is always read with the guidance of the Magisterium of the Church which consists of living, breathing bishops who are guided by the Holy Spirit as they apply the teachings of Scripture to our lives today. Finally, as we saw in Part II, at every Mass the Word of God is brought to life through readings, prayers, the homily, and most perfectly, in the Eucharist itself. The Scripture is ever new, and the Word of God is a living force in the life of the Church.

The principles of Catholic biblical interpretation were explained in a particular way in three important documents. The first of these documents, Pope Pius XII's 1943 encyclical, *Divino Afflante Spiritu*, opened the door to wider use of modern historical methods of biblical interpretation and encouraged the use of the original languages of the Scriptures (Hebrew and Greek) for study and translation. In 1965, the Second Vatican Council gave a definitive account of the Catholic understanding of divine revelation in the Dogmatic Constitution on Divine Revelation known as *Dei Verbum*. Like *Divino Afflante Spiritu, Dei Verbum* emphasizes the need to consider historical and literary context in the interpretation of Scripture. Its teaching is the direct basis for the teaching of the *Catechism of the Catholic Church* on revelation and Scripture, and it continues to inform Catholic biblical interpretation.

Finally, the Pontifical Biblical Commission's 1993 document, *Interpretation of the Bible in the Church*, spelled out the principles of Catholic exegesis in more detail based on the teachings of *Dei Verbum* and the ongoing experience and reflections of Catholic biblical scholars. The document provided guidance on several interpretative methodologies, including what are called textual, historical, literary, source, and redaction methods. It also laid out and described the "senses of Scripture" and listed characteristics of authentic Catholic interpretation. Among these characteristics, it emphasized the role of Sacred Tradition, the role of the interpreter, and the influence of other theological disciplines.

***Dei Verbum* emphasizes the need to consider historical and literary context in the interpretation of Scripture.**

## Lives of Faith

# St. Athanasius

"How far can these persecutions go?" Athanasius asked God.

He had just witnessed his enemies storm their way into his Church and kill members of his congregation. He had fled for his life and only here in the desert had he found safety. The monks were practically hermits, and they would care for and protect him as long as he needed. For now, he was safe. But he could not stop from asking, "Lord, how far can these persecutions go?"

Athanasius was born into a prominent Christian family in Alexandria and seemed to be destined for the priesthood. Alexander, the bishop of Alexandria, saw the boy Athanasius in the streets one day playing with the other boys. The bishop watched as Athanasius pretended to baptize his friends, and he was so amused he gave all the boys an education and told them they could begin to prepare for the priesthood if they wanted.

When Athanasius was ordained a deacon, he was appointed as the personal secretary to Bishop Alexander. Shortly after is when the trouble started. Arius, a priest from Alexandria, began teaching a false interpretation of Scripture: that Jesus was God's son, but not actually God. Rather, He was created by the Father. This false teaching grew in popularity, and soon it was spreading through the early Church like wildfire.

Athanasius opposed Arius—but so did the rest of the Church. He had plenty of support. The Council of Nicaea condemned the teachings of Arius as heresy, but that did not stop Arius and his supporters. When Bishop Alexander died a few months after the council, Athanasius succeeded him as bishop. Arius' supporters had a new target for their attacks on truth.

The rest of Athanasius' life would be marked by persecution for refusing to accept Arius' false teaching on Jesus. Arius' followers falsely accused Athanasius of treason and bribery. They accused him of murder and promoting bloodshed. Again and again they tried to charge him with crimes, and again and again Athanasius was cleared by popes and kings. So, they made their tactics more brutal. They began to physically attack him and his people, and even murdered some of them. Athanasius was exonerated, then charged again; banned, then welcomed back; exiled, then received.

**Persecution lasted for a matter of months, and sometimes it was a matter of years. But Athanasius never lost faith. He never lost hope.**

Sometimes the persecution lasted for a matter of months, and sometimes it was a matter of years. But Athanasius never lost faith. He never lost hope. He would write to his people and care for their concerns as best he could. And as soon as he was able, he would return home.

Over the course of his life, Athanasius was banned five times from Alexandria, received countless accusations against his character, and spent seventeen years of his life in exile. All because he would not stop defending the Truth.

One common theme of all three documents is an encouragement for Catholics to study the Scriptures. For example:

> "This author of salvation, Christ, will men more fully know, more ardently love and faithfully imitate in proportion as they are more assiduously urged to know and meditate the Sacred Letters, especially the New Testament, for, as St. Jerome the Doctor of Stridon says: 'To ignore the Scripture is to ignore Christ'; and again: 'If there is anything in this life which sustains a wise man and induces him to maintain his serenity amidst the tribulations and adversities of the world, it is in the first place, I consider, the meditation and knowledge of the Scriptures'" (*Divino Afflante Spiritu* 57).
>
> This should be so done that as many ministers of the divine word as possible will be able effectively to provide the nourishment of the Scriptures for the people of God, to enlighten their minds, strengthen their wills, and set men's hearts on fire with the love of God" (*DV* 23).

Ultimately, the Magisterium evaluates all new methods of exegesis in light of the faith of the Church. It does this to provide guidance for the work of scholars, but at the same time it exhorts all believers to study the Scriptures. The Scriptures are God's Word to His Church, so when we study them with eyes of faith, it is like having an extended conversation with a friend. Just like we need to spend a great deal of time with a person for a friendship to grow, we need to spend time with the Scriptures if we want to grow in our relationship with God. This desire—to grow in relationship with God—should shape the way we read Sacred Scriptures.

**The Magisterium evaluates all new methods of exegesis in light of the faith of the Church.**

## Criteria for Interpreting Scripture

Now that we know how much the Church desires us to engage Sacred Scripture and how valuable it is to spend time in study with the Bible, we need to look at some practical criteria for interpreting Scripture:

### *Church Teaching and Tradition*

As we discussed above, the home of the Scriptures is the Church. To understand Scripture properly, we need to read it in the context of the Tradition of the Church, which stretches back to the Apostles. We also need to read it in context of the life of the Church, which places Scripture at the heart of her liturgy, preaching, and teaching.

When you approach the Bible, it is important to know you are not the first person who has ever read it. If you struggle to understand it, you are not alone. As a member of the Church, you can learn from others who have read and taught the Scriptures and sometimes struggled to understand them. You can do this by drawing from the Church's tradition of interpretation, built on the experience of the great saints and teachers through the centuries and guided by the authoritative teaching of the Magisterium.

**The work of understanding and handing on the Scriptures continues in the life of the Church today.**

In the Middle Ages, the tradition of interpretation was passed on within the very text of the Bible. Medieval scholars included comments from the fathers of the Church and other important teachers in the margins and between the lines of their Bibles, or they compiled these comments into a chain of commentary called a ***catena***, from the Latin word for "chain."

However, the Church's tradition does not belong only to the past. The work of understanding and handing on the Scriptures continues in the life of the Church today. The research of scholars, the authoritative teaching of the pope and bishops, as well as the preaching and teaching of clergy and catechists draws from and builds on the tradition. God continues to speak to His Church through the Scriptures, and your own reading and study of the Scriptures is a part of this. Your study of the Scriptures will be most fruitful, though, when it is rooted in the Church's tradition, guided by the Church's Magisterium, and enriched by your experience sharing in the life of the Church, especially through the liturgy.

**Aa Vocabulary**

***Catena* (n.):** From the Latin for "chain," the practice of Medieval biblical scholars of including comments from the early Church Fathers and other important teachers in the margins and between the lines of their Bibles, forming a chain of commentary.

### *Historical Context*

Secondly, to understand the Scriptures, we must pay attention to what the inspired authors intended to say. In Unit 2, we learned that the books of the Bible were written by particular people in a particular time and place. To understand what these inspired authors meant by what they wrote, we have to learn about their culture, historical circumstances, and the different styles of writing used. This can be challenging to us today, living thousands of years after the books were written in a very different time and a very different culture. There may be references in a text that a reader 2,000 years ago would have instantly understood without question that today we would not automatically understand. Very often, in order to understand any deeper meaning in a biblical text, we must first understand the historical context—which can include the language the text was written in, the phrases of speech used by the author, the cultural customs at play in the text, the historical circumstances surrounding the event occurring in the text, the manner of dress of the people in the text, the customs surrounding eating and associating with others, and so forth. All of this can make discerning the historical context very challenging to the modern reader.

*Saint Thomas Aquinas* by Carlo Crivelli (1476).

St. Thomas Aquinas wrote many volumes that can help us better understand the unity of Scripture and the truths of our Faith; though it is incomplete, his best-known work is the *Summa Theologiae*.

**Aa Vocabulary**

**Analogy of Faith (n.):** The coherence of the truths of the Faith among themselves and within the whole plan of revelation.

### *The Unity of Scripture and All Truths of the Faith*

To understand the full meaning of the text, we need to do more than try to understand what the inspired human author intended to say in his time. We also need to try to understand what God intends to reveal to us through His words. To do this, we need to read the passage not just in its original historical context, but also in the context of the entirety of Scripture and all the truths of the Faith. The books of the Bible have different human authors and were written in different times and places using different styles of writing, but they were all inspired by the Holy Spirit, so we must read them all together to truly understand what He intends to say to us.

Again, to properly understand a passage of Scripture or a particular Catholic teaching, it is always necessary to see how it relates to the rest of Scripture and the rest of what we believe. The truths of the Faith are both consistent with each other and interconnected. What we learn about one truth helps us understand all the other truths better. Likewise, what we know about the Faith as a whole illuminates how we understand each individual truth. This unity that exists in all Catholic teaching is called the **Analogy of Faith**.

## Senses of Scripture

From what we have just learned in John 6:1–15, we can see that a single passage in Scripture can have multiple layers of meaning. Just like a movie scene filmed with multiple cameras allows us to see the same story from more than one angle and gives a more complete perspective on the scene, we can also look at a Scripture passage through multiple "lenses" that show us different aspects of the biblical account and gives us a more complete perspective on the passage as a whole. Biblical scholars call these "lenses" the **senses of Scripture.** Traditionally, the Church has divided these "senses" into two categories: the "literal sense" and the "spiritual sense."

### *The Literal Sense*

The **literal sense** is the meaning that comes directly from the text and is intended by the inspired author. It is, **"The meaning conveyed by the words of Scripture and discovered by exegesis, following the rules of sound interpretation" (CCC 116)**. As we discussed above, we need to understand the author's historical context and form of writing to discover his intended meaning so these are most important for the literal sense. Also, it is important to note that included in the literal sense are literary

**Aa Vocabulary**

**Senses of Scripture (n.):** The various meanings of the Scripture text.

**Literal Sense (n.):** The meaning that comes directly from the Scripture text and is intended by the sacred author.

Mary and the Apostles await the Holy Spirit whom Jesus had promised to send to them. The Holy Spirit opens our eyes to the truth, goodness, and beauty of Scripture.

*Pentecost* by Unknown Artist (ca. 1504).

techniques used by the sacred authors such as the use of metaphors and analogies. The meaning of the literary techniques employed by the sacred authors are just as important to the meaning of a text as the plain meaning of the words on the page.

Understanding the literal sense correctly is necessary for correctly understanding all other meanings. It is the foundation for everything that follows. The *Catechism*, quoting St. Thomas Aquinas, explains, **"All other senses of Sacred Scripture are based on the literal" (CCC 116).**

### *The Spiritual Sense*

The literal sense of Scripture describes the realities and events of God's plan of salvation. God's plan has an inner unity, so those realities and events themselves are sometimes signs that God uses to point to a deeper meaning. The deeper meaning is the **spiritual sense**.

The spiritual sense of a passage is based on its literal sense, but we can only understand it by seeing how the passage fits into the entirety of God's plan. This is why we need to read the passage with the Church in the context of the entire Bible and all the truths of the Faith. In addition to this, we need grace from the Holy Spirit. The Holy Spirit inspired the Scriptures, and the Holy Spirit helps the Church to understand their full meaning.

> **"The Holy Spirit gives a spiritual understanding of the Word of God to those who read or hear it, according to the dispositions of their hearts. By means of the words, actions, and symbols that form the structure of a celebration, the Spirit puts both the faithful and the ministers into a living relationship with Christ, the Word and Image of the Father, so that they can live out the meaning of what they hear, contemplate, and do in the celebration" (CCC 1101).**

The spiritual sense is broken down further into three senses:

1. The Allegorical Sense: This sense connects the Old and New Testaments by showing how events in the Old Testament prefigure the fulfillment of God's plan in Christ. The Old Testament realities that serve as symbols of New Testament realities are sometimes called **types**, and the study of the connections between the two testaments are referred to as typology. The *Catechism* states: **"We can acquire a more profound understanding of events by recognizing their significance in Christ; thus the crossing of the Red Sea is a sign or type of Christ's victory and also of Christian Baptism" (CCC 117).**

**Aa Vocabulary**

**Spiritual Sense (n.):** The meaning of the Scripture text that reveals the inner unity of God's plan through the realities and events of Scripture, which are signs God uses to point to deeper meaning. The spiritual sense is further broken down into three parts: the allegorical sense, the moral sense, and the anagogical sense.

**Types (n.):** People or things in the Old Testament that foreshadow people or things in the New Testament.

## Isn't the Bible just another piece of literature? It is just myths and fables, right? How do you interpret it, anyway?

The Bible is unique. No other work of writing has ever been so studied, so commented on, so debated. It has been a part of the Church from the beginning, and each generation continues to grapple with it. As we have said many times already, the Bible is not one book among many: it is the Book. Therefore, the Scriptures must be treated with the highest honor and respect.

As we discussed in Unit 2, the Church believes the Bible always teaches the truth, but it does not always do that in a "scientific" way. The Bible is full of many different types of writing. It includes poetry and what we might call literature—fables and allegories—but this does not make it untrue. Inherent in the charge that the Bible is just literature and not worthy of belief is the prejudice that the only truth possible is that gained through scientific investigation and scientific proofs. This is both untrue and an inhuman way of looking at the world.

Of course, music, poetry, paintings, and novels are capable of communicating truth. The ability to make things and the ability to appreciate beauty are part of what it means to be a human being. So, too, is the ability to tell stories and understand the meaning of stories. We communicate truth to each other all the time through beauty—through novels, films, operas, paintings, poetry and statues—and those truths are no less valid because they do not come to us through the scientific communication of exact data. In the Scriptures, God speaks to us as human beings (He actually became human), and so He speaks truth to us using all of the means human beings use to communicate truth.

*The Transfer of the Ark* Attributed to Pieter van Lint (ca. 1650).

Accordingly, we need to approach these different modes of communicating in the way appropriate to them. In our daily lives, we would never listen to a song in the same way that we would read a research paper or study an accounting spreadsheet. The same holds true for the Bible. We need to read the Psalms differently than the Gospels. We need to read the opening chapters of Genesis differently than the letters of St. Paul. Doing that actually makes it easier to perceive the truth being communicated by each.

Even after centuries of active attempts to disprove the biblical accounts of the history of Israel and the life of Christ, nothing has been found "scientifically" that definitively repudiates our biblical understanding of what happened. In fact, the opposite is the case: most evidence supports the biblical narrative.

2. The Moral Sense: This sense reveals what the events in Scripture show us about acting justly and living a moral life. Reading Scripture with an eye to the moral sense reminds us that we can often draw moral lessons from the stories of Scripture. **"The events reported in Scripture ought to lead us to act justly. As St. Paul says, they were written 'for our instruction'" (CCC 117).**

3. The Anagogical Sense: Anagogical comes from the Greek word *anagoge*, meaning "leading." According to the *Catechism*, it helps us **"view realities and events in terms of their eternal significance, leading us toward our true homeland: thus the Church on earth is a sign of the heavenly Jerusalem" (CCC 117).**

**The Church on earth is a sign of the heavenly Jerusalem.**

So, while the allegorical sense ties together the events of Salvation History and the moral sense gives us guidance for our daily lives, the anagogical sense points us to Heaven, our ultimate destiny.

We do not always find every one of these senses in a particular passage of Scripture, but by attempting to look at the Scripture through these different "lenses," we get a more comprehensive perspective, which allows us to draw as much meaning as possible from our reading, prayer, and study of the Bible.

The truths contained within the parable of the Good Samaritan can be understood by considering the various senses of Scripture.

*The Good Samaritan* by David Teniers the Younger (ca. 1656).

# The Truth Is...

Reading and understanding the Bible can be challenging. Often, confusion arises from the misunderstandings that the Bible should be read and analyzed like a book in English class. Many people who try to read the Bible pick a random place and start reading, expecting it to make complete sense. Sometimes they even ask the wrong questions about what they are reading. You would not read Hamlet to learn the ending of Macbeth, but some hope to find an answer where there is none, like expecting to find out what happens to Macbeth in Hamlet.

Ultimately, to read the Bible effectively, we must first know how to read it. That is no easy task. The Bible is unlike any book that has ever been written. With Macbeth you can simply start at the beginning and read to the end and get the complete story. Not so with the Bible. The Bible is more accurately understood as a library of books rather than a single book to be read from cover to cover. In fact, the word *Bible* comes from the Latin word *biblia*, which means "a collection of books." Therefore, to find answers to the right questions about the Bible, we have to know how to read it properly. The Church offers you help in this task so you can grow in holiness and in relationship with the Lord.

Chapter 8

# Focus and Reflection Questions

1. What is exegesis?

2. Why can Scripture not be understood apart from the Church? List at least two reasons.

3. From where/whom does the Church receive her authority to interpret Scripture?

4. What is *Dei Verbum*?

5. What do all the Church documents on interpreting Scripture have in common?

6. What is a *catena*? What does it have to do with the Church's Tradition?

7. Why is it important to understand the historical context of Scripture?

8. What is the "Analogy of Faith"?

9. What are the two broad categories of the senses of Scripture, and how would you define each?

10. What are the three senses into which the spiritual sense of Scripture is broken down?

11. Write a brief reflection in response to this statement from the essay: "We communicate truth to each other all the time through beauty—through novels, films, operas, paintings, poetry and statues—and those truths are no less valid because they do not come to us through the scientific communication of exact data."

12. What does the story of the great lengths St. Athanasius went in order to defend the true teaching about Christ show us regarding the importance of guarding and protecting the Word of God?

# Straight to the Source

ADDITIONAL READINGS FROM PRIMARY SOURCES

*For chapter 8, rather than the usual variety of selections from primary sources, we will look in close detail at the official and dogmatic teaching of the Catholic Church regarding divine revelation found in the Vatican II document* Dei Verbum. *You will read all of* Dei Verbum *in this course.*

## ***Dei Verbum* 12–13—The Dogmatic Constitution on Divine Revelation from the Second Vatican Council, November 18, 1968**

12. However, since God speaks in Sacred Scripture through men in human fashion, the interpreter of Sacred Scripture, in order to see clearly what God wanted to communicate to us, should carefully investigate what meaning the sacred writers really intended, and what God wanted to manifest by means of their words.

    To search out the intention of the sacred writers, attention should be given, among other things, to "literary forms." For truth is set forth and expressed differently in texts which are variously historical, prophetic, poetic, or of other forms of discourse. The interpreter must investigate what meaning the sacred writer intended to express and actually expressed in particular circumstances by using contemporary literary forms in accordance with the situation of his own time and culture. For the correct understanding of what the sacred author wanted to assert, due attention must be paid to the customary and characteristic styles of feeling, speaking and narrating which prevailed at the time of the sacred writer, and to the patterns men normally employed at that period in their everyday dealings with one another.

    But, since Holy Scripture must be read and interpreted in the sacred spirit in which it was written, no less serious attention must be given to the content and unity of the whole of Scripture if the meaning of the sacred texts is to be correctly worked out. The living tradition of the whole Church must be taken into account along with the harmony which exists between elements of the faith. It is the task of exegetes to work according to these rules toward a better understanding and explanation of the meaning of Sacred Scripture, so that through preparatory study the judgment of the Church may mature. For all of what has been said about the way of interpreting Scripture is subject finally to the judgment of the Church, which carries out the divine commission and ministry of guarding and interpreting the word of God.

13. In Sacred Scripture, therefore, while the truth and holiness of God always remains intact, the marvelous "condescension" of eternal wisdom is clearly shown, "that we may learn the gentle kindness of God, which words cannot express, and how far He has gone in adapting His language with thoughtful concern for our weak human nature." For the words of God, expressed in human language, have been made like human discourse, just as the word of the eternal Father, when He took to Himself the flesh of human weakness, was in every way made like men.

# Straight to the Source

ADDITIONAL READINGS FROM PRIMARY SOURCES

## Focus Questions

1. What should the interpreter of Scripture do to see clearly what God wanted to communicate to us?
2. To what should we give attention in order to search out the intention of the sacred writers?
3. What are five things that must be paid attention to in order to find the correct understanding of what a sacred author wanted to assert?
4. Because Scripture must be interpreted in the sacred spirit in which it was written, what three other things must be taken into account when interpreting Scripture?
5. Who has the final authority and judgement on the interpretation of Scripture?
6. To what does *Dei Verbum* compare the way in which God's Word takes form in the Scriptures?

## Reflection Question

If God is the primary author of Scripture, why do you think it is so important to determine what the human authors intended to say? .

Chapter 9

# The Bible in Relation to Science and History

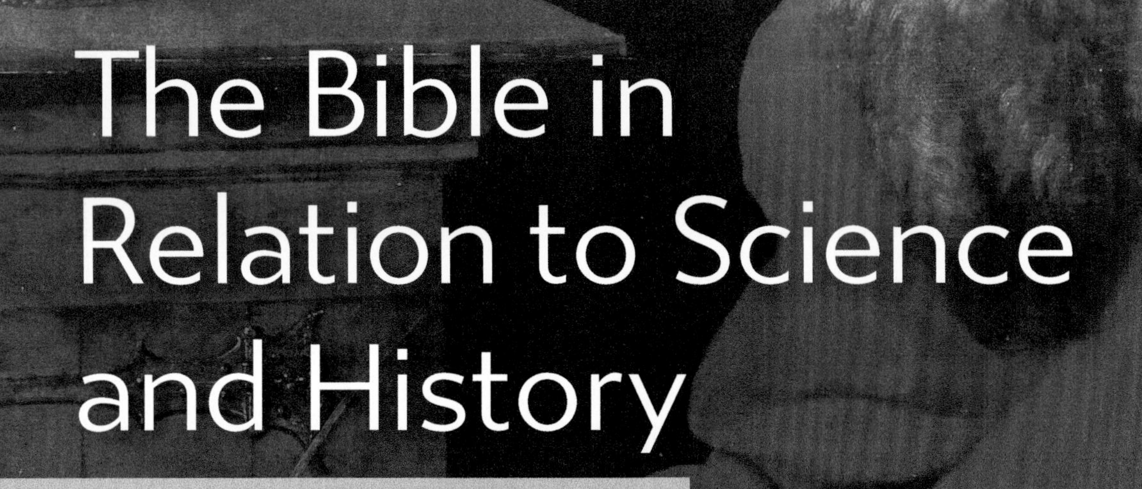

# Chapter Overview

Faith and reason are two paths to the same Truth. Through both, we come to knowledge and a deeper understanding of God who has made Himself known to us. Therefore, there can be no real contradiction between faith and reason because both are involved in knowledge of the same divine Truth. Each has its own proper means of acquiring the Truth, but when properly understood, each assists the other. Knowledge gained from human reason, including the sciences, can help us better understand the truths of Faith and especially the meaning of Scripture. When we consider the discoveries of science, the knowledge available to us through the study of history, and archaeological discoveries, we can come to a deeper and more accurate understanding of the time, place, language, history, and culture of the sacred authors of Scripture. This knowledge is important to knowing what the sacred authors intended to say, and ultimately, what God wanted us to know.

## In this chapter you will learn that …

- Ultimately, faith and reason point to the same Truth.
- Scripture teaches us real truths about the world and the history of the relationship between God and man.
- Catholic exegesis is enriched through the scholarly methods of diverse academic disciplines.
- The discovery of ancient manuscripts continues to enlighten our understanding of the real culture Christ encountered.
- Our understanding of the Truth of Scripture grows richer as we study and pray with it.

### Bible Basics

"Then repay to Caesar what belongs to Caesar and to God what belongs to God."
MATTHEW 22:21

"You believe because you can see me. Blessed are those who have not seen and yet believe."
JOHN 20:29

Aa Vocabulary

**Encyclical (n.):** A pastoral letter written by the pope and sent to the whole Church and even to the whole world, to express Church teaching on some important matter. Encyclicals are expressions of the ordinary papal Magisterium.

## The Bible In Relation to Science and History

People sometimes mistakenly assume that because of the rapid advance of the natural sciences and technology, the study of the Bible and religion are incompatible with science or have little to do with it. However, as we learned in Unit 1, human reason reflecting on the natural world is one of the paths through which we can learn about God. Ultimately, faith and reason, including the natural sciences, point to the same truth, so they cannot contradict one another.

Pope Saint John Paul II put that understanding a different way when he wrote the introduction to his **encyclical**, *Fides et Ratio*: "Faith and reason are like two wings on which the human spirit rises to the contemplation of truth; and God has placed in the human heart a desire to know the truth—in a word, to know himself—so that, by knowing and loving God, men and women may also come to the fullness of truth about themselves."

When we understand the truth we know from faith and the sciences correctly, we see that not only do they not conflict with each other, they actually assist the other. Not surprisingly, we can then find many examples of Christian believers who made great contributions to modern science. For example, Gregor Mendel, the father of modern genetics, and Fr. Georges Lemaître, the author of the Big Bang Theory, were both Catholic priests. Even today, many people working in the natural sciences draw inspiration for their work from their faith in God. Science helps us understand the mechanisms and patterns of the natural world, but it does not reveal the ultimate purpose of things in the natural world or our own role in it. Faith helps us understand these things and give direction and meaning to the findings of science.

**Our knowledge of the sciences informs how we understand the truths of the Faith and the meaning of the Scriptures.**

Likewise, our knowledge of the sciences informs how we understand the truths of the Faith and the meaning of the Scriptures, so Catholic

*Gregor Mendel* by Unknown Photographer.

*Fr. Georges Lemaitre* Photo Credit GL Archive / Alamy stock photo.

Gregor Mendel, the father of modern genetics (left), and Fr. Georges Lemaître, the author of the Big Bang Theory, (right) were both Catholic priests.

*Creation of the World* Attributed to Melchior Bocksberger (ca. 1575).

▲ God created all things, and we can advance in knowledge of His creation though faith and the sciences.

exegesis of the Bible draws on other fields, such as history, anthropology, archeology, and the natural sciences. This means we reject a fundamentalist interpretation of the Bible that insists on a literal interpretation that fails to account for historical context and leads to conflict with the findings of modern science. As we learned in previous chapters, a proper understanding of Scripture takes into account the historical circumstances of the author and the different forms of writing used in that time. This gives us the true literal sense of Scripture as explained above.

Ancient styles of writing are very different from the way a science or history textbook is written today, so many supposed contradictions between Scripture and science are actually due to a misunderstanding of the intended meaning of the ancient text. For instance, the truth taught by the creation story of Genesis 1–2 does not conflict with the findings of modern science that tell us the earth is several billion years old and living things developed through a process of evolution. The author of Genesis was not trying to give a scientific account of how the world was made. That was not his intent. His intent was to help the reader see that God created the world, made man in His image, and did it all out of love. Genesis 1–2 is about the *what* and the *why* of Creation, not the *how*. Recognizing that intent helps us see that no conflict between faith and science exists there.

This does not mean we can reduce the Scriptures to a purely symbolic meaning. As we learned in the last chapter, the literal meaning is the basis of all other senses of the Scriptures, and while the Bible's purpose is not teaching scientific or historical truths in the same manner as a modern-day textbook, it does teach us real truths about the world and the history of the relationship between God and man. Again, we must pay attention to the form of writing. For instance, while the four Gospels do not tell about the life of Jesus in the same way that a modern historian might approach the topic, what we learn about Jesus from the Gospels is still true. Jesus was a real person, who (as we profess in the Creed) was born of the Virgin Mary, suffered under Pontius Pilate, was crucified, died, and was buried, then rose again on the third day. In Jesus, God has truly entered into human history, so the account of His life relayed by the Scriptures is not myth or symbolism. It is historical truth.

## Other Approaches to Scripture

Scholarly exegesis and biblical research draws on modern historical and scientific methods to give us a more accurate understanding of the Bible and to make its meaning more accessible to us today. Two important methods we have already discussed are historical criticism and literary criticism. Historical criticism is the name given to the analysis of the historical context of the text and literary criticism is the name given to the analysis of the literary forms and genres used by the inspired authors. These two methods are essential for establishing the intended meaning of the author.

Two other important methods are:

1. ***Textual criticism***: Before the invention of the printing press, texts had to be copied by hand. Sometimes the copiers made mistakes, which were then reproduced in other copies. Most of these mistakes are minor and have little effect on the meaning of the Bible, but textual criticism examines the development of early manuscripts to more accurately establish the earliest form of the text.
2. ***Source criticism***: The inspired authors sometimes drew on other sources in their writing, both written and oral. Source criticism attempts to determine what these sources are. For example, the similarities between the Gospels of Matthew, Mark and Luke make it clear there is some relationship between them. Biblical scholars have developed a number of theories to explain that relationship. One theory is Mark was written first and Matthew and Luke both drew from Mark and another source of sayings of Jesus that is now lost but has been nicknamed "**Q**." Other theories are that Matthew was written first, and Mark and Luke drew from it, or Mark was written first, followed by Matthew, and Luke drew from both Mark and Matthew.

### Vocabulary

**Textual Criticism (n.):** The name given to the analysis of early manuscripts of Scripture to establish the text's earliest form.

**Source Criticism (n.):** The name given to the analysis of the original sources from where the sacred authors of Scripture may have drawn material for their own writing.

**"Q" Source (n.):** A collection of Jesus' sayings that Matthew, Mark, and Luke are believed by some to have drawn upon for the writing of their Gospels. There is no evidence for the existence of the "Q" source; its existence and purported use by the Evangelists is purely speculation.

*Dead Sea Scroll Caves* Photo Credit: Lux Moundi (November 8, 2012).

▲ The Dead Sea Scrolls were discovered in the caves of Qumran, in 1946.

### *Ancient Manuscripts*

In the last couple of centuries, our understanding of the Bible has also been greatly enriched by archeological discoveries that have given us early manuscripts of biblical texts or physical evidence of the culture of ancient Israel and surrounding nations. A few of the most important of these sources of ancient manuscripts are:

*Qumran and the Dead Sea Scrolls*: The **Dead Sea Scrolls** were discovered in the caves of Qumran by the Dead Sea beginning in 1946. The findings at Qumran give us information about the Essenes, a Jewish sect from the time of Jesus, and the earliest copies of many parts of the Old Testament.

*Nag Hammadi*: In 1945, a collection of Gnostic texts from the 3rd and 4th centuries was found buried in a jar near the Egyptian town of Nag Hammadi. The **Nag Hammadi** texts give us insight into the Gnostic heresy and include the only complete copies of some of their scriptures, such as the so-called Gospel of Thomas.

*The Targumim*: The **targumim** are Aramaic paraphrases of the Hebrew Bible that originated when Hebrew ceased to be the main language of the Jews (not long before the time of Jesus). Some targumim were preserved by the Jewish community and have never ceased to play an important role in how they interpret the Scriptures. More recently, manuscripts of other targumim have been discovered. These targumim help us understand how the Jews around the time of Jesus understood the Scriptures and are important for textual criticism of the Old Testament.

Remember, the sacred authors of the Bible were true authors, not puppets, who wrote using their own powers and abilities. They chose the different writing styles, languages, and details in each story. This means that, like any author, they sometimes intended their writing to be as accurate as

**Aa Vocabulary**

**Dead Sea Scrolls (n.):** Ancient scrolls written by the Jewish sect known as the Essenes found in 1946 in a cave near the Dead Sea. These scrolls contain some of the oldest known versions of Old Testament books.

**Nag Hammadi (n.):** A collection of ancient Gnostic texts found buried in a jar in Egypt in 1946. These texts give unique insight about the Gnostic heresy of the time.

**Targumim (n.):** Aramaic paraphrases of the Old Testament originating from around the time of Christ that help us understand how the Jews of Jesus' time understood Scripture and are important for textual criticism of the Old Testament.

## Lives of Faith

# St. Thomas Aquinas

Everyone loves a good comeback story. Michael Jordan was cut from his high school basketball team. Steven Spielberg was rejected from three different film schools before going on to become one of the greatest film directors of all time. Walt Disney's first animation studio went bankrupt. Steve Jobs was fired from Apple, the company he founded.

But there is a saint who has one of the best comeback stories of them all: St. Thomas Aquinas. When he was still in school, his classmates called him "The Dumb Ox" because he was large in stature, slow moving, and did not speak very often.

However, Pope St. John Paul II called him "a master of thought and a model of the right way to do theology." He is quoted 61 times in the *Catechism of the Catholic Church*, he is a Doctor of the Church, and he is one of the most prolific writers and most influential thinkers in the history of the Catholic Church.

St. Thomas Aquinas lived in the 13th century and traveled to study and teach all over Europe. Aquinas rooted his teaching in the recently revived ancient philosophy of Aristotle. He advised kings, interpreted Scripture, and was incredibly popular with lay people for being able to teach the Truth with simplicity and fervor.

Perhaps he is most famous for his work *Summa Theologiae*. Often referred to as *The Summa*, this lengthy volume provides detailed arguments and counter arguments for various topics within the Faith. St. Thomas intended it as an instructional guide for theology and seminary students, but it has influenced nearly every corner of Christian theology and has been called one of the most influential works in the history of Western literature.

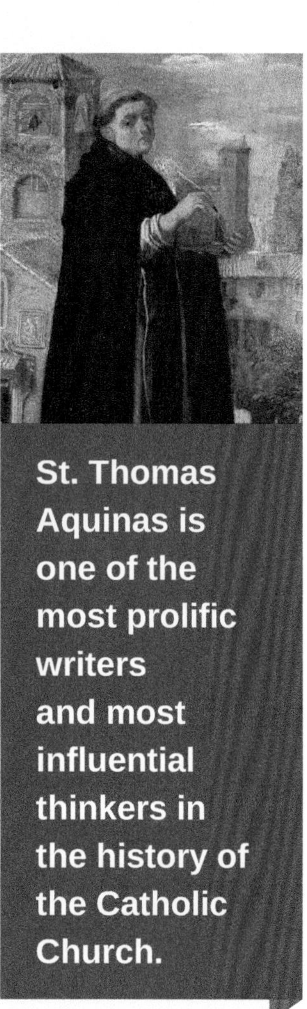

**St. Thomas Aquinas is one of the most prolific writers and most influential thinkers in the history of the Catholic Church.**

However, St. Thomas' greatest contribution to the Church may not be any one of his writings, but one of his dearly held beliefs, namely, that faith and reason were not diametrically opposed, but inseparably linked. You see, Aquinas believed simply that not only could faith and reason coexist, but they were both fundamental to a proper understanding of Catholicism and the world around us.

In the words of Pope Emeritus Benedict XVI, "Aquinas demonstrated that a natural harmony exists between Christian faith and reason. This was Thomas' great achievement. Thomas demonstrated that the two go together: what seemed to be reason incompatible with faith was not reason, and what seemed to be faith was not faith insofar as it was opposed to true rationality."

Thomas Aquinas lived almost 800 years ago, but the importance of his work could not be any clearer than in our world today, where so many people lose their faith or are opposed to any faith at all because they believe faith and reason (or science) simply are not compatible. If ever you are tempted by that false line of thinking—or you hear someone else claim it—remember the teachings of St. Thomas Aquinas, and remember Jesus called Himself "the Truth." Anything that is true points to God!

possible down to the very last detail. Other times, they chose to use poetic or metaphorical language to communicate other kinds of truth. Thus, the Bible contains many styles of writing, including history, poetry, proverbs, and apocalyptic literature. Understanding the intention of the sacred author also requires an understanding of the forms of literature they chose to write in.

As we have seen, Catholic exegesis uses many different approaches to understand the Bible. A proper understanding of the Scriptures is informed by findings of modern scholarship and the truths of the Faith. It is also rooted in the Tradition, life and worship of the Church and guided by the teachings of the Magisterium. Sometimes it is difficult to understand the Bible because its meaning can be complex and containing multiple layers, but when we draw on these sources, we can find the guidance we need to discover the inexhaustible riches of Sacred Scripture. When we read with the eyes of faith, our understanding of Scripture can grow richer and deeper every time we study or pray with them.

▼ The findings at Qumran give us information about the earliest copies of many parts of the Old Testament.

*Great Isaiah Scroll* Photo Credit: Ardon Bar Hama (November 26, 2010).

# The Truth Is...

Truth never contradicts Truth. What God reveals is always true because He cannot lie, contradict Himself, or be in error. Therefore, if human reason reaches some conclusion that contradicts what has been divinely revealed, that conclusion of human reason is in error, either because of the means used to come to the conclusion or because of some other fundamental misunderstanding of what God has revealed. Truth is Truth is Truth.

This may be challenging to accept. We live in a time where we think that because we live today with all of our technologies and sciences that we are "obviously" more advanced and wise than anyone who has lived before us. But this is simply not true. We should not automatically assume this arrogant, modernist position because it biases our interpretation of the past. Applied to Scripture, this point of view can make it very difficult for us to come to know the truth of God's Word, especially in cases of challenging interpretation. We must be open to the possibility that we can be wrong or are capable of misunderstanding. When we do so, we make ourselves humbler and more willing to hear what God wants to speak to us in His Word.

Chapter 9

# Focus and Reflection Questions

1. What is the relationship between faith and the sciences?

2. What does science help us understand?

3. What does faith help us understand?

4. What is Catholic exegesis?

5. What does the Bible teach us?

6. What is the difference between historical criticism and literary criticism?

7. How might a scholar use the method of textual criticism?

8. What is one of the theories about the synoptic Gospels that emerges from source criticism?

9. What is one ancient manuscript that has provided additional cultural or historic context to enrich our exegesis of Scripture?

10. What two elements should inform our proper understanding of Scripture?

11. What did St. Thomas Aquinas believe about the relationship between faith and reason?

# Straight to the Source

ADDITIONAL READINGS FROM PRIMARY SOURCES

## *Dei Filius IV* 5–7, The Dogmatic Constitution of the First Vatican Council on the Catholic Faith, April 24, 1870

5 Even though faith is above reason, there can never be any real disagreement between faith and reason, since it is the same God who reveals the mysteries and infuses faith, and who has endowed the human mind with the light of reason.

6 God cannot deny himself, nor can truth ever be in opposition to truth. The appearance of this kind of specious contradiction is chiefly due to the fact that either the dogmas of faith are not understood and explained in accordance with the mind of the Church, or unsound views are mistaken for the conclusions of reason.

7. Therefore we define that every assertion contrary to the truth of enlightened faith is totally false.

1 How does this document from the First Vatican Council argue that there can never be any real disagreement between faith and reason? Do you agree with this reasoning? Why or why not?

2 Why does it make sense for the Church to define that any assertion or claim that is contrary to the truth of faith is false?

## *Fides et Ratio 9*, an encyclical of Pope St. John Paul II, September 14, 1998

9. The First Vatican Council teaches, then, that the truth attained by philosophy and the truth of Revelation are neither identical nor mutually exclusive: "There exists a twofold order of knowledge, distinct not only as regards their source, but also as regards their object. With regard to the source, because we know in one by natural reason, in the other by divine faith. With regard to the object, because besides those things which natural reason can attain, there are proposed for our belief mysteries hidden in God which, unless they are divinely revealed, cannot be known." Based upon God's testimony and enjoying the supernatural assistance of grace, faith is of an order other than philosophical knowledge which depends upon sense perception and experience and which advances by the light of the intellect alone. Philosophy and the sciences function within the order of natural reason; while faith, enlightened and guided by the Spirit, recognizes in the message of salvation the "fullness of grace and truth" (cf. *Jn* 1:14) which God has willed to reveal in history and definitively through his Son, Jesus Christ (cf. 1 *Jn* 5:9; *Jn* 5:31–32).

1 What are the two kinds of knowledge and what are the "objects" of each?

2 Based upon this excerpt, how could one argue that faith is greater than reason?

# Straight to the Source

ADDITIONAL READINGS FROM PRIMARY SOURCES

## *Divino Afflante Spiritu* 33–35, An encyclical of Pope Pius XII, September 30, 1943

33. As in our age, indeed new questions and new difficulties are multiplied, so, by God's favor, new means and aids to exegesis are also provided. Among these it is worthy of special mention that Catholic theologians, following the teaching of the Holy Fathers and especially of the Angelic and Common Doctor, have examined and explained the nature and effects of biblical inspiration more exactly and more fully than was wont to be done in previous ages. For having begun by expounding minutely the principle that the inspired writer, in composing the sacred book, is the living and reasonable instrument of the Holy Spirit, they rightly observe that, impelled by the divine motion, he so uses his faculties and powers, that from the book composed by him all may easily infer "the special character of each one and, as it were, his personal traits." Let the interpreter then, with all care and without neglecting any light derived from recent research, endeavor to determine the peculiar character and circumstances of the sacred writer, the age in which he lived, the sources written or oral to which he had recourse and the forms of expression he employed.
34. Thus can he the better understand who was the inspired author, and what he wishes to express by his writings. There is no one indeed but knows that the supreme rule of interpretation is to discover and define what the writer intended to express, as St. Athanasius excellently observes: "Here, as indeed is expedient in all other passages of Sacred Scripture, it should be noted, on what occasion the Apostle spoke; we should carefully and faithfully observe to whom and why he wrote, lest, being ignorant of these points, or confounding one with another, we miss the real meaning of the author."
35. What is the literal sense of a passage is not always as obvious in the speeches and writings of the ancient authors of the East, as it is in the works of our own time. For what they wished to express is not to be determined by the rules of grammar and philology alone, nor solely by the context; the interpreter must, as it were, go back wholly in spirit to those remote centuries of the East and with the aid of history, archaeology, ethnology, and other sciences, accurately determine what modes of writing, so to speak, the authors of that ancient period would be likely to use, and in fact did use.

1. Why is it important to discover the intention of the sacred writers of Scripture?
2. Does it surprise you that the Church was an advocate of using discoveries from science and history to help our understanding of the Bible? Why or why not?

UNIT 4

# Overview of the Bible

The Bible is organized into two parts: the Old Testament and the New Testament. The Old Testament refers to the Old Covenant, which is not called "old" because it no longer has meaning for us today. Rather, the Old Testament has great value for our Christian faith, not only as a treasury of spiritual learning, prayer, and wisdom for life, but also as an interpretive key for unlocking the New Testament. In the New Testament, we uniquely encounter the Word of God incarnate, Jesus Christ. The Gospels are our primary source of knowledge of Jesus' life and thus hold a place of primacy among all Scripture. Ultimately, as the *Catechism of the Catholic Church* no. 129 puts it, **"The New Testament lies hidden in the Old, and the Old Testament is unveiled in the New."** Thus, both Testaments of Scripture are essential to each other and to our Christian faith.

Scripture contains the story of our salvation, God's actions in human history. We call this Salvation History. From the very beginning, God has revealed Himself to mankind and entered into relationship with them through a series of covenants. A covenant is a sacred bond of family relationship. In other words, throughout Salvation History, God has invited us to be a part of His divine family and has prepared us gradually and in stages, and in words and deeds to receive the gift of salvation won for us by His only Son, Jesus Christ, who sacrificed Himself on the Cross for our sins. This is our faith, and this is the story of Scripture.

## In This Unit

- **Chapter 10:** Introduction to the Old and New Testaments
- **Chapter 11:** The Unity of the Old and New Testaments

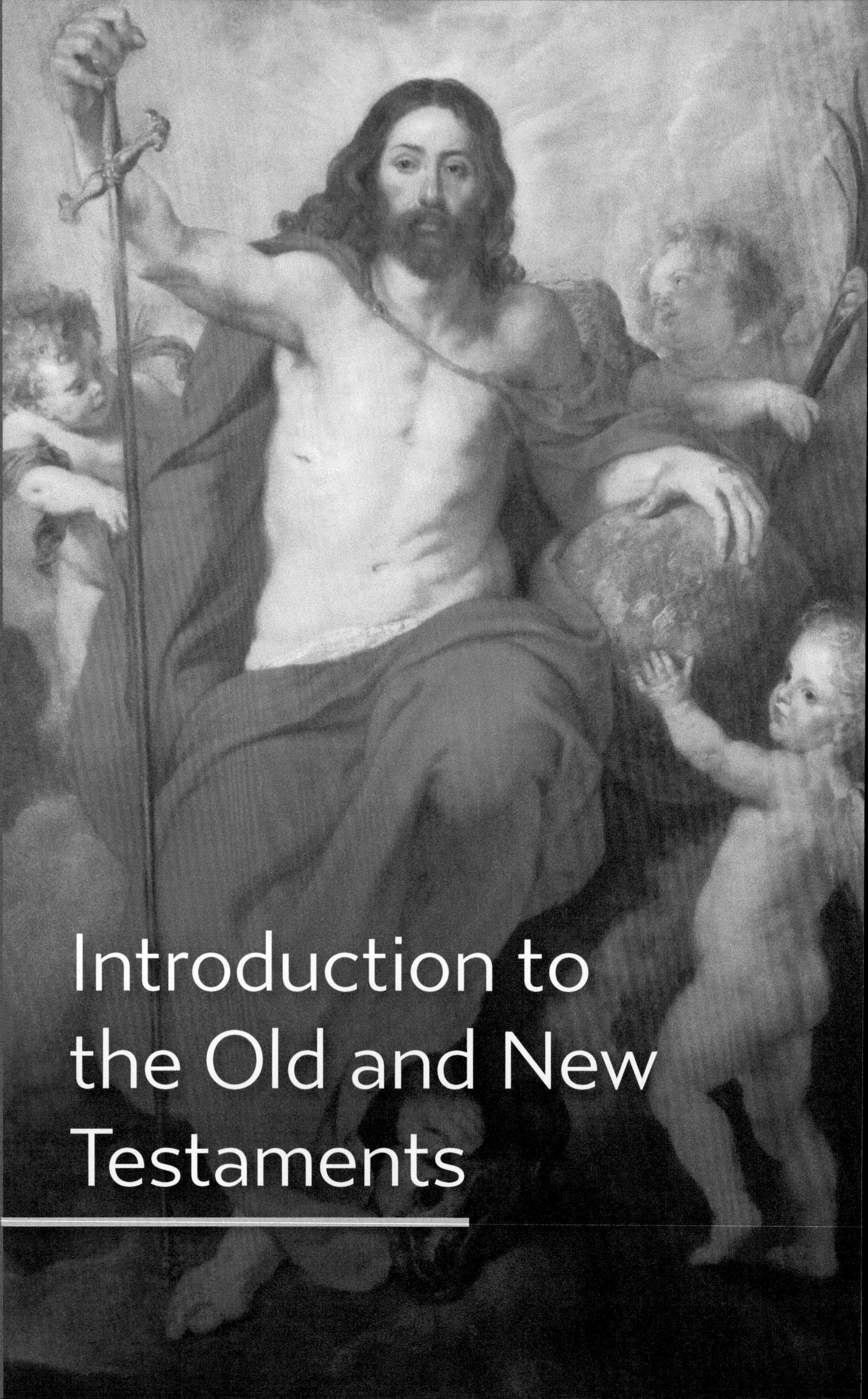

# Introduction to the Old and New Testaments

# Chapter Overview

The Bible is a book unlike any other. In fact, the Bible is made up of 73 books: 46 in the Old Testament and 27 in the New Testament. We can think of Jesus as the "bridge" between these two parts of the Bible. The Old Testament gives us an account of all the ways God revealed Himself to the people of Israel in order to prepare them for salvation. In the New Testament, we meet God's Word incarnate, Jesus Christ. The New Testament tells the story of the New Covenant, which is the story of salvation won for all of humanity by Jesus Christ. Together, the Old and New Testaments form an organic unity of Scripture.

## In this chapter you will learn that …

- Jesus' identity is bound up with the life of Israel, and as their promised Messiah, Jesus fulfilled God's covenant with them.
- The Church is the continuation of Israel. Israel's history is her history.
- Jesus is the hinge around which all of history turns, and all of human history is part of Salvation History.
- The Old and New Testaments are only fully understandable in light of the other.

### Bible Basics

The angel said to them, "Do not be afraid; for behold, I proclaim to you good news of great joy that will be for all the people. For today in the city of David a savior has been born for you who is Messiah and Lord."
LUKE 2:10–11

### Connections to the *Catechism*

CCC 122 (page 143)

Aa Vocabulary

**New Covenant (n.):** The new and everlasting covenant won for us by Christ's Paschal Mystery. In this covenant is the fulfillment of centuries of prophecies and all of God's promises for the forgiveness of sins. We are made members of the New Covenant by our Baptism and we renew and participate in the covenant every time we receive the Eucharist. All people are invited to be members of the New Covenant.

## Introduction to the Old Testament and the New Testament

The Bible is the inspired Word of God. It is also a family history; it is our family history, the history of the people of God. In it, we learn how our spiritual ancestors fell from grace and lost the gift of intimacy with God. We also learn how God worked through many long millennia to bring us back into the life of grace with an even greater outpouring of love and grace than our original parents enjoyed, and into an intimate, familial relationship with Him.

The Old Testament is the beginning of this family history. Made up of forty-six books, it tells the inspired account of the people of Israel and their relationship with God before the coming of Christ. This relationship centers on the covenant God made with Israel.

We will talk more about covenants later in this part of the book. For now, all you need to know is that covenants form sacred and permanent bonds of kinship, or family relationship. Unlike contracts, which form business arrangements, covenants make families. One type of covenant with which we are all familiar is Christian marriage. Another is adoption. When we talk about God making a covenant with Israel, we are talking about Him binding Himself by oath to the descendants of Abraham. He vowed to make them His own people, and they vowed to live in accord with the laws God established.

Jesus was not only an Israelite; He was a descendant of David, Israel's greatest king. So without understanding the Old Testament and God's covenant with Israel, we cannot understand Jesus. His identity is bound up with the life of Israel, and as their promised Messiah, Jesus fulfilled God's covenant with them.

**To know the Old Testament is to know the history of the family of Christ; it is to know the history of the Church.**

However, God's covenant with Israel did not end with Jesus. Rather, with the coming of Jesus, God extended His covenant beyond Israel, offering membership in His family to the Gentiles. This is the story of the New Testament—or the **New Covenant**—and the Church. The Church is the continuation of Israel. Israel's history is her history. Accordingly, to know the Old Testament is to know the history of the family of Christ; it is to know the history of the Church.

Jesus is the hinge around which all of history turns, and all of human history is part of Salvation History. The Old Testament demonstrates this by spanning the history of the world from the first man up to the time of Christ Himself. In doing so, it demonstrates that God never abandoned humanity. Rather, from the Fall of Adam until Jesus (the New Adam), God built up a people, a nation that He cared for, and prepared them in a special way for the coming of the Messiah. In St. Augustine's (AD 354–430) great work, *The City of God*, the North African Doctor of the Church explains how

*The Sacrifice of Noah* Attributed to Antonion de Bellis (between 1640 and 1655).

▲ God made a new covenant with Noah after the flood subsided. The Old Testament tells one coherent story of God's Covenant relationships with mankind.

Sacred Scripture traces the development of this people of God from Adam to Noah, Abraham, Moses, David, the disciples of the New Testament, and ultimately to the baptized in the Catholic Church. For St. Augustine, this was one history, one story of the "City of God."

When thinking about the Old Testament, we need to avoid equating "old" with "out of date" or "obsolete." We call the Old Testament "old" because: 1) It recounts events that took place long before Jesus' birth, so it is actually "old"; and 2) It tells the story of the covenants God made with mankind that were fulfilled with the coming of Christ and His establishment of a "New Testament" or "Covenant." In neither of these cases does "old" mean unimportant or obsolete. In fact, the opposite is true. The Old Testament is enduringly important. We need it to help us make sense of the New Testament. Each is only fully understandable in light of the other.

> **"Indeed, 'the economy of the Old Testament was deliberately so oriented that it should prepare for and declare in prophecy the coming of Christ, redeemer of all men.' 'Even though they contain matters imperfect and provisional,' the books of the Old Testament bear witness to the whole divine pedagogy of God's saving love: these writings 'are a storehouse of sublime teaching on God and of sound wisdom on human life, as well as a wonderful treasury of prayers; in them, too, the mystery of our salvation is present in a hidden way,'" (CCC 122).**

## Vocabulary

**Historical Books (n.):** The books of the Old Testament that are primarily focused on telling the history of Israel from the time of the judges to approximately 150 years before the birth of Christ.

**Prophetic Books (n.):** The books of the Old Testament that are primarily focused on recounting what God communicated to His people through the prophets.

**Wisdom Literature (n.):** The books of the Old Testament that are primarily focused on providing moral exhortation or insights into a well-lived life.

## The Makeup of the Old Testament

The Old Testament is made up of forty-six books divided into the following groupings:

- **Pentateuch or Torah:** Genesis, Exodus, Leviticus, Numbers, and Deuteronomy. Traditionally, the Pentateuch is believed to have been written by Moses himself, but some recent scholarship has called this into question. These five books include the Mosaic Law and the history of the people of God from Adam through its wanderings in the desert.
- **The Historical Books:** Joshua, Judges, Ruth, Samuel 1, Samuel 2, 1 Kings, 2 Kings, 1 Chronicles, 2 Chronicles, Ezra, Nehemiah, 1 Maccabees, 2 Maccabees, Esther, Tobit, and Judith. The primary focus of these books is Israel's history. They recount the story of Israel from the time of the Judges to 150 years before the coming of Christ.
- **The Prophetic Books:** Isaiah, Jeremiah, Lamentations, Baruch, Ezekiel, Daniel, Hosea, Joel, Amos, Obadiah, Jonah, Micah, Nahum, Habakkuk, Zephaniah, Haggai, Zechariah, and Malachi. These books recount what God communicated to His people through the prophets.
- **Wisdom Literature:** Job, Psalms, Proverbs, Ecclesiastes, Song of Songs, Wisdom, and Sirach. These books are mainly concerned with moral exhortation or insights into the well-lived life, and not with key events or institutions in the life of Israel.

The Old Testament was originally recorded in scrolls such as this.

*Open Torah Scroll* Photo Credit: Lawrie Cate (March 9, 2009).

Note that Protestant Bibles often have only thirty-nine books in the Old Testament because the Protestant reformers of the sixteenth century rejected the books of Judith, Tobit, Wisdom, Sirach, Baruch, 1 Maccabees, 2 Maccabees and parts of Esther and Daniel. If Protestant Bibles do include any of these books, they place them in a separate section, calling them *apocryphal* (meaning "doubtful") or **deuterocanonical** (meaning "second canon") because they value them for their historical, spiritual, and theological significance but do not regard them as part of the canon of inspired Scripture. These books are found in the Greek version of the Old Testament that was used by the early Church but not in the Hebrew Old Testament that is used by Jews today. The Council of Trent (1543–1563) confirmed the traditional canon including these books. Unit 2 explains how this canon was formed.

## The New Testament

As we discussed in Unit 2, the New Testament is the name given to the collection of twenty-seven books that recall the life of Jesus and the history of the early Church. Of all the books and writings in the history of humanity, none are more important than these. This is because the books of the New Testament tell us about the most important series of events that has ever happened. They tell us about the Incarnation of God—about God becoming a man and walking among us. They also tell us about the immeasurable implications of that event: how Jesus sent the Holy Spirit down among His Apostles, how He established the Church, and how, through it all, a New Covenant ("testament" is another word for "covenant") was forged between God and man—the covenant through which we receive salvation.

## The Makeup of the New Testament

- **The Gospels:** Matthew, Mark, Luke, and John. The word "gospel" means "good news." The Gospels tell of the Good News of Christ's birth, life, and death, as well as the salvation that these events have made possible for humanity. They are inspired biographies of Jesus, and through them God reveals His nature to us. They are the most important books in both the Bible and human history.
- **The Acts of the Apostles:** Scholars believe Acts was written by St. Luke the Evangelist, who also wrote the Gospel that bears his name. Acts recounts the Ascension of the Lord and the life of the early Church.
- **The Epistles of Paul:** Romans, 1 Corinthians, 2 Corinthians, Galatians, Ephesians, Philippians, Colossians, 1 Thessalonians, 2 Thessalonians, 1 Timothy, 2 Timothy, Titus, and Philemon. Paul is the greatest theologian of the Church. He worked as a missionary to the

### Aa Vocabulary

**Deuterocanonical Books (n.):** Those seven books of the Old Testament and parts of the books of Esther and Daniel that are not considered by most Protestants to be inspired writings, (while remaining valuable for their historical, spiritual, and theological significance). However, these books have always been a part of the Greek version of the Old Testament used by the early Church and were affirmed by the Council of Trent to be inspired writings and part of the traditional canon of Scripture. *Deutercanonical* is Latin for "of the second canon."

**Gospels (n.):** The first four books of the New Testament. They are the heart of the Scriptures and proclaim the Good News of salvation won for us by the Passion, Death, and Resurrection of Jesus Christ. The Gospels are our primary source of knowledge of life of Jesus Christ. The word *Gospel* means "Good News."

**Acts of the Apostles (n.):** The book of the New Testament immediately following the four Gospels that recounts the Ascension of Jesus into Heaven and the life of the early Church.

**Epistles of Paul (n.):** Letters written by St. Paul to communities of early Christians and other individuals to encourage their faith.

### Lives of Faith

## St. Francis Xavier

Two friends were hiking in the woods one day when they came upon a mother grizzly bear on the path. The bear was angry and ready to attack. One of the friends slowly bent down, took off his backpack, took out his tennis shoes, and began replacing his hiking boots with the running shoes.

"What are you doing," the other friend asked, "You can't possibly think you'll outrun the bear!"

"I don't need to outrun the bear," the friend replied. "I only need to outrun you."

It is an old joke, but it raises a good question: Are your friends using you as bear bait? When you dive into the lives of the saints, one of the most fascinating things you will discover is how many of them were close personal friends with one another. They walked with one another, encouraged one another, and called each other to holiness.

One of the best examples of this saintly friendship is St. Francis Xavier.

St. Francis Xavier was born in 1506 in the Navarrese Community in Northern Spain, and studied in Paris where he first met Ignatius of Loyola and Peter Faber. The men became close friends and grew closer to Jesus because of their holy friendship. The three of them, along with four others, were the original seven members and founders of the Society of Jesus—better known as the Jesuits—and all three were eventually beatified as saints.

After his ordination to the priesthood, Saint Francis Xavier's mission took him away from his friends. Pope Paul III asked Francis to travel to India to serve as the Papal Nuncio (an official delegate from Rome). St. Francis Xavier did not hesitate to travel to the East to spread the Gospel, and arrived in the region of Goa, India in 1542.

**Xavier spent his time ministering to the poor, the sick, and children.**

There, Xavier spent his time ministering to the poor, the sick, and children, trying to evangelize the people of the coastal region. As a central part of his ministry, Francis told the native people stories of the Gospel using the mysteries and prayers of the Rosary. Because of language barriers, He spent years in the region, building 40 churches in the process. Before long, he became aware of the plight of the people even further to the east—Japan and China.

Xavier became the first missionary to take Christianity into Japan, and even baptized the first Japanese convert to Christianity. Xavier was not well-received in Japan. The local governments outlawed Christianity quickly, forbade their people from converting, and forced Christians to go underground because of outright persecution. Although St. Francis Xavier was able to travel and meet with local princes and leaders, he was not able to overcome the barriers easily. But this did not stop him.

Xavier eventually left Japan to travel back to India and planned to visit China as well to plead for Portuguese prisoners being held captive there. However, he never made it to mainland China because he fell ill and died.

St. Francis Xavier traveled far during his life. He and his fellow Jesuits—his friends—changed the landscape of Christianity throughout the world.

Gentiles, spreading the Gospel beyond the Jews. His letters were written to communities of Christians.

- **The Catholic Epistles:** James, 1 Peter, 2 Peter, 1 John, 2 John, 3 John, and Jude. These letters are called "catholic" because they were written to the entire Church rather than to a particular community. The word *catholic* means "universal."
- **Letter to the Hebrews:** Hebrews offers a complex discussion of who Christ is and the implications of the Incarnation. It was long believed to have been written by St. Paul. This is no longer generally accepted and the authorship is undecided.
- **Book of Revelation** (*the Apocalypse*): The Book of Revelation is a highly symbolic account of the visions of John. Tradition maintains that this was St. John the Apostle. The Book of Revelation is a difficult book to interpret, but the consensus is that it reveals the events of the end of this world and the second coming of Christ. It also gives us insights into the Mass, helping us understand the connections between the liturgy we celebrate on earth and the worship the angels and saints offer to God in Heaven.

### Aa Vocabulary

**Catholic Epistles (n.):** The seven letters written to the entire Church by Apostles. They are the epistles of James, 1 and 2 Peter, 1, 2, and 3, John, and Jude.

**Book of Revelation (n.):** The final book of the New Testament and the Bible that is a highly symbolic account of a vision of Heaven granted to St. John the Evangelist.

*St. John on Patmos* by Gaspar de Crayer (between 1649 and 1669).

St. John the Evangelist was the youngest of Christ's Apostles, and the only one of them who was not martyred.

# The Truth Is...

Throughout this course you have been learning about God. However, the study of God is different from the study of other things. Coming to know God is more like coming to know a good friend. It involves far more than just memorizing facts about that friend. It means to learn about them, to grow in love for and trust of them, and to build a relationship with them. The same is true with the study of God. It is about more than "learning things about Him." It is about growing in relationship with Him. And that involves learning to trust and love Him. But you cannot do that without knowing Him. This is why we sometimes say theology is "faith seeking understanding."

To know and understand God, we must listen to Him. The good news is God speaks to us! That is what we encounter in the pages of Scripture—the Word of God spoken in human language. When we grow deeper in understanding of Scripture, we grow deeper in understanding of God, and deeper in relationship with Him. Knowing how God revealed Himself in the Old Testament is kind of like learning about our best friend, the stories of their past, their family, the formative events that helped shape them into the person they are today. In the New Testament, we meet God face-to-face in His Son Jesus Christ, which is like being with that same best friend in the present, being in their presence, and experiencing relationship with them. God has revealed Himself so we can know Him, and He invites us to be in relationship with Him.

Chapter 10

# Focus and Reflection Questions

1. Of which covenant does the Old Testament tell the history?
2. Of which great King of Israel was Jesus a descendant?
3. Why must we understand the Old Testament to understand Jesus?
4. To whom did God extend His covenant after the coming of Jesus?
5. What teachings does the Pentateuch include?
6. What history is recounted in the historical books?
7. What do the prophetic books contain?
8. What do we learn from the wisdom literature in the Bible?
9. What are the Gospels?
10. Which book recounts the Ascension of the Lord and the life of the early Church?
11. To whom were St. Paul's epistles originally written?
12. How do the Catholic epistles differ from St. Paul's epistles?
13. What does the author of the Letter to the Hebrews discuss?
14. What events is the Book of Revelation about?
15. How were the stories of Scripture, especially the Gospels, a central part of St. Francis Xavier's ministry?

# Straight to the Source

ADDITIONAL READINGS FROM PRIMARY SOURCES

*For chapter 10, rather than the usual variety of selections from primary sources, we will look in close detail at the official and dogmatic teaching of the Catholic Church regarding divine revelation found in the Vatican II document* Dei Verbum*. You will read all of* Dei Verbum *in this course.*

### ***Dei Verbum*** **14–16—The Dogmatic Constitution on Divine Revelation from the Second Vatican Council, November 18, 1968**

14. In carefully planning and preparing the salvation of the whole human race the God of infinite love, by a special dispensation, chose for Himself a people to whom He would entrust His promises. First He entered into a covenant with Abraham (see Gen. 15:18) and, through Moses, with the people of Israel (see Ex. 24:8). To this people which He had acquired for Himself, He so manifested Himself through words and deeds as the one true and living God that Israel came to know by experience the ways of God with men. Then too, when God Himself spoke to them through the mouth of the prophets, Israel daily gained a deeper and clearer understanding of His ways and made them more widely known among the nations (see Ps. 21:29; 95:1–3; Is. 2:1–5; Jer. 3:17). The plan of salvation foretold by the sacred authors, recounted and explained by them, is found as the true word of God in the books of the Old Testament: these books, therefore, written under divine inspiration, remain permanently valuable. "For all that was written for our instruction, so that by steadfastness and the encouragement of the Scriptures we might have hope" (Rom. 15:4).
15. The principal purpose to which the plan of the old covenant was directed was to prepare for the coming of Christ, the redeemer of all and of the messianic kingdom, to announce this coming by prophecy (see Luke 24:44; John 5:39; 1 Peter 1:10), and to indicate its meaning through various types (see 1 Cor. 10:12). Now the books of the Old Testament, in accordance with the state of mankind before the time of salvation established by Christ, reveal to all men the knowledge of God and of man and the ways in which God, just and merciful, deals with men. These books, though they also contain some things which are incomplete and temporary, nevertheless show us true divine pedagogy. These same books, then, give expression to a lively sense of God, contain a store of sublime teachings about God, sound wisdom about human life, and a wonderful treasury of prayers, and in them the mystery of our salvation is present in a hidden way. Christians should receive them with reverence.
16. God, the inspirer and author of both Testaments, wisely arranged that the New Testament be hidden in the Old and the Old be made manifest in the New. For, though Christ established the new covenant in His blood (see Luke 22:20; 1 Cor. 11:25), still the books of the Old Testament with all their parts, caught up into the proclamation of the Gospel, acquire and show forth their full meaning in the New Testament (see Matt. 5:17; Luke 24:27; Rom. 16:25–26; 2 Cor. 14:16) and in turn shed light on it and explain it.

# Straight to the Source

ADDITIONAL READINGS FROM PRIMARY SOURCES

## Focus Questions

1. Why did God choose a people for Himself?
2. What did God manifest to the people of Israel through His words and deeds?
3. What did He do through the mouths of the prophets? What did Israel gain by this?
4. What does *Dei Verbum* teach about the value of the Old Testament books?
5. What is the principal purpose of the plan of the Old Covenant?
6. What do the books of the Old Testament contain and reveal?
7. What is the relationship between the Old and New Testaments?

## Reflection Question

*Dei Verbum* makes the case that the Old Testament is a sort of road map, or foundation for the New Testament. There are plenty of things in our human experience that require road maps, foundations, and other preparation in order to be fully realized. What are some examples of these other things in our human experience? Why do you think God chose to reveal Himself and His plan for salvation in this way?

Chapter II

# The Unity of the Old and New Testaments

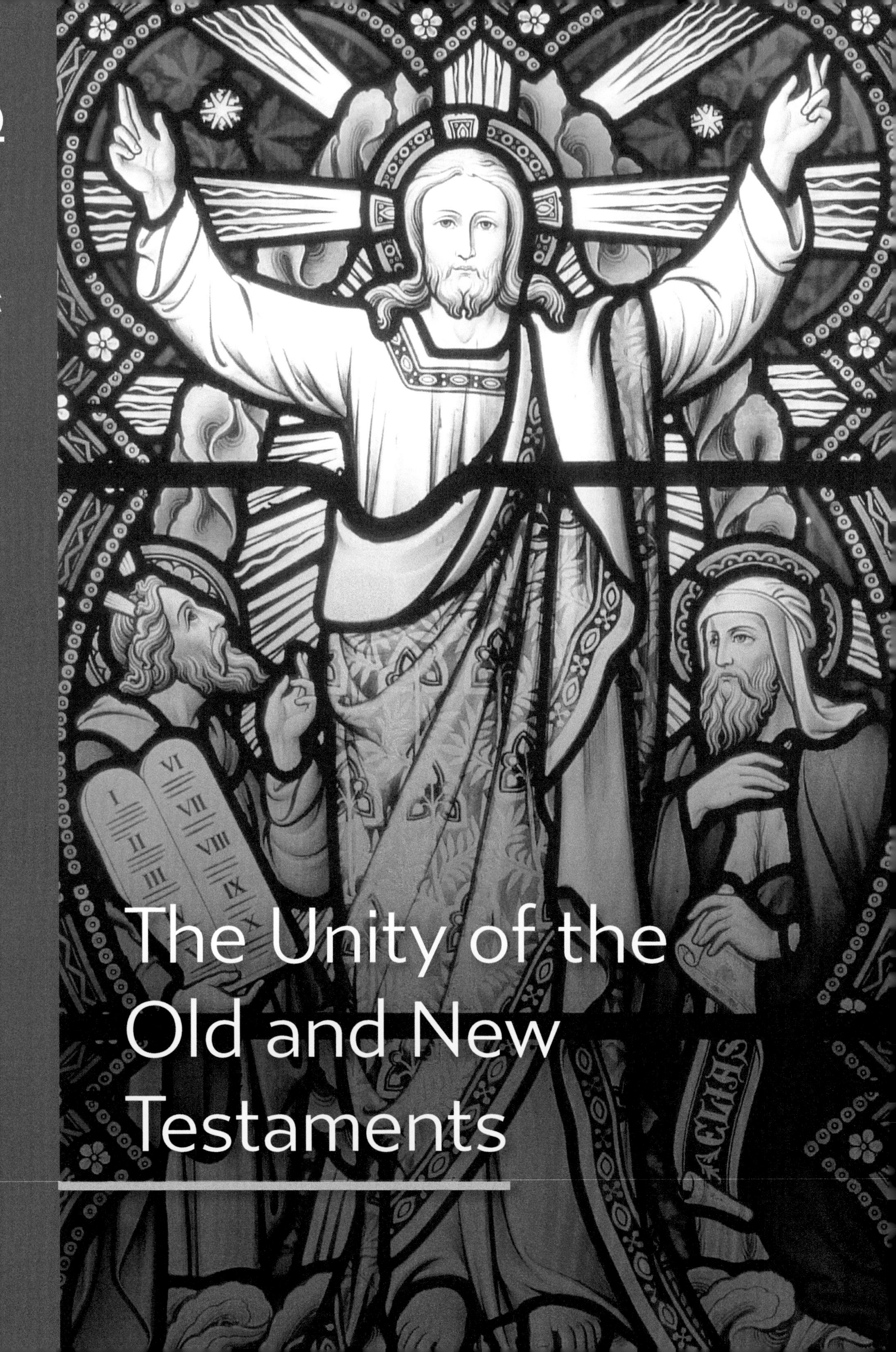

# Chapter Overview

Together, the Old and New Testaments form an organic unity of Scripture. That means they are interconnected and interdependent, each essential for understanding the other. The Old Testament tells of how God prepared His people for a Savior through a series of five major covenants. Jesus revealed the Father to humanity through His life and teaching, offering a New Covenant in His Blood. Millennia have passed since the Bible was written, and almost 2000 years since it was compiled by the Church, but we are as much a part of God's family as the people we read about in it. We participate in the New Covenant through reception of the Sacraments, given to us in the Church established by Christ when He lived on earth.

## In this chapter you will learn that …

- Neither the Old nor the New Testament can be understood in isolation from the other.
- Revelation unfolded in history through real events.
- The Old Testament is often divided into five major covenants. Taken together, these five covenants are considered the Old Covenant.
- Despite the Old Covenant, a vast gap between man and God existed.
- Everything changed with the coming of Jesus and the establishment of the New Covenant.
- In the New Covenant, the people of God promise to have faith, do as Jesus taught, and live a divine life made possible by the Sacraments.

### Bible Basics

In the beginning was the Word, and the Word was with God, and the Word was God. He was in the beginning with God. All things came to be through him, and without him nothing came to be.
JOHN 1:1–3

"Do not think that I have come to abolish the law or the prophets. I have come not to abolish but to fulfill. Amen, I say to you, until Heaven and earth pass away, not the smallest letter or the smallest part of a letter will pass from the law, until all things have taken place."
MATTHEW 5:17–18

### Connections to the *Catechism*

CCC 405 (page 158)
CCC 783 (page 158)

## The Unity of the Old and New Testaments

The Old and New Testaments together form the Sacred Scriptures. Both Testaments are indispensable, and both are inspired by the Holy Spirit. It is the constant teaching of the Church that neither the Old nor the New Testament can be understood in isolation from the other. As St. Augustine wrote: "The New Testament lies hidden in the Old and the Old Testament is unveiled in the New." Let's look at an example of what this means in practice.

**The New Testament lies hidden in the Old and the Old Testament is unveiled in the New.**

## Typology

The Old Testament begins with the creation of the world: **"In the beginning, when God created the heavens and the earth" (Gen. 1:1)**. The creation story relates that God "spoke" the world into being. The New Testament reveals that the Word that God spoke in Genesis was itself a person, His Son. St. John writes, **"In the beginning was the Word, and the Word was with God, and the Word was God. He was in the beginning with God. All things came to be through him, and without him nothing came to be" (John 1:1–3)**. Because we have St. John's Gospel, we read the account in Genesis differently; we know Genesis reveals something about the inner workings of the Trinity.

In this sense, the Old Testament becomes "unveiled" by the New. It is not "corrected" by the New Testament or "replaced" by the New Testament. The Genesis account of creation remains as true after the New Testament as it was before. However, the New Testament uncovers a new layer of depth, a new layer of meaning. The meaning itself is not new; it had always been there. But without the light of the New Testament, it was obscured. What is new is that in light of Christ, we can now see that meaning. Likewise, without the book of Genesis we cannot fully understand what John tells us about Jesus Christ. John helps us see us that Christ is the same Word who created the heavens and the earth "in the beginning" and with His Incarnation, He came to make a new creation of humanity and the earth.

This example from Genesis and John is just one of many connections uniting the Old and New Testaments. As we learned in Unit 3, when we read the Old Testament and New Testament together, the persons and events of the Old Testament are unveiled in the allegorical sense, as "types" that point to Jesus and the New Covenant. For instance, the Passover prefigures Christ's sacrifice on the Cross and the Eucharist. Jesus is the lamb that is slain in atonement for our sins, and the Eucharist is the meal we eat that saves.

Typology—reading the Old Testament and New Testament in light of the other and seeing how events, people, places, and things from one Testament, point to or are illuminated by the other— shows us this. It helps us see the unity of the Old and New Testaments. However, this unity is

Abraham and the Three Angels by Giovanni Battista Tiepolo (ca. 1770).

Abraham is visited by three angels, who reveal that God will grant him and his wife, Sarah, a son in their old age.

more than a matter of literary connections in the inspired text. The unity is rooted in the Salvation History recounted by those texts.

We need to remember that revelation unfolded in history, through real events that actually happened. Sacred Scripture is an inspired account of that revelation, and the unity of the two Testaments is rooted in the continuity of the events of Salvation History. This revelation, from Adam to the life of the early Church, forms a consistent narrative—a single, long, and dramatic story of the relationship between God and His people.

## The Covenants of the Old Testament

Covenants are central to this relationship between God and man. As we mentioned at the outset of this part of the book, a covenant creates a family bond between two people or groups of people. It is a sort of deal, with each side agreeing to certain conditions and obligations. However, a covenant is not a contract. The two differ in several important ways.

First, in a contract, people exchange goods or services under very narrow conditions. The reason you enter into a contract is because you want something from someone else and the only way to get it is to give up something of value. For example, you give the clerk at the store a dollar because you want the soda that he has. In a sense, contracts are a compromise; you would rather have both the dollar and the soda, but you cannot have both. You must choose. Since, at that moment you would rather have the soda, you give up the dollar.

However, in a covenant what you want is the other person; you want to be united to them in the most intimate way possible, and what you are willing to give in exchange is yourself. This is what happens when a man and a woman get married. They agree to certain provisions—they will be faithful, they will love each other, they will welcome children—but, what they actually exchange is themselves, and what they have afterwards is a family, not a compromise. In fact, they actually have more than they had before, because a family is bigger than the sum of its parts.

The history of salvation is the history of covenants between God and humanity, culminating in the ultimate covenant offered by Christ. (Remember "testament" is just another word for "covenant.") The Old Testament is often divided into five major covenants, each focused on a different important person (often referred to as a covenant **mediator**). Each covenant also includes a **covenantal sign**, a visible, outward representation of the interal realities of the covenant. Taken together, these five covenants are considered the Old Covenant.

### Vocabulary

**Mediator (n.):** The person whom God chose to represent all those entering into a covenant with Him. Adam, Noah, Abraham, Moses, David, and Jesus Christ are the mediators of the six primary covenants throughout Salvation History.

At the creation of the world God made man to be in total communion with Him. Salvation History tells the story of the renewal of man's relationship with God.

*God Creating the Animals of the World* by Izaak van Oosten (17th century).

1. **Adam and Eve (Genesis 1:26–2:17):** God gave the first humans an earthly paradise—the Garden of Eden—and walked in it with them. In return for the gift of their life and the many blessings God poured out on them, Adam and Eve promised they would not eat of the tree of the knowledge of good and evil. That was the law of the first covenant. There also was a sign of the first covenant between God and man: the Sabbath Day.
2. **Noah and his family (Genesis 6:18; 9:8–17):** After the sin of Adam and Eve, humanity's first covenant with God was broken. God restored it with Noah and his family, though, after the flood. He gave them a New Law to obey, and a new symbol of the renewed covenant: the rainbow.
3. **Abraham and his descendants (Genesis 12:1–3; 17:1–14; 22:16–18):** God's covenant with Abraham began with three promises: 1) God would give Abraham's descendants land (the Promised Land) and make them a great nation; 2) Abraham's descendants would have a great name, or become a dynasty of great kings; and 3) Abraham's descendants would be more numerous than the stars and the world would be blessed through them. Both the law God asked Abraham to obey and the symbol that represented this covenant were one and the same: circumcision.
4. **Moses and the Israelites (Exodus 19:5–6; 3:4–10; 6:7):** God made His covenant with Abraham's descendants, the people of Israel, by promising them they will be His chosen people and He will be their God. In turn, Israel promised they would worship no other god. To help them honor their promise, God gave them the law, which includes the 10 Commandments. This law is also the sign of the covenant.
5. **David and the Kingdom of Israel (2 Samuel 7:8–19):** God's covenant with David centers on two promises; King David's royal house will rule forever and through David's heirs, wisdom will come to all humanity. The sign of this covenant was the temple that David's son Solomon built.

Collectively, we call these covenants the Old Covenant or the Old Testament. Through them, God sought to bring His people together in worship and prepare them for the coming of Jesus. However, the Old Covenant was always an anticipatory covenant. It always pointed forward towards something more. It pointed towards a Sabbath where man and God rested in harmony together towards a true peace, a vast family of God, a nation of priests, and a lasting kingdom.

**Aa Vocabulary**

**Covenantal Sign (n.):** An external representation of the interior reality occurring within a covenant. Every covenant included a sign taken from human experience to represent the depth of God's love and mercy present at the heart of the covenant.

**Through [the Old Covenant], God sought to bring His people together in worship and prepare them for the coming of Jesus.**

Aa **Vocabulary**

**Grace (n.):** The free and undeserved gift of His own divine life that God gives to human persons.

However, with each covenant something was missing: humanity's ability to honor their end of the bargain. This is because through the sin of Adam, humanity lost the life of God in their souls; they lost God's **grace**. Not only did Adam and Eve lose the grace of God, but because of the Fall, Original Sin is transmitted to every human being as a wounded human nature. The *Catechism* explains that Original Sin **"is a deprivation of original holiness and justice, but human nature has not been totally corrupted: it is wounded in the natural powers proper to it; subject to ignorance, suffering, and the dominion of death; and inclined to sin— an inclination to evil that is called 'concupiscence'" (CCC 405)**. This wounded nature and tendency to sin made it impossible for humankind to fulfill their part of the covenants on their own. They lacked the intimate communion with God they had been created to know, and no matter how much mankind desired to give itself to God, they could not love God as He deserved to be loved, and they could not make up for all the covenant laws they broke—for all the ways they sinned. Despite the old covenants, a vast gap between man and God existed.

## The New Covenant

**To establish this New Covenant, God became a man and walked among us.**

Everything changed with the coming of Jesus and the establishment of the New Covenant. To establish this New Covenant, God walked among us. This bridged the gap that had opened with the Fall. Jesus taught us the true law—a law not written on stone tablets like the law of Moses but written rather in our hearts (Hebrews 8:8–11). He also helped us see that only the keeping of this definitive law, expressed particularly in the Sermon on the Mount (Matthew 5–7; Luke 6:20–49), satisfies our covenantal obligations to God.

Likewise, when Jesus was crucified and resurrected, He acted as both high priest and sacrificial victim, doing what fallen man never could do on his own with the animal sacrifices of the Old Covenant: atone for humanity's sins. Through Jesus' Church, the people of God have truly become the international, enduring people of God, the nation of **"priests, prophets, and kings" (CCC 783)** promised to Abraham and David. Indeed, Jesus, as the heir to David, satisfied God's promise to make the House of David rule forever.

In the New Covenant, the people of God promise to have faith, to do as Jesus taught, and to live a life rooted in the sacraments. These Sacraments, especially the Eucharist, are the signs of the New Covenant. They were given to us by Jesus, and they are the primary means through which God lavishes His grace upon humanity, a grace that far exceeds the original grace given to Adam and Eve. This grace is necessary for true union between God and man and is given to us first in Baptism. Grace is what was missing from man's soul after the Fall and, along with the wounded human nature inherited by all human beings by Original Sin, is what made keeping the Old Covenant law impossible.

This grace is given to us first in Baptism. Baptism takes the place of circumcision; through it we enter into the New Covenant, becoming the adopted sons and daughters of God.

Once baptized, we can participate in the Church's communion with Jesus through the Eucharist. Importantly, the only time Jesus uses the words "New Covenant" in the Gospels is during the Last Supper, when referencing the Eucharist: **"Then he took the bread, said the blessing, broke it, and gave it to them, saying, 'This is my body, which will be given for you; do this in memory of me.' And likewise the cup after they had eaten, saying, 'This cup is the new covenant in my blood, which will be shed for you.'" (Luke 22:19–20)**.

Through the Eucharist, Jesus gives Himself to us and we give ourselves to Him. This exchange is real. It is intimate. It is physical. In feeding us with his flesh and blood, His Body actually becomes a part of our bodies. This is one of the reasons St. Paul compared the relationship between Jesus and the Church to that between a husband and wife (Ephesians 5:23–33).

This union of Jesus and the Church is the perfect marriage, the completely satisfied covenant, repeatedly renewed in every celebration of the Eucharist and totally fulfills the promises of the Old Covenant, re-establishing and exceeding the communion with God that we lost through the first sin. This is why Jesus said: **"Do not think that I have come to abolish the law or the prophets. I have come not to abolish but to fulfill. Amen,**

Jesus gives us His Body, Blood, Soul, and Divinity in the Holy Sacrament of the Eucharist, which He established at the Last Supper.

*The Last Supper* by Maerten de Vos (between 1550 and 1603).

## Lives of Faith

# St. Mark

How well do you know Jesus?

That is a question everyone should ask themselves from time to time. Not how much do you know *about* Jesus, but how well do you know *Him*? The truth is, it is easy to learn a lot about Jesus without actually knowing Him, and there is a big difference between the two. So, how do we get to know Jesus better?

Thankfully, God gave us the gift of Sacred Scripture so we can know Him more. And thanks to men like St. Mark, we can know more about Jesus and get to know Him at the same time.

You might recognize St. Mark from his most famous work: The Gospel according to Mark. Many scholars believe St. Mark's Gospel was the first Gospel written and was probably used as source material for the Gospels of Matthew and Luke, although there are other theories that Matthew was perhaps written first.

We know from the New Testament that Mark was a disciple of Jesus, he was friends with St. Peter and St. Paul, and he was an active member of the early Church. His mother's house was used as a place for prayer and meeting in the early Church and St. Mark spent much of his time after Jesus' resurrection traveling and spreading the Gospel. He is regarded as the founder of the Church in Africa and was the first Bishop of Alexandria.

At some point during his travels, St. Mark felt the inspiration of the Holy Spirit to begin recording the life and ministry of Jesus. Imagine for a moment what it was like for St. Mark as he sat in prayer and felt the urge to begin writing. Do you think he knew that billions of people would read what the Holy Spirit was urging him to put down? Do you think he knew what God planned to do with his humble work?

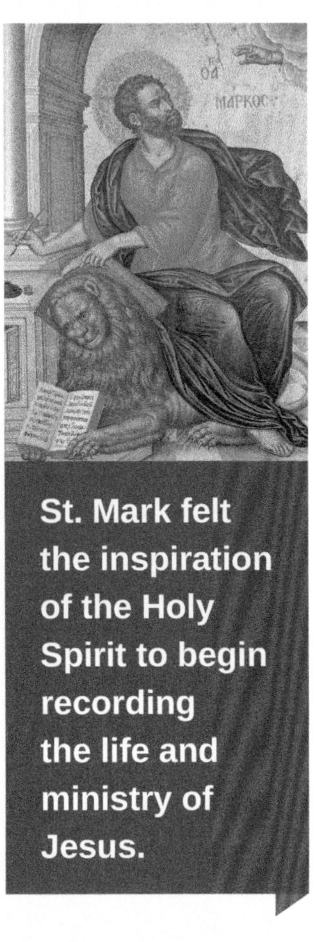


**St. Mark felt the inspiration of the Holy Spirit to begin recording the life and ministry of Jesus.**

St. Mark is a classic example of the truth that God can do a lot with our humble efforts. We do not know what St. Mark expected when he began writing, but because he allowed himself to be used by God men and women have been getting to know Jesus through Mark's Gospel for nearly two thousand years.

**I say to you, until Heaven and earth pass away, not the smallest letter or the smallest part of a letter will pass from the law, until all things have taken place." (Matthew 5:17–18)**.

Jesus' mission was to complete the story, not start a new one. As such, St. Paul describes the New Covenant as lifting the veil from the eyes of the people of God so they could see clearly what was already there in the Old Covenant:

> **"Therefore, since we have such hope, we act very boldly and not like Moses, who put a veil over his face so that the Israelites could not look intently at the cessation of what was fading. Rather, their thoughts were rendered dull, for to this present day the same veil remains unlifted when they read the old covenant, because through Christ it is taken away. To this day, in fact, whenever Moses is read, a veil lies over their hearts, but whenever a person turns to the Lord the veil is removed" (2 Corinthians 3:12–16)**.

We can then see why the Church teaches that the Old Testament and the New Testament form a single body of Scripture. Only together do they show us the full story of God and His people. Only together do they give us the full account of Salvation History, of God bringing humanity back into communion with Him. As Pope Benedict XVI wrote:

> "The mystery of the Covenant expresses this relationship between God who calls man with his word, and man who responds, albeit making clear that it is not a matter of a meeting of two peers; what we call the Old and New Covenant is not a contract between two equal parties, but a pure gift of God. By this gift of his love God bridges every distance and truly makes us his "partners," in order to bring about the nuptial mystery of the love between Christ and the Church" (*Verbum Domini* 22).

Jesus Christ is the hinge, the center, of this story of salvation. All the history of Israel in the Old Testament points towards him; He is the one who will fulfill the covenants of the Old Testament. Similarly, the life of the Church after Jesus points back to Him, its very life is communion with Christ. Therefore, all history turns around Jesus.

**Through the Sacraments, we participate directly in the communion with God that the New Covenant initiated.**

In pointing back to Christ, the Church does not look to Jesus simply as a person who lived long ago. Nor does it view Salvation History as a story that ended with His Ascension into Heaven. Through the Sacraments, we participate directly in the communion with God that the New Covenant initiated. This is what the Mass is all about: we read from the Old Testament, we read from the New Testament, and then we participate directly in the promise of the New Covenant in the Eucharist.

The covenantal union between God and all creation reveals how much God loves His creation. In turn, we are meant to share God's love and express it through our relationships with others. This mutual sharing builds up the Church.

# The Truth Is...

Reading the New Testament and seeing how Jesus fulfills the covenants and prophecies can be relatively easy to do. This is especially true when the Gospel writers, St. Paul, and even Christ Himself directly tell us about it, essentially doing the Scriptural analysis for us! But these connections may also be especially easy to doubt. After all, given that the authors of the New Testament had access to the Old, how hard would it have been to craft stories about a Savior that seemed to fulfill the prophecies?

More challenging (and more rewarding) to find are those signs of Jesus hidden in the accounts of the old covenants. Recognizing Him there can be harder to do, but those signs of Jesus in the Old Testament—written many centuries before His coming—can sometimes provide those "aha" moments that bring things into focus when it comes to our faith.

Chapter 11

# Focus and Reflection Questions

1. With what event does the Old Testament begin?

2. How does the New Testament help us understand this event more fully? How does this fuller understanding help us understand God more fully?

3. In what ways does the Genesis account of creation help us understand the opening lines of John's Gospel?

4. Biblical typology is not merely literary analysis, but is rooted in what?

5. With whom did God make the first covenant?

6. What was the sign of God's covenant with Noah and his family?

7. What law was given through the covenant with Moses?

8. Collectively, what do we call the five covenants in the Old Testament?

9. What was missing in all these covenants?

10. How do we participate directly in the communion with God that the New Covenant initiated?

11. The **Lives of Faith** section of this chapter asks you to ponder whether St. Mark knew what God planned to do with his humble work, the Gospel of Mark. This same pondering can be applied to all of the Gospel writers. How do you think the Gospel writers would react today knowing the full affect of the Gospels they wrote?

# Straight to the Source

ADDITIONAL READINGS FROM PRIMARY SOURCES

*For chapter 11, rather than the usual variety of selections from primary sources, we will look in close detail at the official and dogmatic teaching of the Catholic Church regarding divine revelation found in the Vatican II document* Dei Verbum. *You will read all of* Dei Verbum *in this course.*

## *Dei Verbum* 17–20—The Dogmatic Constitution on Divine Revelation from the Second Vatican Council, November 18, 1968

17. The word of God, which is the power of God for the salvation of all who believe (see Rom. 1:16), is set forth and shows its power in a most excellent way in the writings of the New Testament. For when the fullness of time arrived (see Gal. 4:4), the Word was made flesh and dwelt among us in His fullness of graces and truth (see John 1:14). Christ established the kingdom of God on earth, manifested His Father and Himself by deeds and words, and completed His work by His death, resurrection and glorious Ascension and by the sending of the Holy Spirit. Having been lifted up from the earth, He draws all men to Himself (see John 12:32, Greek text), He who alone has the words of eternal life (see John 6:68). This mystery had not been manifested to other generations as it was now revealed to His holy Apostles and prophets in the Holy Spirit (see Eph. 3:4–6, Greek text), so that they might preach the Gospel, stir up faith in Jesus, Christ and Lord, and gather together the Church. Now the writings of the New Testament stand as a perpetual and divine witness to these realities.

18. It is common knowledge that among all the Scriptures, even those of the New Testament, the Gospels have a special preeminence, and rightly so, for they are the principal witness for the life and teaching of the incarnate Word, our savior.

The Church has always and everywhere held and continues to hold that the four Gospels are of apostolic origin. For what the Apostles preached in fulfillment of the commission of Christ, afterwards they themselves and apostolic men, under the inspiration of the divine Spirit, handed on to us in writing: the foundation of faith, namely, the fourfold Gospel, according to Matthew, Mark, Luke and John.

19. Holy Mother Church has firmly and with absolute constancy held, and continues to hold, that the four Gospels just named, whose historical character the Church unhesitatingly asserts, faithfully hand on what Jesus Christ, while living among men, really did and taught for their eternal salvation until the day He was taken up into Heaven (see Acts 1:1). Indeed, after the Ascension of the Lord the Apostles handed on to their hearers what He had said and done. This they did with that clearer understanding which they enjoyed after they had been instructed by the glorious events of Christ's life and taught by the light of the Spirit of truth. The sacred authors wrote the four Gospels, selecting some things from the many which had been handed on by word of mouth or in writing, reducing some of them to a synthesis, explaining some things in view of the situation of their churches and preserving the form of proclamation but always in such fashion that they told us the honest truth about Jesus. For their intention in writing was that either from their own memory and recollections, or from the witness of

# Straight to the Source

ADDITIONAL READINGS FROM PRIMARY SOURCES

> those who "themselves from the beginning were eyewitnesses and ministers of the Word" we might know "the truth" concerning those matters about which we have been instructed (see Luke 1:2–4).
>
> 20. Besides the four Gospels, the canon of the New Testament also contains the epistles of St. Paul and other apostolic writings, composed under the inspiration of the Holy Spirit, by which, according to the wise plan of God, those matters which concern Christ the Lord are confirmed, His true teaching is more and more fully stated, the saving power of the divine work of Christ is preached, the story is told of the beginnings of the Church and its marvelous growth, and its glorious fulfillment is foretold.
>
> For the Lord Jesus was with His apostles as He had promised (see Matt. 28:20) and sent them the advocate Spirit who would lead them into the fullness of truth (see John 16:13).

## Focus Questions

1. What is set forth in a most powerful way in the New Testament?
2. What does Dei Verbum tell us that Christ did?
3. What does the New Testament stand as?
4. What books of the Bible have a special preeminence? Why?
5. What does the Church affirm about the Gospels?
6. What did the Gospel writers select to include in the Gospels?
7. Besides the Gospels, what other kinds of books does the New Testament contain and what are they about?

## Reflection Question

Throughout this course you have learned much about the ways the Truths of the Catholic Faith have been handed on through Scripture and Tradition through apostolic succession and under the faithful care of the Magisterium. Why is it important the Gospel writers derived the content for their Gospels directly from the Apostles?

UNIT 5

# The Gospels

The four Gospels, Matthew, Mark, Luke, and John, hold a place of primacy among the Scriptures. They are our primary source of knowledge about Jesus Christ. In the Gospels we truly meet Jesus. The sacred authors of each Gospel wrote for a specific audience to communicate a a different point of view of Jesus, His ministry, and the meaning of His saving actions. The Gospels of Matthew, Mark, and Luke are called the synoptic Gospels. The word *synoptic* means "to see together." These three Gospels "see" the story of Christ's life similarly, and even borrow stories and the structure of their Gospels from each other. John's Gospel is unlike the others and is not concerned with telling a chronological account of Christ's life. Written last, John's Gospel assumes that his reader is familiar with the other Gospels and is concerned with the deeper theological realities of Christ's ministry and with presenting Jesus as the incarnate Word of God who has always existed with God. Together, the four Gospels are a reliable historical and theological resource not simply for knowledge of Christ, but for encountering Christ as He is and hearing His Word spoken to us, living and effective, as an invitation to enter the Kingdom of God.

## In This Unit

Chapter 12

# The Gospels' Central Place in Scripture

# Chapter Overview

The Gospels are the heart of the Bible. In them we meet Jesus, who is the Good News itself. Each Gospel takes a different point of view on the story of Jesus, each sharing different details of the same story. The Gospels of Matthew, Mark, and Luke are very similar to one another and see the story of Christ in a similar way. Their accounts of the life of Christ are solid and reliable so we can believe in and depend upon them to give us the Truth for our salvation.

## In this chapter you will learn that …

- The Gospels are the heart of Scripture and in them we meet Jesus, who is the Good News itself.
- Matthew, Mark, and Luke are the synoptic Gospels because they see the story of Jesus in a similar way.
- There are many parallels in the synoptic Gospels, but each adds their own unique details.
- Scholars are unsure exactly why the synoptic Gospels are so similar, theorizing that they may have used each other's Gospels as templates, shared ideas, or shared common sources.

### Bible Basics

Now I want you to know, brothers, that the gospel preached by me is not of human origin. For I did not receive it from a human being, nor was I taught it, but it came through a revelation of Jesus Christ.

GALATIANS 1:11–12

For I am not ashamed of the gospel. It is the power of God for the salvation of everyone who believes: for Jew first, and then Greek. For in it is revealed the righteousness of God from faith to faith; as it is written, "The one who is righteous by faith will live."

ROMANS 1:16–17

### Connections to the *Catechism*

CCC 516 (page 171)

CCC 638 (page 183)

## The Gospels' Central Place in Scripture

As we have seen, Jesus Christ stands at the center of Salvation History. And fittingly, the Gospels—Matthew, Mark, Luke, and John—stand at the center of Sacred Scripture. They are the heart of the entire biblical story, for through the Gospels we encounter God telling us about Himself. Prayerfully read, these Gospels provide Christians with a true encounter with God.

## The Proclamation of the Good News

Remember, Jesus Himself is God's definitive revelation because He is God. He is God walking around with us, touching us, and talking with us. He is the Good News. He is the Gospel—the Word of God. As St. Paul states, **"Now I want you to know, brothers, that the gospel preached by me is not of human origin. For I did not receive it from a human**

Jesus Christ, the Word of God, is the icon of God's self-revelation; He said "Whoever has seen me has seen the Father" (Jn. 14:9b).

*Christ Pantocrator* by the Master of Cefalù (ca. 1150).

**being, nor was I taught it, but it came through a revelation of Jesus Christ" (Gal. 1:11–12).**

Notice St. Paul attributes his reception of the Gospel to an encounter with Jesus. This reveals an important truth which is often overlooked; namely, the Gospel is not merely a collection of writings about Jesus, it is Jesus Christ Himself. He is the definitive Revelation of God. He is the Word become flesh that lived among us (John 1:14). He Himself is the Good News! He did not just tell us about God. He actually is God, and His whole life is a revelation of who God is. **"Christ's whole earthly life—his words and deeds, his silences and sufferings, indeed his manner of being and speaking—is Revelation of the Father" (CCC 516).**

Even more than that, because Jesus was also a man, He reveals mankind perfectly to us. He shows us ourselves. The Vatican II document, *Gaudium et Spes*, explained: "The truth is that only in the mystery of the incarnate Word does the mystery of man take on light. For Adam, the first man, was a figure of Him Who was to come, namely Christ the Lord. Christ, the final Adam, by the revelation of the mystery of the Father and His love, fully reveals man to man himself and makes his supreme calling clear" (22).

We call the four Gospels of the Bible "Gospels" because they are directly about Jesus, they tell us about what He taught and what He did. They tell us about the Good News that is Christ Himself: God revealing God to us and showing us what it means to be perfectly human. In turn, the Church relates this Gospel, the truth of Christ, to the faithful. The Gospel can be related in many forms, from preaching, to the liturgy, to Scriptural writings, but no matter how the Gospel comes to us, it is always from Jesus, and is always about Jesus.

When prayerfully approached, the books of the Gospels lead us to accept Jesus Christ in faith, to apply His teachings to our lives, and so "work out" our salvation (Phil. 2:12). St. Paul explains: **"For I am not ashamed of the gospel. It is the power of God for the salvation of everyone who believes: for Jew first, and then Greek. For in it is revealed the righteousness of God from faith to faith; as it is written, 'The one who is righteous by faith will live'" (Rom. 1:16–17)**.

Encountering Jesus through the eyes of the New Testament authors, and within the tradition of the Church, gives us knowledge of Him for our salvation. At the same time, it leads to a personal relationship with God. It helps us to not just know about God's existence, but to know Him, as intimately and as personally as we know our parents or closest friends.

**"Christ's whole earthly life—his words and deeds, his silences and sufferings, indeed his manner of being and speaking—is Revelation of the Father"**

CCC 516

## The Synoptic Gospels: Matthew, Mark, & Luke

As we saw in Unit 2, the Gospels were formed over a period of time in three stages: the life and teaching of Jesus, the oral tradition, and the written tradition (CCC 76, 126). But what do we know about the individual Gospels themselves?

In order to answer that question, we need to divide up the Gospels, first looking at the Gospels of Matthew, Mark, and Luke. These are often referred to as the **Synoptic Gospels**.

**Aa Vocabulary**

**Synoptic Gospels (n.):** The Gospels of Matthew, Mark, and Luke, which present the story of Christ's life in a similar way and even borrow stories and the structure of their Gospels from each other. The word *synoptic* comes from the Greek for "viewed together."

**The Gospel of Matthew:** Written c. AD 55–70, by Matthew the Apostle, for Jewish Christians. Main Focus: The "Kingdom of God" and how Jesus brings the Kingdom into the world.

**The Gospel of Mark:** Written c. AD 50–70, by St. Mark, a companion of Sts. Peter and Paul, for Gentile Christians in Rome. Main Focus: The gradual revelation of Jesus' identity and a call to imitate Jesus' sacrifice in discipleship.

**The Gospel of Luke:** Written in the early AD 60s, by St. Luke, a companion of St. Paul's, for Gentile Christians. Main Focus: Salvation is from the Jews and extends to embrace the whole world (especially the lowly, broken, and outcast).

The Synoptic Gospels recall many of the same stories and miracles of Jesus. Because of their similarities, the three are called *synoptic*, which means, "seeing the whole together."

At first, the similarity of Matthew, Mark, and Luke's Gospels can strike us as repetitive or unnecessary. But, if we think of Jesus' life as a game-ending touchdown catch to win the Super Bowl, we can see that is not the case. Consider thousands of people are eyewitnesses to the event. The Synoptic Gospel authors are positioned in different places throughout the stadium. They all see the catch, and they can confirm it happened, but they all tell the story a bit differently. Those differences are important to capturing the essence of that great moment in time. The slight differences reveal not only the authors' different lines of sight but also differences in how they evaluate the significance of aspects of the story, differences in the audiences to which they write, and differences in what they want to communicate to those audiences. Taken together, we learn more by having multiple accounts of the same event than if we had only one. Let us look at some examples of this from the Gospels.

# Why do some people want to change what the Church teaches about Jesus?

Even in the apostolic age, St. Paul had to face opposition to the teaching of Christ:

> **"[...] so that we may no longer be infants, tossed by waves and swept along by every wind of teaching arising from human trickery, from their cunning in the interests of deceitful scheming. Rather, living the truth in love, we should grow in every way into him who is the head, Christ, from whom the whole body, joined and held together by every supporting ligament, with the proper functioning of each part, brings about the body's growth and builds itself up in love" (Eph. 4:14–16).**

There have always been people who try to change or bend what the Church teaches. Sometimes they do this to justify their particular belief or lack of belief. Sometimes they do this because the Church's teaching makes demands on them they would rather not face. Sometimes the attempt to change or alter Church teaching comes from sincere but misguided or misinformed efforts at trying to explain mysteries about Christ or God's revelation.

For example, in the early Church the doctrines of the Trinity and Incarnation were sometimes unclear. Accordingly, Christians who sincerely thought the Catholic Church's solutions were inadequate sought to formulate their own. However, in doing so they created heresies. Likewise, sometimes people find doctrines such as the suffering and Death of Christ to be disturbing, so they try to re-tell the story in a way that satisfies their understanding of who God is. This was what the writers of the Gnostic Gospels did. In modern times, some people have become so convinced that only science is capable of discovering truth and scientific laws are absolute, they have felt it necessary to explain away or just outright deny the miracles of the Bible.

*Saint Paul and Saint Barnabas in Lystres* by Michel Corneille the Elder; Photo Credit: VladoubidoOo (March 28, 2012).

These are all mistakes. Avoiding them begins with remembering that we are called to conform to God. God does not have to conform to us. **"Do not conform yourselves to this age but be transformed by the renewal of your mind, that you may discern what is the will of God, what is good and pleasing and perfect" (Rom. 12:2)**.

## Parallels in the Synoptic Gospels

### *Infancy Narrative*

In the world of Scriptural studies, the Christmas story is often referred to as the **Infancy Narrative**. Both the Gospel of Matthew and the Gospel of Luke present an infancy narrative. Each is different from the other, but they are not contradictory. Rather, when we read both accounts, we get a fuller vision of what happened.

Matthew's account of the birth of Jesus is very brief, but we can learn more about many of the key events it relates by looking to Luke's Gospel. For example, Matthew says Mary **"was found with child through the holy Spirit" (Mt. 1:18)**. Luke gives us a full description of how this happened: the Annunciation.

Obviously, Matthew was right that Mary became pregnant through the Holy Spirit, but he left out so much concerning Mary's experience. On the other hand, Luke is extremely interested in the experiences of Mary and explains in detail what happened to her. After the Annunciation, Luke goes on to tell of Mary's Visitation to Elizabeth, and he quotes in full Mary's beautiful monologue, the *Magnificat* (Luke 1:39–56). On the other hand, Matthew's account focuses on the concerns and visions of Joseph (Mt. 1:19–25), information totally absent from Luke's Gospel.

Likewise, the story of Christ's birth, Christmas, offers a great example of the way the Synoptic Gospels complement each other, giving us a fuller picture of what happened when read together. The account of Christmas we know so well—the account represented by nativity sets and seen in Christmas pageants—is actually drawn from two different books in the Bible.

Concerning the actual birth of Jesus, Matthew states simply that Jesus was born in Bethlehem (Mt. 2:1). However, Luke gives a long narrative account of how and why Mary and Joseph were in Bethlehem (Luke 2:1–7). Luke also tells us what happened on the night of Jesus's birth. He tells of the shepherds and of the chorus of angels that appeared in the heavens singing **"Glory to God in the highest" (Lk. 2:14)**. It is Matthew who tells us about the wise men from the East who followed a star to adore the infant Christ (Mt. 2:1–12). Importantly, the Gospel of Mark does not mention the birth of Jesus at all. Think how much less we would understand about Jesus if we only had Mark as a source!

### *The Baptism of the Lord*

Let us look at another important event from the life of Jesus: His Baptism in the Jordan River by John the Baptist. This event is recounted in all three of the Synoptic Gospels:

**Aa Vocabulary**

**Infancy Narrative (n.):** The name given to the Gospel stories of Christ's birth and infancy.

The Baptism of Christ by Joachim Patinir (ca. 1520).

Saint Ambrose wrote that "[t]he Lord was Baptized, not to be cleansed Himself, but to cleanse the waters, so that those waters, cleansed by the flesh of Christ which knew no sin, might have the power of Baptism."

- Matthew 3:13–17: **Then Jesus came from Galilee to John at the Jordan to be baptized by him. John tried to prevent him, saying, "I need to be baptized by you, and yet you are coming to me?" Jesus said to him in reply, "Allow it now, for thus it is fitting for us to fulfill all righteousness." Then he allowed him. After Jesus was baptized, he came up from the water and behold, the heavens were opened [for him], and he saw the Spirit of God descending like a dove [and] coming upon him. And a voice came from the heavens, saying, "This is my beloved Son, with whom I am well pleased."**
- Mark 1:9–11: **It happened in those days that Jesus came from Nazareth of Galilee and was baptized in the Jordan by John. On coming up out of the water he saw the heavens being torn open and the Spirit, like a dove, descending upon him. And a voice came from the heavens, "You are my beloved Son; with you I am well pleased."**

**"This is my beloved Son; with whom I am well pleased."**
**MATT. 3:13–17**

- Luke 3:21–22: **After all the people had been baptized and Jesus also had been baptized and was praying, heaven was opened and the holy Spirit descended upon him in bodily form like a dove. And a voice came from heaven, "You are my beloved Son; with you I am well pleased."**

The bulk of each Gospel's account is the same: Jesus came to John and was baptized; the Holy Spirit then descended upon Him like a dove, and the Father announced that Jesus was His Son—revealing the mystery of the Trinity. However, there are significant differences. Only Matthew recounts the conversation Jesus had with John, giving us Jesus' explanation for why He, too, ought to be baptized even though He was without sin. Luke tells us the Holy Spirit did not simply descend onto Jesus but that Jesus was actually in the midst of prayer—in the midst of a conversation with His Father in Heaven—and that the descent of the Holy Spirit was a part of this conversation.

Up to this point, the three Gospels paint a fuller picture of the event—just like with the Christmas story. But what about the apparent contradiction at the end? Did the Father speak to Jesus as recounted by Mark and Luke or did He address the crowd as Matthew tells us? Did the Father say "This is my beloved son" or "You are my beloved son"? Not surprisingly, this question has been much discussed, but because we believe all three Gospels were inspired by God and so inerrant, this apparent contradiction must somehow not be a contradiction at all. How is this possible?

St. Luke's Gospel is one of the three Synoptic Gospels, along with Matthew and Mark.

*St. Luke the Evangelist* by Vladimir Borovikovsky (ca. 1809).

## Lives of Faith
# St. Luke

*He does not have basketball practice at 6 tomorrow.*

What does this sentence mean? It depends on which part of the sentence you emphasize.

> ***He** does not have basketball practice at 6 tomorrow.*
>
> *He **does not** have basketball practice at 6 tomorrow.*
>
> *He does not have **basketball** practice at 6 tomorrow.*
>
> *He does not have basketball **practice** at 6 tomorrow.*
>
> *He does not have basketball practice at **6** tomorrow.*
>
> *He does not have basketball practice at 6 **tomorrow**.*

See how the meaning of the sentence changes, depending on what you emphasize?

The written word is a beautiful and complicated way to communicate. And that is why St. Luke wrote his Gospel.

St. Luke was a Greek physician who converted to Christianity, likely as a result of the ministry of St. Paul. It is believed that St. Luke met St. Paul around the year 51—about twenty years after Jesus' public ministry, Death, Resurrection, and Ascension. St. Luke traveled with St. Paul for some time on his missionary journeys, and at some point during their journeys began recording and writing down the story of Jesus. Luke wrote the Gospel with his name as well as the Acts of the Apostles.

St. Luke's Gospel is the most complete of the synoptic Gospels, and it tells some of the most well-known stories of Jesus, some of which are not included in the other Gospels. The story of the Prodigal Son, the story of Lazarus and the Rich Man, Mary's Magnificat and the Annunciation of Mary, as well as over a dozen other miracles and parables only appear in Luke's Gospel.

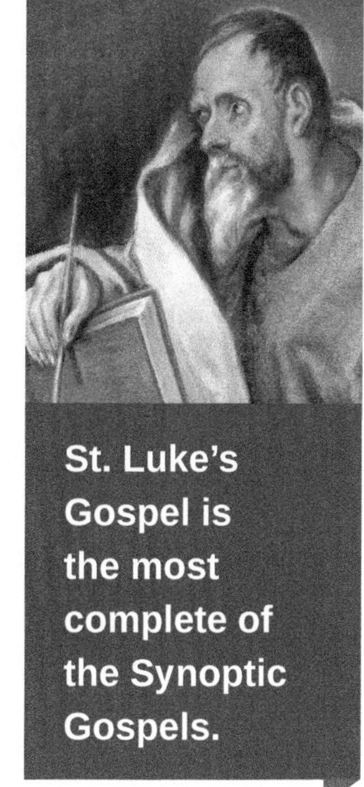

**St. Luke's Gospel is the most complete of the Synoptic Gospels.**

St. Luke lived in a very particular point in the history of the Church. He did not walk with Jesus or see Him, and he did not hear His words. But he would have met many men and women who did. He would have heard from eye witnesses of Jesus' ministry and learned from them. He would have been able to ask questions and get clarification. His perspective is much like ours. He needed to come to know and love Jesus without seeing Him. And that is his primary motivation for writing his Gospel.

He writes in the very beginning of his Gospel: **"Since many have undertaken to compile a narrative of the events that have been fulfilled among us, just as those who were eyewitnesses from the beginning and ministers of the word have handed them down to us, I too have decided, after investigating everything accurately anew, to write it down in an orderly sequence for you, most excellent Theophilus, so that you may realize the certainty of the teachings you have received" (Luke 1: 1–4).**

St. Luke wants you to know that he gave you a complete, accurate and investigated account of the life of Jesus, putting it into an orderly sequence so you can feel assured of the accuracy of what you hear. And through that accurate account, you can come to know and love Jesus.

The key to answering that question is remembering we do not believe the Gospels are necessarily word-for-word depictions of exactly what happened—like we might have if someone had recorded Christ's life on video. The Evangelists wrote to communicate the Good News to their audience. They made decisions about what stories and words were most important, and sometimes they needed to summarize, paraphrase, or add explanations in order to effectively communicate the truth of what happened. For example, Jesus and the other Jews depicted in the Gospels likely spoke Aramaic, but the Gospels translate their words into Greek.

Consequently, there are sometimes small differences between how the Gospels depict a scene. These differences do not detract from their inerrancy. The Gospels do not misrepresent what happened or deceive us about it. They are completely accurate in the sense that they always convey the truth of what happened. In this case, the truth is that God the Father was speaking, and He was speaking for others to hear. Whether He said "This" or "You," He was announcing to the world that Jesus was His beloved Son. Of course Jesus already knew this about Himself.

### *The Temptation of Jesus*

All three Synoptic Gospels depict how, following His Baptism, Jesus went into the wilderness, where He experienced temptations and trials from Satan. Mark is the shortest Gospel, so he has a short summary of what happened. Matthew and Luke go into more detail, and their accounts are nearly identical, although they list the order of the temptations differently. All three note that He spent forty days in the desert. This detail is important because these forty days and nights are reminiscent of the Exodus, when the Israelites spent forty years enduring trials and hardships in the desert after they left Egypt and before they entered the Promised Land. These two events together—Jesus' temptation and Israel's wanderings—inspire the Catholic practice of prayer and penance during the forty days of Lent.

**"For we do not have a high priest who is unable to sympathize with our weaknesses, but one who has similarly been tested in every way, yet without sin"**

HEB. 4:15

Of course, the very idea of Jesus being "tempted" in the desert can strike some of us as strange. After all, He is the Son of God. Is it even possible for the Son of God to be tempted to sin? The Letter to the Hebrews gives us some insight into this question when it says, **"For we do not have a high priest who is unable to sympathize with our weaknesses, but one who has similarly been tested in every way, yet without sin" (Heb. 4:15)**. So the short answer is yes, Jesus was truly tested, but no, He never could have succumbed to that testing.

This is possible because Jesus is fully God and fully man. He has our human nature and as a man could endure temptation. Because He also has a divine nature, he did not endure it in quite the same way we do. As

*The Temptation of Christ* by Sandro Botticelli (1482).

Jesus' temptation in desert shows us that, if we call upon Him and ask for grace, we too are capable of saying no to sin.

God, He possessed by His very nature all the grace necessary to withstand temptation. It is also important to note how He withstood it: by rebuking the Devil with the words of Holy Scripture. The Word of God used the Word of God to silence Satan.

The lesson for us in this is two-fold. First, Jesus' time in the wilderness reveals His solidarity with us. When we, too, are tested and tempted, He understands what we are enduring. However, His refusal to give into temptation shows us that with His grace, we too are capable of enduring hardship and temptation. If we call upon Him, if we ask Him to share His strength with us, we are capable of saying no to sin. Moreover, we can say no to sin in the same way He did: by recalling the words of Sacred Scripture. The better we know the Bible, the better we know both the nature and truth of God's promises and commandments, the more readily we can choose what is right and avoid what is wrong.

**Jesus' refusal to give into temptation shows us that with His grace, we too are capable of enduring hardship and temptation.**

### *The Sermon on the Mount and the Sermon on the Plain*

Both Matthew and Luke include a story of Jesus delivering a sermon to a large gathering of people, during which Jesus presents some form of the Beatitudes (and, especially in Matthew, a number of other essential

**Aa Vocabulary**

**Parables (n.):** Short stories that convey unfamiliar or complex truths in a simple and easy to understand way by using characters and situations that are familiar.

teachings). Matthew depicts Jesus delivering eight Beatitudes in a sermon on a mountain (Matt 5–7), while Luke depicts Jesus delivering only four Beatitudes in a sermon on a plain (Luke 6:17–49). The four Beatitudes that Luke writes about parallel four of the Beatitudes Matthew includes, while using slightly different language. These differences in language can help to deepen our understanding of what Jesus meant by each teaching. It is likely that the Beatitudes were a central part of Jesus' standard message. In other words, wherever Jesus went and taught, some form of the Beatitudes would have been presented. Hence, the Gospels record two separate occasions where Jesus taught the Beatitudes. This is similar to how a politician will have a collection of standard talking points they will incorporate into every stump speech when travelling from place to place.

### *Jesus's Parables*

After His time in the desert, Jesus leaves the wilderness and launches into His public ministry, a ministry which would be defined by His teaching, miracles, and **parables**. Those parables are particularly important because of the insights they give us into the Kingdom Christ proclaimed. In sum, they are short stories that convey complex truths in a simple and easy to understand form, even if they did not themselves actually happen.

Let us look at two of Jesus' best-known parables:

**The Prodigal Son:** In this parable, found only in Luke's Gospel, Jesus tells the story of a son who demands his inheritance while his father is still living. Though it pains the father, he gives into the son's request. The son then goes off to a foreign land and spends all his inheritance on frivolous pleasures that do not last. He soon becomes poor and destitute. Eventually, he comes to his senses and returns to the father to ask forgiveness. The father surprises him with his generosity, not only forgiving his son but also celebrating his return with a great feast.

The situation Jesus paints in this parable would sound as familiar to His original audience as it does to us. Back then, families broke up and children abused their parents' gifts, just as they do today. Knowing the sadness of such situations, most people would welcome an end where father and son reconcile, but Jesus's ending goes beyond mere reconciliation. The father does not just forgive his son; he rejoices at his son's return. He runs to meet him and throws a feast. In this parable, as in others, Jesus challenges us to look at reality through God's eyes, not our own, and in the process, see how God's love and generosity exceeds our expectations.

*The Raising of Lazarus* by Jean Jouvenet (ca. 1711).

▲ Christ performed a variety of miracles as a witness to His divinity, and to reveal the Kingdom of God to the world.

**The Mustard Seed:** In a parable found in all three Synoptic Gospels, Jesus compares the Kingdom of God to a mustard seed, saying the seed is among the smallest of all seeds, but when it grows, it grows into the largest of plants.

There are many applicable meanings here. In one sense, Jesus is speaking about the growth of the Kingdom of God within us through our lives of faith. In another sense, Jesus is speaking about the growth of the Church as the sign and instrument of the Kingdom of God in the world. Jesus' parables are always multilayered in that they can be seen from many different angles. This is why Jesus' parables are timeless stories that convey spiritual and ethical truths.

**Aa Vocabulary**

**Miracle (n.):** A supernatural act of God that demonstrates His power over all things and are signs of the Kingdom of God.

### *Jesus' Miracles*

Jesus' **miracles** were another way for Him to reveal the Kingdom of God. Jesus entered into a world of brokenness and sin; we can see this in the types of miracles He performs. He casts out demons (Mark 1:32–34, Luke 4:40–41); He heals and cleanses those who are sick (Matt. 8:1–4, Lk. 5:12–16); he overcomes the disorder of nature (Matt. 8:23–27, Mark 6:45–52);

**Aa Vocabulary**

**Paschal Mystery (n.):** Christ's work of redemption accomplished by His Passion, Death, Resurrection, and Ascension.

**Last Supper (n.):** The last meal, a Passover, Jesus ate with His Apostles, on the night before He died during which He instituted the Eucharist.

▼ The climax of Jesus' Paschal Mystery begins with the the Last Supper in which Jesus Gives us His own Body and Blood, Soul and Divinity in the Eucharist.

and He raises the dead and restores their life (Mark 5:21–24, 35–43, Luke 7:11–17). All of Jesus' miracles not only witness to His divine power, but also reveal the Kingdom of God coming into the world and healing its brokenness.

These miracles are similar to His parables in that we have multiple accounts for many of them. Just like with the parables, reading the different accounts together helps us to better understand the significance of the event.

### *The Paschal Mystery*

Following Jesus' public ministry, we enter into the climax of the Gospels with the events of Jesus' Passion, Death, Resurrection, and Ascension. These events are collectively known as **The Paschal Mystery**. They are central to the Gospel because they reveal and communicate God's salvation to us.

This climax begins with the **Last Supper** when Jesus gives us His own Body and Blood as the New Covenant (Matt. 26:20–35). It is this New Covenant that we celebrate and memorialize at every Mass. After the Last Supper, Jesus' agony in the Garden of Gethsemane (Matt. 26:36–46) reveals His human fright at the prospect of the Cross, coupled with His determination to endure death for our sake. His betrayal and trial before the Roman

*Stained Glass Window Depicting the Last Supper* Photographer Unknown.

and Jewish authorities then testify to the universality of sin and our collective complicity in turning away from God. Next, His Death on the Cross reveals His supreme selfless gift of love. It is not easy to look at the violence of the Cross and call it beautiful, but understanding that on it, Jesus takes on the sins and brokenness of the world and gives His own life so that we might have eternal life, makes us see the Cross as the center of the Christian Faith.

However, the story of Jesus would have been deemed a failure without the Resurrection. The Resurrection of Jesus **"is the crowning truth of our faith in Christ" (CCC 638)** because it validates the truth of His life and ministry, it brings about the victory of life over death, and it points forward to our own resurrection and life in God's eternal Kingdom. Finally, the Ascension of Jesus reveals the beginning of God's new creation and points forward to the day when we will rejoice with God in the **"new heaven and a new earth" (Rev. 21:1)**.

As with the other events from the life of Jesus, when we read the accounts of the three Synoptic Gospels together, we see how they tell the same story, but emphasize different themes by focusing on different details. For instance, at the crucifixion of Jesus, only Luke reports His words, **"Father, forgive them, they know not what they do" (Lk. 23:34)**, and His conversation with the repentant thief (Luke 23:40–43). In this way, Luke emphasizes the forgiveness Jesus offers from the Cross.

### *The Synoptic Problem*

The **Synoptic Problem** is the name given to the questions surrounding the similarities of the Synoptic Gospel and their relationship to one another. Scholars want to know which Gospel was first. Are the Gospels of Mark and Luke similar to that of Matthew because Matthew's was written first and Mark and Luke used it as a source? Or, perhaps it was the other way around. Perhaps Mark's Gospel was first, and Matthew and Luke used it. Perhaps there was a fourth source, sometimes called "Q," that was used by the Evangelists to inform all of their Gospels.

While these are fascinating questions and well worth the effort of the many scholars who tackle them, their answers do not change the fact that all four Gospels are inspired by the Holy Spirit and are just as God wanted them to be. When the Gospels tell us about the same event in slightly different ways, they do so for a reason. We always need to enter into these differences with that in mind.

**Aa Vocabulary**

**Synoptic Problem (n.):** The name given to the questions surrounding the similarities between the synoptic Gospels such as who wrote first, did the Gospel writers borrow or share information from each other's Gospels, or did they have a common source.

# The Truth Is...

We meet Jesus in the Gospels, plain and simple. Sure, the Gospels are books written by men under the inspiration of the Holy Spirit. We could look at them, as some do, as simply historical texts, biographies of a man who lived long ago and who claimed to be God. But, they are more than that. They are the living account of our God and Savior who became man, dwelt among us for a time to show us His love for us and to speak to us in a human way, and then, when the time was right, He freely gave His life for ours. The Gospels are not just words on a page in an old dusty book. Rather, through them, we encounter Jesus, our Savior Himself.

Have you ever looked through an old photo album from when you were a child? Have you seen pictures from when you were little that you could not possibly remember the event captured in the photo, but still, because of the power of the picture, you are vividly transported to that moment in time and made present to that event again? This is like the Gospels. Their powerful and life-changing account of the life of Christ, a life you and I were not alive to witness with our own two eyes, has the power to vividly and transformatively make Christ present to us today. However, the question is will you take the time to meet Him?

Chapter 12

# Focus and Reflection Questions

1. Why is Jesus the "Good News"?

2. What else, other than God Himself, does Jesus reveal to us?

3. Why do we call the four Gospels of the Bible "Gospels"?

4. Why is it important for us to encounter Jesus in the Gospels?

5. Why are Matthew, Mark, and Luke called the synoptic Gospels?

6. Why is it good that we have multiple accounts of the same events in the Gospels?

7. What is unique about Luke's account of Mary's pregnancy with Jesus?

8. What is key for understanding seeming contradictions between the Gospels, as in the accounts of Jesus' baptism?

9. How is it possible that Jesus was tempted? What do we learn about ourselves through Jesus' temptation?

10. What do we learn about the Beatitudes from the Gospel accounts of the Sermon on the Mount and the Sermon on the Plain?

11. Why did Jesus teach in parables?

12. What was the purpose of Jesus' miracles?

13. What event do all the Gospels agree upon that is the "crowning truth of our faith in Christ"?

14. What is the synoptic problem?

15. In the long history of the Church, why have some people tried to change the teaching about Jesus?

16. Why is Luke's Gospel so reliable? Luke's Gospel is the most complete of the synoptic Gospels, and he relied on the testimony of many eye witnesses to Jesus' ministry.

# Straight to the Source

ADDITIONAL READINGS FROM PRIMARY SOURCES

### Quote from Venerable Fulton Sheen

The Old Testament is like a radio with its hidden voice announcing the One to come. The New Testament is like a television because the Word became both audible and visible.

1. Put this quote from Venerable Fulton Sheen in your own words.
2. Think about what you have learned in this course so far. Why is the Old Testament like a radio? Why is the New Testament like a television?
3. Do you agree or disagree with this analogy? Why?

### *Evangelii Gaudium* 5—An Apostolic Exhortation of Pope Francis, November 24, 2013

The Gospel, radiant with the glory of Christ's cross, constantly invites us to rejoice. A few examples will suffice. "Rejoice!" is the angel's greeting to Mary (Lk 1:28). Mary's visit to Elizabeth makes John leap for joy in his mother's womb (cf. Lk 1:41). In her song of praise, Mary proclaims: "My spirit rejoices in God my Saviour" (Lk 1:47). When Jesus begins his ministry, John cries out: "For this reason, my joy has been fulfilled" (Jn 3:29). Jesus himself "rejoiced in the Holy Spirit" (Lk 10:21). His message brings us joy: "I have said these things to you, so that my joy may be in you, and that your joy may be complete" (Jn 15:11). Our Christian joy drinks of the wellspring of his brimming heart. He promises his disciples: "You will be sorrowful, but your sorrow will turn into joy" (Jn 16:20). He then goes on to say: "But I will see you again and your hearts will rejoice, and no one will take your joy from you" (Jn 16:22). The disciples "rejoiced" (Jn 20:20) at the sight of the risen Christ. In the Acts of the Apostles we read that the first Christians "ate their food with glad and generous hearts" (2:46). Wherever the disciples went, "there was great joy" (8:8); even amid persecution they continued to be "filled with joy" (13:52). The newly baptized eunuch "went on his way rejoicing" (8:39), while Paul's jailer "and his entire household rejoiced that he had become a believer in God" (16:34). Why should we not also enter into this great stream of joy?

1. What does Pope Francis make clear in this excerpt about what the Gospel invites us to do?
2. What does it mean to rejoice? When and why do we rejoice? Why is the Gospel message reason to rejoice?

# Straight to the Source

ADDITIONAL READINGS FROM PRIMARY SOURCES

### *Divino Afflante Spiritu* 58, An encyclical of Pope Pius XII, September 30, 1943

There those who are wearied and oppressed by adversities and afflictions will find true consolation and divine strength to suffer and bear with patience; there—that is in the Holy Gospels—Christ, the highest and greatest example of justice, charity and mercy, is present to all; and to the lacerated and trembling human race are laid open the fountains of that divine grace without which both peoples and their rulers can never arrive at, never establish, peace in the state and unity of heart; there in fine will all learn Christ, "Who is the head of all principality and power" and "Who of God is made unto us wisdom and justice and sanctification and redemption."

1. Who will find consolation in Christ? Why? Where is this consolation found?
2. What does it mean to be consoled? Why do the Gospels offer us consolation?

Chapter 13

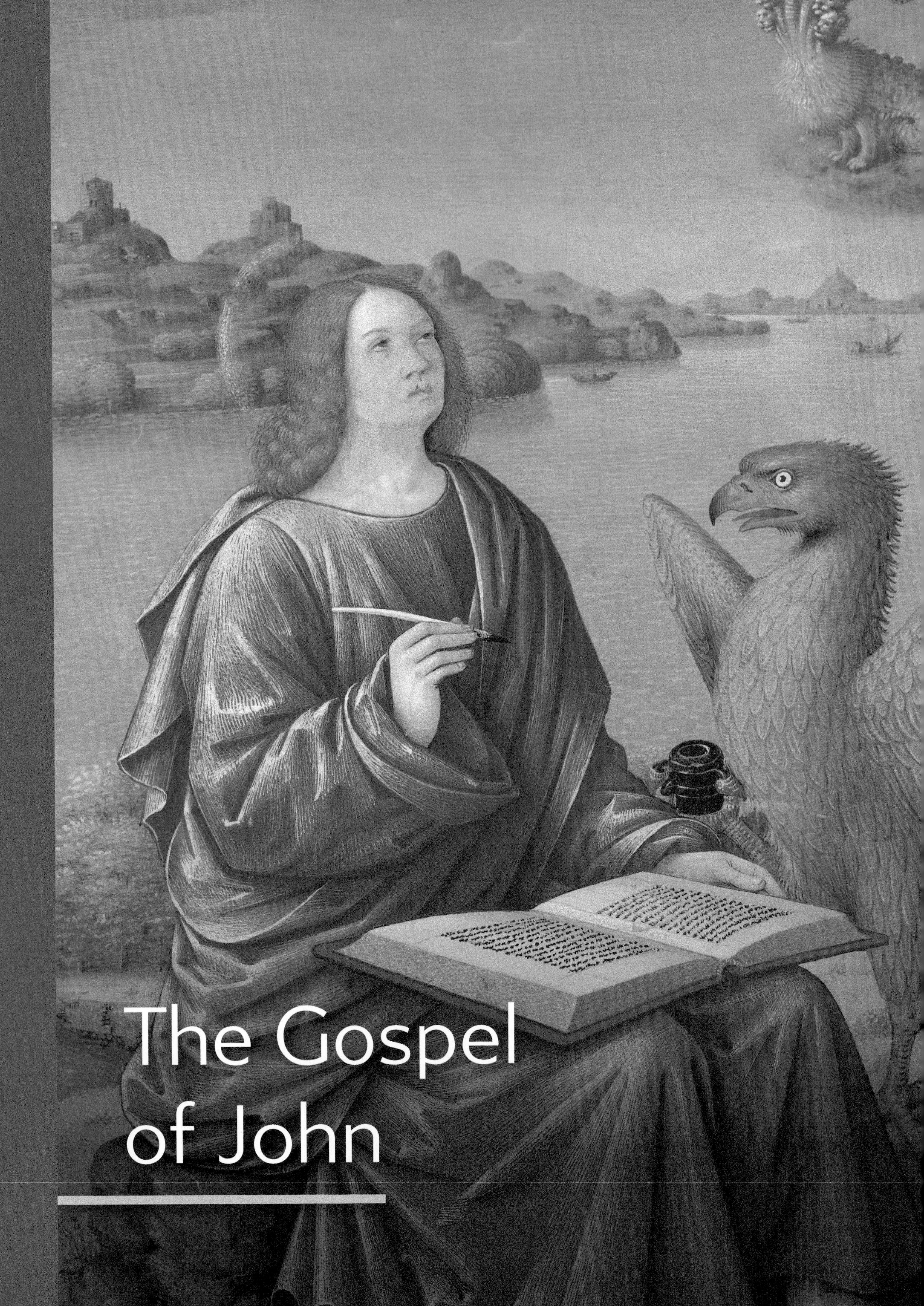

# The Gospel of John

# Chapter Overview

When you read the Gospel of John, you are reading something written by someone who loved Jesus more than we can imagine. And we know Jesus loved John in a special way—trusting John so much He gave the care of His mother Mary to him. John was truly the beloved Apostle of Jesus.

Perhaps because of how much he loved his teacher, John does not want to tell us about the events of Jesus' life and stop there. In fact, John assumes we have already read the other Gospels, so we already know these basic, important facts. He communicates the events plus deeper theological realities, helping us to see Jesus as the incarnate Word of God. He especially centers on seven signs or wondrous deeds of Jesus that point to the greater reality and goal of Jesus' mission.

## In this chapter you will learn that ...

- The traditional author of John's Gospel is St. John the beloved Apostle.
- John's Gospel combines biography with deep, prayerful, and theological reflections on the meaning of those events.
- John includes seven signs or wondrous deeds of Jesus and the seven "I AM statements" of Jesus.
- John tells us at the end of his Gospel that the life of Jesus could never be contained with a book.

**Bible Basics**

In the beginning was the Word, and the Word was with God, and the Word was God.
JOHN 1:1

And the Word became flesh and made his dwelling among us, and we saw his glory, the glory as of the Father's only Son, full of grace and truth.
JOHN 1:14

Aa Vocabulary

**Divine Logos (n.):** The Divine Word of God. *Logos* is Greek for "word."

## The Gospel of John

**The Gospel of John:** Written c. AD 60–90, by St. John the Apostle, primarily for Jewish Christians. Main Focus: **"But these are written that you may [come to] believe that Jesus is the Messiah, the Son of God, and that through this belief you may have life in his name" (Jn. 20:31).**

John's Gospel is unique in that it combines the raw biographical facts of Jesus' life with John's deep, prayerful, and theological reflections on the meaning of those events. The Gospel of John is not one of the Synoptic Gospels because it differs from them to such an extent that it is most often considered on its own. Tradition has it that the Gospel was written by St. John the Apostle, one of the sons of Zebedee. St. John was one of Jesus's twelve chosen Apostles. In his Gospel, John refers to himself as the **"one whom Jesus loved" (Jn. 13:23)**, and John portrays himself as laying on Jesus's chest during the Last Supper in an act of true friendship. John's Gospel is a rich theological portrait of Jesus told through the eyes of a man who was deeply changed by his encounter with Christ.

One of John's theological concerns is showing that Jesus is at the center of creation and Salvation History.

In his Gospel, one of John's theological concerns is showing that Jesus is at the center of creation and Salvation History. He does this especially in the prologue to his Gospel, where he identifies Jesus as the **Divine Logos** or Word. John takes us back before creation, echoing Gen. 1:1: **"In the beginning was the Word, and the Word was with God, and the Word was God" (Jn. 1:1)**. The Word or Son of God exists from all eternity with God the Father. All things were created through Him.

He later writes: **"And the Word became flesh and made his dwelling among us, and we saw his glory, the glory as of the Father's only Son, full of grace and truth" (Jn. 1:14)**. Here, we can see that by taking on flesh as a man, Jesus, the Word, is at the center of our redemption. Jesus is the person who brings together Heaven and earth, God and man, the Old and the New Covenants. Jesus bridges the "gap" between man and God: **"No one has ever seen God. The only Son, God, who is at the Father's side, has revealed him" (Jn. 1:18)**.

To illustrate that Jesus is the **"Word become flesh" (Jn. 1:14)**, John gives us seven "signs" (or miracles) worked by Jesus.

1. The miracle at Cana (Jn. 2:1–11);
2. The healing of the official's son (Jn. 4:46–54);
3. The healing of the paralytic (Jn. 5:1–9);
4. The multiplication of the loaves (Jn. 6:1–14);

5. The restoration of the blind man (Jn. 9:1–41);
6. The raising of Lazarus (Jn. 11:17–44), and, most important of all,
7. The Resurrection of Jesus (Jn. 20:1–10).

Each of the seven signs featured in John's Gospel makes theological points about who Jesus is and what He has come to do. They all point to God's glory and to the reality of Jesus as God Himself. That they number seven is important. John starts his Gospel with an account of creation that obviously points back to Genesis 1. In Genesis, creation happens in seven days. In John's Gospel, the seven signs point to the new creation being worked by Christ.

Seven is also the biblical number of completion, so it is fitting that in addition to the seven signs, John includes seven "I AM statements" of Jesus. "I AM" was the name God gave Himself in the Old Testament (Ex. 3:14). In the Gospel of John, God himself tells us who he is:

**"I am the bread of life" (Jn. 6:35),**

**"I am the light of the world" (Jn. 8:12),**

**"I am the gate for the sheep" (Jn. 10:7),**

**"I am the good shepherd" (Jn. 10:11),**

**"I am the resurrection and the life" (Jn. 11:25),**

**"I am the way and the truth and the life" (Jn. 14:6),**

**"I am the true vine" (Jn. 15:1).**

▼ The miracle at the wedding feast in Cana is the first of the seven miracles of Christ that St. John records in his Gospel.

*The Marriage Feast at Cana* by Bartolomé Esteban Murillo (ca. 1672); Photo Credit: DeFacto (January 28, 2018).

### Lives of Faith

## St. John the Evangelist

What do the next few years of your life have in store for you?

For many of you, you are working towards high school graduation and then going to college. Some of you will work, others might travel. You will make friendships and you may find someone to date. You will see more of the world than you have seen before, figure out what you are hoping to do with your life, learn a lot, make some mistakes, and you will start the process of "growing up." But for St. John, the outlook could not have been more different when he was your age.

St. John the Evangelist is best known for writing the Gospel with his name, the Letters of John, and the Book of Revelation. He was around fifteen years old when Jesus called him to be one of the first Apostles. He was an eye witness to Jesus' public ministry and was the only Apostle present at the Crucifixion.

John and James, both fishermen, were brothers, and were known as the Sons of Thunder. This title likely referred to their personalities. In one story from the Gospel of Luke, a Samaritan village refused to welcome Jesus while He traveled to Jerusalem. The story says James and John asked Jesus, **"Lord, do you want us to call down fire from heaven to consume them?" (Luke 9:54).** Sons of Thunder indeed!

But despite (or because of) his potentially impetuous personality, St. John was referred to in the Gospel of John as "the beloved disciple." At the Last Supper, John reclined at the table with his head resting on Jesus' chest. At the Crucifixion it is John who Jesus speaks of when He says to His mother, Mary, **"woman, behold, your son,"** and—turning to John—**"behold, your mother." (John 19:26–27)**. John was also the first Apostle present at the empty tomb of Jesus.

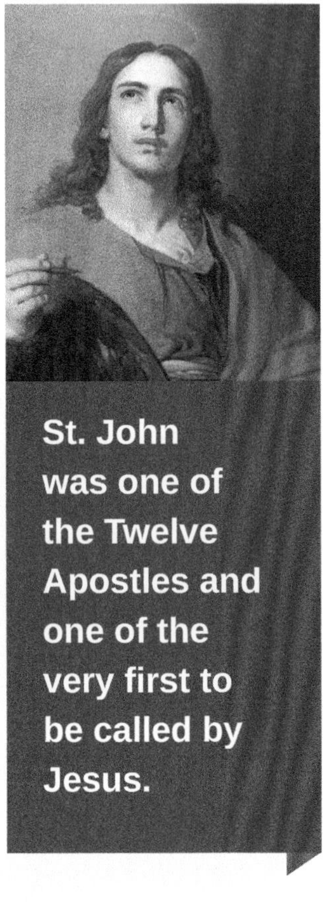

**St. John was one of the Twelve Apostles and one of the very first to be called by Jesus.**

After Jesus' Ascension into Heaven and the descent of the Holy Spirit at Pentecost, St. John traveled to fulfill his mission to evangelize all the world. He traveled with St. Peter to Rome and other cities throughout the region, took care of Mary until she was assumed into Heaven, and—like many other Apostles—suffered imprisonment and persecution for his beliefs.

However, unlike all the other Apostles, St. John did not die a martyr. According to tradition, he lived until a very old age, eventually being exiled to the island of Patmos. It was on this island he received the visions which he recorded for the Book of Revelation, and it was on this island that he died around 100 AD.

John was your age when he encountered Jesus. If you had asked him what life had in store for him before he met Jesus, he likely would have said he would be a fisherman like his father and brother, raise a family, and live a typical life for a Jewish man at his point in history. But when he met Jesus, everything changed. God had incredible things in store for him, and He has incredible things in store for you, too.

Many scholars describe the Gospel of John as presenting a **high Christology**. Christology is the theological exploration of who Christ is. By a "high Christology," these scholars mean that John focuses on Christ's divinity, emphasizing that Jesus was totally God. St. John's Gospel is also sometimes described as being more mystical or spiritual than the Synoptic Gospels.

However, it would be a mistake to take this idea too far, for St. John also relates solid and clear teachings about things in this world. For example, in John 6 he relates Christ's explicit teaching on the Eucharist, known as the **Bread of Life Discourse**.

### The Bread of Life Discourse and the High Priestly Prayers

The importance of the Eucharist for John is clear: it is Christ's Body and Blood, Soul and Divinity, and through receiving the Eucharist, we have eternal life.

The Eucharistic teaching in John's Gospel serves as a bridge to the drama of the Paschal Mystery and Jesus' Last Supper discourses. St. John's account of the Last Supper differs from that of the Synoptic Gospels. His does not provide the **Institution Narrative** concerning the Eucharist; John's Eucharistic teaching was instead presented in chapter 6. Rather, over the course of four chapters (John 13–17), John relates Jesus's teachings and prayers of that night.

These are some of the most powerful and profound passages in the entirety of Scripture. In them, Jesus washes the Apostles' feet, giving them

*Christ the Saviour* by Juan de Juanes (16th century); Photo Credit: Quinok (August 26, 2015).

**Aa Vocabulary**

**High Christology (n.):** A theological exploration of Christ's divinity.

**Bread of Life Discourse (n.):** The name given to Jesus' explicit teaching about the Eucharist in John 6:22–71.

**Institution Narrative (n.):** The name given to the Gospels' accounts of the Last Supper when Jesus gave the Eucharist for the first time.

When Our Lord declares Himself to be the Bread of Life, He is speaking of His Body, Blood, Soul, and Divinity in the Sacrament of the Eucharist. St. John emphasizes this truth in his Gospel narrative.

an example of service (Jn. 13:4–9). He also expounds upon His unity with the Father and invites the Apostles to join Him in the communion of the Trinity: **"As the Father loves me, so I also love you. Remain in my love" (Jn. 15:9)**. At John's account of the Last Supper, Jesus, in effect, summarizes the entirety of His actions and teachings for the Apostles, preparing them for His departure.

At the end of the Last Supper discourses, Jesus then offers what is known as the **High Priestly Prayer**. This prayer is a powerful sequence of petitions from Jesus to His Father through which He passes His mission onto the Apostles and asks God to protect them and strengthen them, so they might remain united with each other and with God: **"And I have given them the glory you gave me, so that they may be one, as we are one, I in them and you in me, that they may be brought to perfection as one, that the world may know that you sent me, and that you loved them even as you loved me" (Jn. 17: 22–23)**.

### Vocabulary

**High Priestly Prayer (n.):** The name given to Jesus' prayer at the end of the Last Supper discourse in John's Gospel. It includes a sequence of petitions from Jesus to the Father through which He passes His mission on to the Apostles and asks God to protect and strengthen them so they might remain united with each other and with God.

> **"And I have given them the glory you gave me, so that they may be one, as we are one, I in them and you in me, that they may be brought to perfection as one, that the world may know that you sent me, and that you loved them even as you loved me."**
>
> JN. 17: 22–23

Through Jesus' High Priestly Prayer, we receive a glimpse of how He sees us and learn that the persons of the Trinity are inviting us into their life of unity and love. We also receive an example of how to pray. In this regard, John 17 is worth special attention.

John's account of the Last Supper pulls all the threads and themes of His Gospel together. In it, we encounter Jesus as the "Logos," the all-creating Word, issuing forth from the Father for all eternity, praying for unity among the Apostles (Jn. 17:6–19) and all believers.

John's Gospel likewise gives us a unique vantage point of the events of the Passion, Death, and Resurrection of Jesus. John has a unique perspective on these events because he was the only one of Jesus' Apostles who witnessed the crucifixion. From the foot of the Cross, he witnessed the flow of blood and water from Jesus' side (Jn. 19:35), which the Church has long seen not only as a physical sign of death, but also as a spiritual sign of the sacraments of Baptism and the Eucharist. John is also a unique witness to the Resurrection of Jesus. John testifies that Mary Magdalene alerts the Apostles to the stone being rolled away (Jn. 20:1), John and Peter investigate further and believe based on the empty tomb (Jn. 20:8). We too believe in the Resurrection, in part, because of the empty tomb. John testifies to this and to the many post-Resurrection appearances of Jesus (Jn. 20:19–25; Jn. 20:26–29; Jn. 21:1–23).

John's unique theological perspective based on eye-witness testimony complements the Synoptic Gospels. As John tells us at the end of his Gospel, the life of Jesus is a subject that could never be exhausted by books (Jn. 21:25), but together, the four Gospels—written by four different human authors, but all inspired by the same Holy Spirit—give us a rich and true understanding of who Jesus is and what He did during His life on earth.

# The Truth Is...

When you are in high school, you are often assigned to read textbooks about other written works instead of going straight to those works themselves. For example, you might read what Professor So-and-So thinks about the Federalist Papers without ever reading a single page of James Madison or Alexander Hamilton's words for yourself.

This once-removed approach is too bad when it happens in history class, but it is downright tragic in religion class. If you only read what a textbook's authors think about the Bible, you might know about the Bible but you will not know the Bible. You will never encounter God Himself in the Scriptures.

The bottom line is that the essay in this chapter on the Gospel of John may be informative, and hopefully it will be a help along your spiritual journey, but it can never replace reading the Gospel of John—and all of Sacred Scripture—for yourself.

## Chapter 13

# Focus and Reflection Questions

1. When was John's Gospel written?

2. By whom was it written?

3. Why is John's Gospel often considered on its own, separately from the three other Gospels?

4. With what does John begin his Gospel? Does this surprise you? Explain.

5. What was the name God gave Himself in the Old Testament?

6. Why would it be wrong to characterize John's Gospel as completely mystical or spiritual?

7. What does the Bread of Life discourse in John's Gospel teach us?

8. How does John's description of the Last Supper differ from the account in the synoptic Gospels? What does he emphasize?

9. Why is John uniquely able to write about the Crucifixion?

10. How does the fact that John was a teenager during the events of the Gospel change the way you understand him?

# Straight to the Source

ADDITIONAL READINGS FROM PRIMARY SOURCES

### Excerpt from the General Audience of Pope Benedict XVI, July 5, 2006

Let us dedicate our meeting today to remembering another very important member of the Apostolic College: John, son of Zebedee and brother of James. His typically Jewish name means: "the Lord has worked grace." He was mending his nets on the shore of Lake Tiberias when Jesus called him and his brother (cf. Mt 4: 21; Mk 1: 19).

John was always among the small group that Jesus took with him on specific occasions. He was with Peter and James when Jesus entered Peter's house in Capernaum to cure his mother-in-law (cf. Mk 1: 29); with the other two, he followed the Teacher into the house of Jairus, a ruler of the synagogue whose daughter he was to bring back to life (cf. Mk 5: 37); he followed him when he climbed the mountain for his Transfiguration (cf. Mk 9: 2).

He was beside the Lord on the Mount of Olives when, before the impressive sight of the Temple of Jerusalem, he spoke of the end of the city and of the world (cf. Mk 13: 3); and, lastly, he was close to him in the Garden of Gethsemane when he withdrew to pray to the Father before the Passion (cf. Mk 14: 33).

Shortly before the Passover, when Jesus chose two disciples to send them to prepare the room for the Supper, it was to him and to Peter that he entrusted this task (cf. Lk 22: 8).

His prominent position in the group of the Twelve makes it somewhat easier to understand the initiative taken one day by his mother: she approached Jesus to ask him if her two sons—John and James—could sit next to him in the Kingdom, one on his right and one on his left (cf. Mt 20: 20–21).

As we know, Jesus answered by asking a question in turn: he asked whether they were prepared to drink the cup that he was about to drink (cf. Mt 20: 22). The intention behind those words was to open the two disciples' eyes, to introduce them to knowledge of the mystery of his person and to suggest their future calling to be his witnesses, even to the supreme trial of blood.

A little later, in fact, Jesus explained that he had not come to be served, but to serve and to give his life as a ransom for many (cf. Mt 20: 28).

In the days after the Resurrection, we find "the sons of Zebedee" busy with Peter and some of the other disciples on a night when they caught nothing, but that was followed, after the intervention of the Risen One, by the miraculous catch: it was to be "the disciple Jesus loved" who first recognized "the Lord" and pointed him out to Peter (cf. Jn 21: 1–13).

1. As Pope Benedict notes at the beginning of the audience, the typical Jewish name John means "the Lord has worked grace." Reflecting on John's involvement in Jesus' ministry and his closeness to Jesus, how did Jesus work grace through him?
2. Does it surprise you to know that Jesus had friends to whom He was closer (like John or Peter) than others? Why or why not?

# Straight to the Source

ADDITIONAL READINGS FROM PRIMARY SOURCES

### *Dominum et Vivificantem* 8—Encyclical letter of Pope St. John Paul II, May 18, 1986

It is a characteristic of the text of John that the Father, the Son and the Holy Spirit are clearly called Persons, the first distinct from the second and the third, and each of them from one another. Jesus speaks of the Spirit-Counselor, using several times the personal pronoun "he"; and at the same time, throughout the farewell discourse, he reveals the bonds which unite the Father, the Son and the Paraclete to one another. Thus "the Holy Spirit . . .proceeds from the Father" and the Father "gives" the Spirit. The Father "sends" the Spirit in the name of the Son, the Spirit "bears witness" to the Son. The Son asks the Father to send the Spirit-Counselor, but likewise affirms and promises, in relation to his own "departure" through the Cross: "If I go, I will send him to you," Thus, the Father sends the Holy Spirit in the power of his Fatherhood, as he has sent the Son; but at the same time he sends him in the power of the Redemption accomplished by Christ-and in this sense Holy Spirit is sent also by the Son: "I will send him to you."

1. Why do you think St. John emphasized the reality of the Trinity so much in his Gospel?
2. As you have learned over the course of this chapter, John's Gospel clearly presents Jesus as claiming to be God (as evidenced by the "I AM" statements of Jesus). How does John's treatment of the Trinity in his Gospel enrich our understanding of Jesus' claims to be God?

# Glossary

**Acts of the Apostles (n.):** The book of the New Testament immediately following the four Gospels that recounts the Ascension of Jesus into Heaven and the life of the early Church. *(pg. 145)*

**Ambo (n.):** A raised podium or lectern in a Church sanctuary from which the Scripture readings are proclaimed during Mass. *(pg. 94)*

**Analogy of Faith (n.):** The coherence of the truths of the Faith among themselves and within the whole plan of revelation. *(pg. 117)*

**Anthropology (n.):** The study of the origins and nature of the human person. *(pg. 6)*

**Apocryphal Books (n.):** Those seven books of the Old Testament and parts of the books of Esther and Daniel that are not considered by most Protestants to be inspired writings but are still considered valuable for their historical, spiritual, and theological significance. Also called the "apocrypha". See also Deuterocanonical. *(pg. 80)*

**Apostolic Succession (n.):** The handing on of apostolic preaching and authority from the Apostles to their successors, the bishops, through the laying on of hands, as a permanent office in the Church. *(pg. 49)*

**Arianism (n.):** An influential heresy of the early Church that taught that Jesus, the Son of God, was created by God the Father, and therefore not truly equal to Him or of the same substance. *(pg. 79)*

**Bishops (n.):** A successor to the Apostles, who has received the fullness of the Sacrament of Holy Orders. He is the leader of a particular church, or diocese, entrusted to him. *(pg. 49)*

**Book of Revelation (n.):** The final book of the New Testament and the Bible that is a highly symbolic account of a vision of Heaven granted to St. John the Evangelist. *(pg. 147)*

**Bread of Life Discourse (n.):** The name given to Jesus' explicit teaching about the Eucharist in John 6:22-71. *(pg. 193)*

**Canon of Scripture (n.):** The official list of inspired books that make up the Bible. *(pg. 77)*

***Catena* (n.):** From the Latin for "chain," the practice of Medieval biblical scholars of including comments from the early Church Fathers and other important teachers in the margins and between the lines of their Bibles, forming a chain of commentary. *(pg. 116)*

**Catholic Epistles (n.):** The seven letters written to the entire Church by Apostles. They are the epistles of James, 1 and 2 Peter, 1, 2, and 3, John, and Jude. *(pg. 147)*

**Council of Trent (n.):** An ecumenical council held from 1545-1563 in Trent, Italy that sought to affirm Church teaching, answer Protestant heresies, and end abusive practices within the Church. *(pg. 80)*

**Covenant (n.):** A sacred permanent bond of family relationship. God entered into a series of covenants with His People throughout Salvation History to invite us to be part of His divine family and to prepare us gradually and in stages, words and deeds to receive the gift of salvation. *(pg. 34)*

**Covenantal Sign (n.):** An external representation of the interior reality occurring within a covenant. Every covenant included a sign taken from human experience to represent the depth of God's love and mercy present at the heart of the covenant. *(pg. 157)*

**Creed (n.):** A brief summary or profession of our Christian Faith, such as the Nicene Creed and the Apostles' Creed. *(pg. 20)*

**Dead Sea Scrolls (n.):** Ancient scrolls written by the Jewish sect known as the Essenes found in 1946 in a cave near the Dead Sea. These scrolls contain some of the oldest known versions of Old Testament books. *(pg. 131)*

**Deposit of Faith (n.):** The full content of divine revelation communicated by Christ, contained in Sacred Scripture and Sacred Tradition, handed on in the Church from the time of the Apostles, and from which the Magisterium draws all that it proposes for belief as being divinely revealed. *(pg. 48)*

**Deuterocanonical Books (n.):** Those seven books of the Old Testament and parts of the books of Esther and Daniel that are not considered by most Protestants to be inspired writings, (while remaining valuable for their historical, spiritual, and theological significance). However, these books have always been a part of the Greek version of the Old Testament used by the early Church and were affirmed by the Council of Trent to be inspired writings and part of the traditional canon of Scripture. *Deutercanonical* is Latin for "of the second canon". *(pg. 145)*

**Divine Inspiration (n.):** The gift of the Holy Spirit that God gave to the human authors of the Bible which enabled them to write that which He wanted committed to writing for the sake of our salvation. *(pg. 62)*

**Divine Logos (n.):** The Divine Word of God. Logos is Greek for "word." *(pg. 190)*

**Divine Revelation (n.):** God's communication of Himself, by which He makes known the mystery of His divine plan by deeds and words over time, and most fully by sending His Son, Jesus Christ. *(pg. 9)*

**Dynamically Equivalent Translation (n.):** A translation of the Bible that uses different words or different figures of speech from those in the original in the attempt to preserve the actual, deep meaning of the original. *(pg. 83)*

**Ecumenical Council (n.):** A meeting of all the world's bishops together in union with the pope. *(pg. 25)*

**Encyclical (n.):** A pastoral letter written by the pope and sent to the whole Church and even to the whole world, to express Church teaching on some important matter. Encyclicals are expressions of the ordinary papal Magisterium. *(pg. 128)*

**Enlightenment (n.):** A philosophical movement of the eighteenth century that denied the value of faith and maintained that reason alone leads us to truth and holds the potential to solve the problem of evil. *(pg. 25)*

**Epistles of Paul (n.):** Letters written by St. Paul to communities of early Christians and other individuals to encourage their faith. *(pg. 145)*

**Exegesis (n.):** An interpretation or anlysis of a scriptural text. *(pg. 110)*

**The Fall (n.):** When Adam and Eve, due to the temptation and lies of Satan, disobeyed God and rejected His love. Also called the Fall of Man. *(pg. 9)*

**Fathers of the Church (n.):** The bishops and teachers of the early Church. *(pg. 20)*

**Five Proofs for the Existence of God (n.):** Arguments developed by St. Thomas Aquinas that use human reason and observation of the created world to conclude that God exists. Also called the "five ways." *(pg. 21)*

**Fundamentalist (n.):** An exclusive and overly literal reading of the words of Scripture. *(pg. 64)*

**Garden of Eden (n.):** The place where Adam and Eve originally dwelled in perfect harmony with themselves, with all of creation, and with God. Paradise. *(pg. 8)*

**Gentiles (n.):** People of non-Jewish ethnicity. *(pg. 19)*

**Gnostic Gospels (n.):** Ancient books about the life of Christ that are infused with theology that reflects the Gnostic heresy rampant at the time. Two are falsely attributed to St. Thomas the Apostle and St. Mary Magdalene. *(pg. 79)*

**Gnosticism (n.):** The name given to a heresy of the early Church that taught, among other things, that Jesus was not fully human, the material world was evil, and salvation was achieved through secret knowledge, or gnosis. *(pg. 79)*

**Gospels (n.):** The first four books of the New Testament. They are the heart of the Scriptures and proclaim the Good News of salvation won for us by the Passion, Death, and Resurrection of Jesus Christ. The Gospels are our primary source of knowledge of life of Jesus Christ. The word "Gospel" means "Good News." *(pg. 145)*

**Grace (n.):** The free and undeserved gift of His own divine life that God gives us to human persons. *(pg. 158)*

**High Christology (n.):** A theological exploration of Christ's divinity. *(pg. 193)*

**High Priestly Prayer (n.):** The name given to Jesus' prayer at the end of the Last Supper discourse in John's Gospel. It includes a sequence of petitions from Jesus to the Father through which He passes His mission on to the Apostles and asks God to protect and strengthen them so they might remain united with each other and with God. *(pg. 194)*

**Historical Books (n.):** The books of the Old Testament that are primarily focused on telling the history of Israel from the time of the judges to approximately 150 years before the birth of Christ. *(pg. 144)*

**Historical-critical method (n.):** The name given to the method of Scripture analysis that considers the historical context of Scripture. *(pg. 112)*

**Homily (n.):** A preaching by an ordained minister to explain the Scriptures proclaimed at Mass. *(pg. 95)*

**Immaculate Conception (n.):** The dogma that from the first moment of her conception, by the grace of God, Mary was preserved from Original Sin. *(pg. 94)*

**Incarnation (n.):** The fact that the Son of God assumed human nature and became man in order to accomplish our salvation. Jesus Christ, the Son of God, the second Person of the Trinity, is both true God and true man. *(pg. 11)*

**Inerrant (adj.):** Without error. Scripture is inerrant: it teaches without error the truth God wanted known for the sake of our salvation. *(pg. 65)*

**Infallible (adj.):** Incapable of error. *(pg. 51)*

**Infancy Narrative (n.):** The name given to the Gospel stories of Christ's birth and infancy. *(pg. 174)*

**Institution Narrative (n.):** The name given to the Gospel's accounts of the Last Supper when Jesus gave the Eucharist for the first time. *(pg. 193)*

**Israel (n.):** Hebrew word meaning "He who strives with God." God changed Jacob's name to Israel after he wrestled with an angel. God's Chosen People became known as the People of Israel. *(pg. 34)*

**Last Supper (n.):** The last meal, a Passover, Jesus ate with His Apostles, on the night before He died during which He instituted the Eucharist. *(pg. 182)*

**Latin (n.):** The universal language of the Roman empire, which, until modern times, was read and understood by most educated people in the Western world. To this day, it is the official language of the Catholic Church. *(pg. 81)*

***Lectio Divina* (n.):** An ancient form of praying with Scripture that is a slow and thoughtful encounter with the Word of God. Latin for "divine reading." *(pg. 97)*

**Lectionary (n.):** The official liturgical book from which the reader proclaims the Scripture readings during Mass. *(pg. 94)*

**Literal Sense (n.):** The meaning that comes directly from the Scripture text and is intended by the sacred author. *(pg. 118)*

**Literal Translation (n.):** A straightforward translation of the Bible that replaces words in the original language with words in the secondary language that have the same simple meaning and without regard for figures of speech of nuances in meaning. *(pg. 83)*

**Liturgy (n.):** The public work or worship of the Church. It is the participation of the people of God in the "work of God," which is our salvation from sin. *(pg. 93)*

**Liturgy of the Eucharist (n.):** The second part of the Mass in which we receive the Body and Blood, Soul and Divinity of Jesus Christ in the Eucharist. Here, the priest prays the words of consecration and changes the bread and wine into the Body and Blood of Christ. Those well disposed also come to the altar to receive Holy Communion. *(pg. 97)*

**Liturgy of the Hours (n.):** The public prayer of the Church which sanctifies the whole course of the day and night. It consists of a variety of prayers, Scripture readings, most especially the Psalms, and writings of the saints, divided into "hours," which are prescribed to be prayed at specific times of day. *(pg. 93)*

**Liturgy of the Word (n.):** The first part of the Mass in which we receive the written word of God. Here, the Scriptures are proclaimed and the priest teaches in a homily. We also join together in prayer for others and profess our faith. *(pg. 97)*

**Magisterium (n.):** The living teaching authority of the Catholic Church whose task it is to give authentic interpretation of the Word of God found in Scripture and Tradition, and to ensure the faithfulness of the Church to the teachings of the Apostles in matters of faith and morals. This authority is exercised by all of the world's bishops in union with the pope, and by the pope alone when he defines infallibly a doctrine of faith or morals. *(pg. 49)*

**Mediator (n.):** The person whom God chose to represent all those entering into a covenant with Him. Adam, Noah, Abraham, Moses, David, and Jesus Christ are the mediators of the six primary covenants throughout Salvation History. *(pg. 156)*

**Messiah (n.):** The Hebrew word for "anointed one" and the title given to the Savior God promised to the people of Israel. *(pg. 19)*

**Miracles (n.):** A supernatural act of God that demonstrates His power over all things and are signs of the Kingdom of God. *(pg. 181)*

**Nag Hammadi (n.):** A collection of ancient Gnostic texts found buried in a jar in Egypt in 1946. These texts give unique insight about the Gnostic heresy of the time. *(pg. 131)*

**Natural Revelation (n.):** God's communication of Himself to us through the created order. *(pg. 9)*

**New Covenant (n.):** The new and everlasting covenant won for us by Christ's Paschal Mystery. In this covenant is the fulfillment of centuries of prophecies and all of God's promises for the forgiveness of sins. We are made members of the New Covenant by our Baptism and we renew and participate in the covenant every time we receive the Eucharist. All people are invited to be members of the New Covenant. *(pg. 142)*

**New Testament (n.):** The 27 books of the Bible written by the sacred authors in apostolic times, which have Jesus Christ, the incarnate Son of God as their central theme. *(pg. 11)*

**Old Testament (n.):** The 46 books of the Bible, which record the history of salvation from creation through the old covenant with Israel, in preparation for the appearance of Christ as Savior of the World. *(pg. 11)*

**Original Sin (n.):** The state of human nature deprived of the original holiness and justice Adam and Even enjoyed before the fall. *(pg. 9)*

**Pagan (n.):** A person who practices polytheism, or the worship of many gods. *(pg. 20)*

**Parables (n.):** Short stories that convey unfamiliar or complex truths in a simple and easy to understand way by using characters and situations that are familiar. *(pg. 180)*

**Paschal Mystery (n.):** Christ's work of redemption accomplished by His Passion, Death, Resurrection, and Ascension. *(pg. 182)*

**Patriarchs (n.):** The fathers of the People of Israel: Abraham, Isaac, and Jacob. *(pg. 35)*

**Pentateuch (n.):** The Greek name for the first five books of the Old Testament: Genesis, Exodus, Leviticus, Numbers, and Deuteronomy. Also known as the Books of Moses. *(pg. 37)*

**Pope (n.):** The successor of St. Peter as bishop of Rome and Supreme Pontiff of the universal Catholic Church. The pope exercises a primacy of authority as the vicar of Christ on earth and the shepherd of the whole Church. *(pg. 49)*

**Prophetic Books (n.):** The books of the Old Testament that are primarily focused on recounting what God communicated to His people through the prophets. *(pg. 144)*

**Protestant Reformation (n.):** A 16th century revolt began by Martin Luther that divided and eventually splintered Christianity. Many Christian churches formed as a result of this split, which are known as Protestant churches, or denominations. Though Jesus desires that His Church be one, all baptized Christians are brothers and sisters in Christ. *(pg. 100)*

**"Q" Source (lost source of Jesus' sayings) (n.):** A collection of Jesus' sayings that Matthew, Mark, and Luke are believed by some to have drawn upon for the writing of their Gospels. There is no evidence for the existence of the "Q" source; its existence and purported use by the Evangelists is purely speculation. *(pg. 130)*

**Relativism (n.):** A dangerous philosophy that says moral principles are a matter of individual preference based on personal experience, socioeconomic status, education, and particular culture, rather than based on absolute objective moral truths. Relativism denies the existence of good and evil and harms our ability choose the good. *(pg. 26)*

**Rosary (n.):** A prayer in honor of the Blessed Virgin Mary, which repeats the "Hail Mary" prayer in "decades" of ten prayers, each preceded by an "Our Father" and concluded by a "Glory Be," accompanied by meditation on the mysteries of Christ's life. It is typically prayed using a chain of beads. *(pg. 98)*

**Sacred Scripture (n.):** The written record of God's revelation of Himself contained in the Old and New Testaments. It was composed by human authors inspired by the Holy Spirit. The Bible. The Word of God. *(pg. 11)*

**Sacred Tradition (n.):** The living transmission of the Gospel message in the Church. *(pg. 48)*

**Scholasticism (n.):** An intellectual method originating in medieval Europe that sought to integrate classical philosophy and Christian thought in order to understand and explain revealed truths. *(pg. 21)*

**Second Vatican Council (n.):** The most recent ecumenical council of the Church held at the Vatican between 1963 and 1965. Also called Vatican II. *(pg. 92)*

**Senses of Scripture (n.):** The various meanings of the Scripture text. *(pg. 118)*

***Sensus Fidei* (n.):** The supernatural appreciation of faith on the part of the whole people of God, when, from the bishops to the last of the faithful, they manifest a universal consent in matters of faith and morals and cannot in such a case err in belief. Latin for "sense of the faithful." *(pg. 52)*

**Septuagint (n.):** The pre-Christian Greek translation of the Old Testament books made by Jewish scholars and later adopted by Greek speaking Christians. *(pg. 78)*

***Sola Scriptura* (n.):** The belief that the Bible is the only source of divine revelation held by most non-Catholic Christian churches. Latin for "by Scripture alone." *(pg. 100)*

**Source Criticism (n.):** The name given to the analysis of the original sources from where the sacred authors of Scripture may have drawn material for their own writing. *(pg. 130)*

**Spiritual Sense (n.):** The meaning of the Scripture text that reveals the inner unity of God's plan through the realities and events of Scripture, which are signs God uses to point to deeper meaning. The spiritual sense is further broken down into three parts: the allegorical sense, the moral sense, and the anagogical sense. *(pg. 119)*

**Synod (n.):** A meeting of bishops of a particular region, of the whole world, or of bishops and priests and other members of the faithful within a particular diocese to address the doctrinal and pastoral needs of the Church. *(pg. 79)*

**Synoptic Gospels (n.):** The Gospels of Matthew, Mark, and Luke, which present the story of Christ's life in a similar way and even borrow stories and the structure of their Gospels from each other. The word synoptic comes from the Greek for "viewed together." *(pg. 172)*

**Synoptic Problem (n.):** The name given to the questions surrounding the similarities between the synoptic Gospels such as who wrote first, did the Gospel writers borrow or share information from each other's Gospels, or did they have a common source. *(pg. 183)*

***Targumim* (n.):** Aramaic paraphrases of the Old Testament originating from around the time of Christ that help us understand how the Jews of Jesus' time understood Scripture and are important for textual criticism of the Old Testament. *(pg. 131)*

**Textual Criticism (n.):** The name given to the analysis of early manuscripts of Scripture to establish the text's earliest form. *(pg. 130)*

**Theology (n.):** The study of God based on divine revelation. *(pg. 93)*

**Theopneustos (adj.):** Greek for "God-breathed." *(pg. 62)*

**Types (n.):** People or things in the Old Testament that foreshadow people or things in the New Testament. *(pg. 119)*

**Vulgate (n.):** The 4th century Latin translation of the Bible that was mostly completed by St. Jerome. It became the official Latin translation of the Bible for the Catholic Church in the 16th century. The Latin word vulgata means "commonly used." *(pg. 81)*

**Way of the Cross (n.):** A traditional devotional prayer that focuses on the Passion of Jesus. It follows Jesus' path as He carried His Cross and was crucified. Most parishes have a series of plaques, icons, or other works of art that present the 14 stations for devotion, meditation, and prayer. *(pg. 101)*

**Wisdom Literature (n.):** The books of the Old Testament that are primarily focused on providing moral exhortation or insights into a well-lived life. *(pg. 144)*

# Index

Page numbers in color indicate illustrations. References to specific citations from Scripture and the *Catechism* will be found in the separate **INDEX OF CITATIONS**.

## D

## E



## F



## G



## H

## I



## J

## K



## L

## P



## Q



## R



## S

## U



## V



## W

# Index of Citations

## Scripture

### Old Testament

## New Testament

# *Catechism of the Catholic Church* (CCC)